'Teschers introduces the reader to the work of Wilhelm Schmid, a German theorist who urges us to develop our own art of living in order to live a *beautiful* life. With this pedagogical aspiration in mind, Teschers takes seriously the idea that we are individuals living in a social context and that learning is something we do throughout our lives, and not solely in the classroom. Using a clear and accessible writing style, Teschers offers practical and theoretical suggestions as to what a contemporary education should look like, and invites us to reflect upon individual and societal values as we aim at developing practical wisdom. This book will be of interest to a wide audience, particularly those interested in philosophy, education, psychology and well-being.'

—*Laura D'Olimpio, Senior Lecturer in Philosophy,*
The University of Notre Dame, Australia

'Teschers' *Education and Schmid's Art of Living* is a welcomed perspective to education at a time that tends to be dominated by narrow economic interests. Teschers' book reinvigorates the ancient but perennial quest to seek a happy and good life – or in today's terms, a sense of well-being. This rich and holistic notion of the good life involves engaging philosophically with emotions, feelings, attitudes, cognition, meaning-making, purposefulness, wisdom and spirituality, both for individuals and for society more generally. He explores these mainly through a dialogue between positive psychology and Schmid's approach to a beautiful life. The result is a formulation of an art of living for education which is able to empower individual persons and all of society. Not only does an art of living require students to take a responsible role, but Teschers also explains how teachers might be able to offer a pedagogy that is able to educate for such an artful enterprise. I thoroughly recommend this book for those who are seeking how to make human life more meaningful and how education may once again serve this quest.'

—*Scott Webster, Senior Lecturer in Curriculum and*
Pedagogy, Deakin University, Australia

'In this scholarly and readable work, Christoph Teschers brings the thoughts and ideas of contemporary German philosopher Wilhelm Schmid to an English-speaking audience. Drawing on rich philosophical traditions, which include the classical thinkers, Kant, and Foucault, Teschers argues that an education for the art of life is valuable, as it challenges the instrumentalist and economistic discourses dominating education, particularly at school level. Teschers builds a convincing case for showing that suffering and despair are part of human life, and can indeed be educative. The context of twenty-first century life that challenges traditional approaches to knowledge, opens the way to thinking differently about how to live life. How one may wish to live, rather than what it is one will do in life, is a central concern for Christoph Teschers, and this book makes a commendable contribution to addressing that concern.'

—*Leon W. Benade, Senior Lecturer and Coordinator of Research,*
School of Education, AUT University, New Zealand

Education and Schmid's Art of Living

Instead of simply following the current neoliberal mantra of proclaiming economic growth as the single most important factor for maintaining well-being, *Education and Schmid's Art of Living* revisits the idea of an education focused on personal development and the well-being of human beings. Drawing on philosophical ideas concerning the good life and recent research in positive psychology, Teschers argues in favour of shifting the focus in education and schooling towards a beautiful life and an art of living for today's students.

Containing a thorough discussion of the ideas of contemporary German philosopher Wilhelm Schmid, this book considers the possible implications of developing a more humanistic and life-centred approach to educational policy, research and practice, showing that Schmid's concept of *Lebenskunst* provides a firm philosophical basis for this endeavour. Among others, this book draws on analytical and continental traditions to challenge current views and assumptions with regard to education and the role of schooling for contemporary societies. As a result, Teschers' work is sure to spark a debate about the direction of educational policy and practice in the 21st century.

Education and Schmid's Art of Living is essential reading for academics and students with an interest in education. Given the importance of such topics as the relationship between education and society, teacher education and how best to structure schools and learning environments, Teschers' work will appeal to academics and students in a diverse range of fields, including education, philosophy, sociology and psychology.

Christoph Teschers has held a range of positions at New Zealand tertiary institutions since 2012 and is currently faculty member at the College of Education, University of Canterbury. Following a period of study at the Friedrich-Alexander University, Germany, he completed a Doctor of Philosophy in education at the University of Canterbury, New Zealand. Dr Teschers' research interests include well-being, the art of living, positive psychology and philosophy for children.

New Directions in the Philosophy of Education Series
Series Editors
Michael A. Peters, University of Waikato, New Zealand;
University of Illinois, USA Gert Biesta, Brunel University, UK

For a full list of titles in this series, please visit www.routledge.com

This book series is devoted to the exploration of new directions in the philosophy of education. After the linguistic turn, the cultural turn, and the historical turn, where might we go? Does the future promise a digital turn with a greater return to connectionism, biology, and biopolitics based on new understandings of system theory and knowledge ecologies? Does it foreshadow a genuinely alternative radical global turn based on a new openness and interconnectedness? Does it leave humanism behind or will it reengage with the question of the human in new and unprecedented ways? How should philosophy of education reflect new forces of globalization? How can it become less Anglo-centric and develop a greater sensitivity to other traditions, languages, and forms of thinking and writing, including those that are not rooted in the canon of Western philosophy but in other traditions that share the "love of wisdom" that characterizes the wide diversity within Western philosophy itself? Can this be done through a turn to intercultural philosophy? To indigenous forms of philosophy and philosophizing? Does it need a post-Wittgensteinian philosophy of education? A postpostmodern philosophy? Or should it perhaps leave the whole construction of "post"-positions behind?

In addition to the question of the intellectual resources for the future of philosophy of education, what are the issues and concerns that philosophers of education should engage with? How should they position themselves? What is their specific contribution? What kind of intellectual and strategic alliances should they pursue? Should philosophy of education become more global, and if so, what would the shape of that be? Should it become more cosmopolitan or perhaps more decentred? Perhaps most importantly in the digital age, the time of the global knowledge economy that reprofiles education as privatized human capital and simultaneously in terms of an historic openness, is there a philosophy of education that grows out of education itself, out of the concerns for new forms of teaching, studying, learning and speaking that can provide comment on ethical and epistemological configurations of economics and politics of knowledge? Can and should this imply a reconnection with questions of democracy and justice?

This series comprises texts that explore, identify, and articulate new directions in the philosophy of education. It aims to build bridges, both geographically and temporally: bridges across different traditions and practices and bridges towards a different future for philosophy of education.

In this series

Education and Schmid's Art of Living
Philosophical, Psychological and Educational Perspectives on Living a Good Life
Christoph Teschers

Education and Schmid's Art of Living

Philosophical, Psychological and Educational Perspectives on Living a Good Life

Christoph Teschers

LONDON AND NEW YORK

First published 2018
by Routledge
2 Park Square, Milton Park, Abingdon, Oxon OX14 4RN

and by Routledge
711 Third Avenue, New York, NY 10017

Routledge is an imprint of the Taylor & Francis Group, an informa business

© 2018 Christoph Teschers

The right of Christoph Teschers to be identified as author of this work has been asserted by him in accordance with sections 77 and 78 of the Copyright, Designs and Patents Act 1988.

All rights reserved. No part of this book may be reprinted or reproduced or utilised in any form or by any electronic, mechanical, or other means, now known or hereafter invented, including photocopying and recording, or in any information storage or retrieval system, without permission in writing from the publishers.

Trademark notice: Product or corporate names may be trademarks or registered trademarks, and are used only for identification and explanation without intent to infringe.

British Library Cataloguing-in-Publication Data
A catalogue record for this book is available from the British Library

Library of Congress Cataloging-in-Publication Data
A catalog record for this book has been requested

ISBN: 978-1-138-68044-9 (hbk)
ISBN: 978-1-315-56384-8 (ebk)

Typeset in Galliard
by Apex CoVantage, LLC

Contents

List of figures   x
Acknowledgements   xi
Preface   xii

1 Introduction   1

2 Philosophical concepts of the art of living   6
   2.1 Various interpretations of the art of living 6
   2.2 Relevant philosophical concepts explored 9
      The philosophic life – Socrates 9
      Hedonism – Epicurus 13
      Eudaimonia – *Aristotle* 16
      The morally good life – Kant 18
      The care of the self – Foucault 20

3 Emotions and the good life   23
   3.1 Defining feelings, emotions and affects 23
   3.2 A classification of emotions – past, present, future 25
   3.3 Defining relevant emotional concepts 26
      Sensational and attitudinal pleasures 27
      Happiness and eudaimonia 28
      Joy and enjoyments 29
      Satisfaction and contentment 30
      Well-being and subjective well-being 30
   3.4 Positive and negative emotions 31
   3.5 Suffering and despair 33
   3.6 The good life 34

4 Positive psychology and the art of living   38
   4.1 The relevance of positive psychology for an art of living 38
   4.2 The usage of terms 39

    4.3 Subjective well-being and positive emotions 40
        Emotions about the past 42
        Emotions about the future 42
        Emotions about the present 43
    4.4 Enhancing positive emotions and enduring happiness 45
        Positive emotions 45
        Enduring happiness 46
        Signature strengths and the six core virtues 47
    4.5 Flow 48
        Why flow? 48
        What is flow? 49
        Social and cultural perspectives 50
        Limitations of optimal experience 51
    4.6 Meaning in life and harmony 52
        Purpose 53
        Resolve 54
        Harmony 55

5 *"Lebenskunst"* – Schmid's concept of the art of living   58
    5.1 Schmid's approach 59
    5.2 Choice and freedom 62
        Problems of choice 63
        Choice and the art of living 65
        Education and choice 67
    5.3 The quest for a new art of living 68
        Philosophy of the art of living 69
        Ethical considerations 71
        Descriptions of the art of living 73
        Fundamental questions 74
    5.4 The care of the self 77
        The subject of the care of the self 77
        The labour of care 78
    5.5 An educational perspective 82
        Hermeneutics 82
        Techniques for an art of living 84
        Education for the art of living 89

6 *Lebenskunst* and positive psychology in dialogue   94
    6.1 The relevance of the art of living and positive psychology
        today 94
    6.2 Concepts and definitions of a "good life" 97
    6.3 Concepts of the self 98

6.4 Social influences on individual human beings 103
6.5 Control over consciousness and the care of the self 105

7 An educational approach to the art of living 109
7.1 Reasons for an educational approach 109
7.2 An end of education 110
7.3 The importance of the art of living for education 115
7.4 An educational critique of Schmid's concept
  Lebenskunst *118*

8 Beyond schooling 123
8.1 Education and schooling – a German perspective 123
8.2 De-schooling and the art of living 126
  The de-schooling critique 126
  Possible ways out 128
8.3 The art of living and schooling 130

9 Life pedagogy – an education for life concept 133
9.1 Pedagogical content and practice 134
  Skills and knowledge 134
  Hermeneutics 136
  Bildung 138
  Wisdom 140
  Spirituality and education 142
  Mind-sets and attachments 145
9.2 Requirements for teaching the art of living 147
  The teacher, his or her personality and developing an art of living 147
  Pedagogical approaches for teaching the art of living 149
  Teaching settings and school context 151
  Implications for teacher education 153

10 Conclusion 157

Bibliography 161
Index 167

Figures

5.1 Hierarchy of ethics as proposed by Schmid   72
6.1 Example: John's self-concept   101

Acknowledgements

As most projects of this scope, writing a book is hardly ever a solitude undertaking, and many people have supported me and contributed to the development of this book. First, I would like to thank the series editors, Professor Michael Peters and Professor Gert Biesta, as well as Routledge Editor Heidi Lowther and the Routledge Editorial Board, for their support in accepting and publishing this book in the *New Directions in the Philosophy of Education* series.

Further, I would like to express my gratitude to a number of colleagues who have been most influential through their feedback, comments and ongoing discussion and support: Professor Peter Roberts, Associate Professor Kathleen Quinlivan, Dr John Calvert, Dr Filipe Santos, Dr Louise Tapper, Dr Scott Webster, Dr Leon Benade and Dr Laura D'Olimpio. Thank you all for supporting me during the writing process of this book and for your ongoing professional support through collegial discussions and the collaborative development of new ideas. I would also like to thank the many colleagues I have met on the way and who have impacted in smaller and larger ways to the completion of this book through their collegiality and the one or other philosophical discussion in hallways or in the campus café.

I also thank my family who have supported me in so many ways over the years and continue to stand behind me despite the demands of academia and the challenges involved. A special thanks to my wife Barbara, who not only put up with me spending many hours on this project but who also supported this book by reading early drafts and providing feedback on clarity and expression. I also want to thank my parents (it does not matter how old one gets, one will always be a child in some sense, I guess), who have played a key role in my embarking on this academic journey in the first place that led to this and hopefully many more books in the future.

All of you and the many other people who supported me and I did not mention individually, please accept my deepest thanks and gratitude.

Preface

Before delving into the main content of this book, I would like to briefly explain why this topic is of personal importance to me and how my exploration of the art of living in relation to education commenced.

The starting point and motivation for this research topic traces back to my own upbringing and experiences during adolescence in a German middle-class environment; in particular, from my personal struggle to figure out which direction to take in life after school. It seemed that any support given at the time revolved around deciding on a career path, not so much considering *how one might want to live*. This experience is not unique to myself. Having worked with young people in different settings for many years, I have observed similar struggles faced by adolescents thinking about life as they search for their path, which indicates that there might be a structural issue in terms of young people being (ill-)prepared for making significant life choices. This problem of contemporary societies, where informed and prudent decision-making in relation to fundamental life choices is limited by a lack of supporting structures to think about the larger questions in life, and by too many career options available in our mostly flexible and changing economy and industry, is one reason why I consider it important for educationists to explore ways of better supporting young people to find their way and to make significant life choices. Combining philosophical theories in relation to the art of living and psychological findings around well-being and happiness with educational theory and practice is one way that might lead to possible answers, as proposed in this book.

One aspect that can help young people to find their bearing in life, I would argue, is to strengthen a student's faculty of hermeneutics: the ability to make sense of, and give meaning to, the world one is living in (Gadamer 1975). As will be discussed later on in this book, the hermeneutic circle of perception, interpretation (giving meaning to what one perceives), shaping one's own self and view of the world through this interpretation, and a subsequent altered perception based on one's overall view of the world, is an important aspect of developing one's own art of living. The process of hermeneutics is also significant to the understanding of education and learning processes for the discussion in this book. An example of this hermeneutic circle in my own learning and development is that, after having spent many years on this topic, I came to see that my initial desire to make life easier for young people might actually not be the best way to support them. As will be discussed later on, personal development and growth are strongly related to struggle, trying times and even despair. If everything is easy and effortless, there is no need to strive, grow and evolve. However, I believe that certain knowledge, skills and understanding can help to develop one's own art of living and, in the end, to live a good and beautiful life more readily than without. Although I am sure that many people manage well in finding their way in life and might even live a life they consider good and beautiful, I would venture to say that no small amount of young people are not that lucky and that too many people might experience life periods that are closer to survival than purposeful living. If we as educationists and teachers can make a difference by helping young people to make reflected life decisions towards what they perceive a good and beautiful life to be earlier rather than later, it is my belief that we ought to do so.

However, as can be seen in the theory of the art of living, leading a good and beautiful life is not only a question for adolescents, but a journey people might struggle with throughout their life cycle. Therefore, and due to a broad understanding of education as a never-ending journey that takes place nearly everywhere and all the time, the scope of this topic widens beyond schooling to include a person's full lifespan. Of course, not all aspects of lifelong education can be explored fully here, but some considerations for an *education for life* concept that builds on ideas of the art of living, positive psychology and education are discussed in this book, which hopefully provides a foundation for further research and for a more detailed educational theory in the future.

1 Introduction

In his book *Erfahrung und Verantwortung* [Experience and Responsibility] Eckard Liebau (1999) points out that a question commonly asked today is: "Which Education is needed for [. . .] society?" (p. 5, my translation). This question prioritises society above education, which is a way of thinking that seems to dominate modern societies and, therefore, exploits education as a tool to shape young people into useful elements of industry and economy. The focus of school curricula today often seems to be on the instruction of knowledge and skills deemed necessary to function in society and not on education understood in the way of providing far-ranging knowledge and enabling individuals to engage in critical thinking and (self-)reflection. But, Liebau continues,

> educational thinking can invert this hierarchy; it can also ask for the structure a society must have, to be capable and willing to provide for people's educational demands. [. . .] Obviously, this inversion has an impact on the question of schooling: What does schooling contribute to education – and what can and should it contribute?
>
> (p. 5, my translation)

This inversion and the resulting questions are the starting point of this study. Today's modern societies are mostly characterised by a host of opportunities and challenges alike. The pace of life is quicker than ever before, and the changes and developments in societies, science and technology come about faster every day. One of the major challenges for human beings is to make a myriad of decisions on a daily basis, which will define their place in society, in life and in the world altogether. To make prudent and sensible decisions is, therefore, a key competence for a successful and good life. One of the difficulties, however, is to acquire this key competency in time. In a fast-moving and changing world, where children's life experiences are very different from everything their parents encountered; in schools, where curricula are overloaded with facts and scientific knowledge; and in societies that are globalised and influenced by dozens of cultures, the challenge to find – and define – the way one wants to live has reached an intensity where people need help to learn the skills and knowledge necessary to live a good and beautiful life.

Introduction

The question of how to live a good life has been discussed in philosophy for thousands of years, and answers have been given in many cultures over time. Nevertheless, as Csikszentmihalyi (2008, 20–2) points out, the answers today might be the same as those discovered in the past, but they need to be rephrased, as people in different cultures and with changing historical backgrounds no longer understand the former wisdom. Scholars such as Martha Nussbaum (2001), Alexander Nehamas (1998), Fred Feldman (2004), Mihaly Csikszentmihalyi (2008) and Wilhelm Schmid (2000a; Schmid 2000b) are only some who have been interested in formulating an understanding of *an art of living* for people today.

There are various philosophical approaches to leading a good life. One of them, and the one favoured in this book, is the *Lebenskunst* [art of living] concept from Schmid (2000a; Schmid 2000b).[1] Schmid describes the art of living as the art of taking responsibility for one's own life in an attempt to make it a "beautiful" one. Schmid does not present this concept as a prescription for how everybody should live, but as a way to enable individuals to find their own way to live a good and beautiful life based on their own norms, values and beliefs. Some of the key points of his philosophy are a focus on the individual, the care of the self (cf. (Foucault 1984)) at the heart of the art of living, the importance of prudence and practical wisdom and the emphasis that each human being is always part of a social structure.

Schmid focuses on the individual, as each human being has a core, an essence or a self that is more accessible and closer to what one experiences as one's own consciousness than any other being or object one can perceive.[2] Each human being has, to a certain extent, some kind of autonomy over his or her own body, mind and actions in the world, which results in the experience of self-identity and in a feeling of distinction from the bodies, minds and actions of other human beings (see Section 6.3). Accepting this level of individuality, which is a strong concept in Western culture, an art of living approach practically has to focus on the individual, as the final judgement about his or her own life as being a good and beautiful one can only be made by the individual living and experiencing this life (Schmid 2000a; Schmid 2000b).

However, the relationship between individuals and society is quite contested in philosophical and sociological theory. It will not be argued here that an individual can develop independently of society and the social context he or she is living in. On the contrary, a person's development and growth are always dependent on the society he or she is living in and the experiences he or she is exposed to. Schmid also acknowledges that each human being is a social animal and nearly always part of a social structure and community. Therefore, strong reciprocal dynamics influence not only the individual, but also the people one is in contact with and society as a whole (see Sections 5.3 and 6.4). Some of the aspects of social interaction involve ethical and moral values and considerations. Schmid bases his ethical concept, originating from the individual, on the qualities of prudence and practical wisdom. These qualities will allow an individual not only to find his or her place in social settings, but also to transform selfishness into a reflective form of self-interest, which takes into account the desires and the benefit of the Other[3] and of society as a whole.

One aspect of living a good life is the notion of happiness, which has boomed in the public as well as in the academic domain over the last decade but has not reached its peak yet: Martin Seligman presented the "happiness formula" in his book *Authentic Happiness* in 2002; research about happiness, subjective well-being and life satisfaction began to form the field of positive psychology (see Chapter 4); more than 600,000 books[4] are available concerning the topics of happiness and/or well-being; and organisations and indices have been founded, including *The Happy Planet Index*,[5] *The World Values Survey*[6] and the *World Database of Happiness*.[7] Recently, governments – Britain (Easton 2006) and Bhutan are two examples – have started to shift their focus to include individual happiness when evaluating the state of the country and the living situation of its people. To support this development, Suntum, Prinz and Uhde (2010) developed a so-called "Glücks-BIP" [happiness-GDP], which combines a country's gross domestic product (GDP) with additional indicators for measuring happiness, which are based on positive psychology research. Even some schools and colleges have taken up the task of improving their pupils' happiness and life skills. Examples are the "well-being centre" at Geelong Grammar School in Australia and happiness classes at the Wellington College in Berkshire, UK. In the United States, resilience classes have been introduced to the curriculum in some schools.[8] However, Jules Evans (2008) pointed out that these programmes are mainly based on the findings of positive psychology and cognitive behavioural therapy, and Suissa (2008) voiced concerns about the lack of an underlying educational theory for these kinds of happiness classes.

As the field of the art of living is rather vast, including all fundamental aspects of a human's life cycle, and the scope of this book is limited, many areas of interest can only be touched on. The decision to focus on Schmid's philosophy of the art of living is based on three factors. First, it is a relatively recent concept, including considerations about current social settings, but it also takes into account various historical concepts of the art of living. Second, through Schmid's self-limiting approach to refrain from normative definitions of a good life (i.e. explicit definitions of what to do to live a good life; a catalogue of checkpoints to determine if one's life is a good one or not), it has the potential of being universally applicable. And, finally, Schmid discusses educational requirements on the basis of his philosophical considerations, which provide a good starting point for an underlying educational theory towards the art of living.

The main objectives of this book are (i) to argue for a general shift in the focus of educational research, policy and practice towards a more humanistic and life-centred approach, combined with the economic development of society[9]; (ii) to argue for Schmid's art of living concept as a well-suited philosophical basis for this endeavour; (iii) to support this argument with positive psychology research outcomes and critique the shortcomings of the latter despite its current popularity; and, finally, (iv) to set the foundations for an education for life concept that promotes "the best possible realization of humanity as humanity" (Dewey 2001, 100) through the personal growth and development of each individual.

To accomplish these aims, this book will start with a review of various philosophical concepts and understandings of the art of living in Chapter 2. A discussion of various significant concepts and terms regarding emotions and the good life will follow in Chapter 3. Having established the interpretation of these basic terms that are relevant for philosophical and psychological considerations alike, Chapter 4 will then be a review of recent positive psychology research in relation to the art of living.

Schmid's concept *Lebenskunst*, as the main philosophical art of living concept used in this book, will be summarised and discussed from an educational point of view in Chapter 5. Chapter 6 will then engage more closely with parallels and differences between positive psychology and philosophical concepts of the art of living, especially with Schmid's concept *Lebenskunst*. This dialogue between the disciplines will be presented from an educational point of view; a more thorough discussion of the art of living and education will be conducted in the following chapters.

Chapter 7 marks a turning point in this study from establishing a philosophical and psychological background to the development of an educational approach to the art of living. This approach includes arguments for the importance of a shift of educational focus towards the art of living and the good life of students, as well as an educational critique of Schmid's concept. In Chapter 8, the relations between education, schooling and the art of living will be explored on the basis of the German understanding of education, which is a combination of *Erziehung* [upbringing], *Bildung* [self-formation] and *Entfaltung* [flourishing]. It will be argued that, although predominant in public discourse, schooling is only a part of education, and not necessarily the most important one. The discussion will be pointed beyond schooling and towards an *education for life*.

Finally, Chapter 9 will introduce various aspects of an "education for life" concept, which builds on the insights gained in the previous chapters. This chapter is not meant to propose a complete concept, but rather to be a starting point for the development of such an approach. Some previously mentioned aspects, such as *Bildung*, wisdom and spirituality, will be revisited and added to the spectrum of necessary considerations for a holistic educational concept. Additionally, this chapter will address some of the practical implications for teachers, schools and teacher training.

It needs to be mentioned that, despite the notion of an art of living being a lifelong process, the focus of this book in terms of practical implications will be mainly on education in schools. The scope of this book already limits the discussion of this one area of education and does not allow me to engage significantly with the vast body of knowledge in other areas, such as early childhood, adult education or education in other social institutions (e.g. youth centres). These areas will be left to further research.

Notes

1 Schmid is a contemporary German philosopher whose work has not yet been translated into English. However, a summary of his philosophy will be given in Chapter 5.

2 Relations between the individual, others and society will be discussed in Section 6.4; different interpretations of the self and its role in the art of living can be found in Section 6.3.
3 "The Other" (with capital "O") is used in this book as a translation for the German term *der Andere*, which refers to a singular, non-specific person one interacts with in a certain situation, instead of the whole body of "others", or "other people" in general. This term is used frequently in Schmid's text, and the Other is an attempt to capture Schmid's original meaning.
4 Search for 'happiness' (about 47,000 hits) combined with search for 'well-being' (about 573,000 hits) on www.amazon.com, 24.08.2011.
5 www.happyplanetindex.org
6 www.worldvaluessurvey.org
7 http://worlddatabaseofhappiness.eur.nl
8 All three examples here are developments over recent years, where predominantly findings from positive psychology research have been used to inform educational content and practice in an attempt to help students become more resilient and 'happy'. More details can be found on the institutions' websites. Also, a term recently used in this context is *positive education*, which is based on positive psychology, but quite questionable from an educational perspective, as it could imply that all other education might not be positive, which is highly contestable to say the least.
9 Some national examples in this direction are the humanistic focus of the national school system of Finland, an attempt of the British government to support the development of happiness for its people through happiness classes and the declaration of the government of Bhutan to measure its success mainly at the happiness of its people, not the GDP. However, despite these localised attempts, economic pressure and neo-liberal ideology seem to often undermine this trend on a global scale, as can be seen, for example, in New Zealand and Australia (Ozolins 2011).

2 Philosophical concepts of the art of living

There is a wide range of definitions and conceptualisations of the term *the art of living*. In this chapter, a walk-through of various definitions of the art of living will be provided, followed by a more detailed discussion of some of the major concepts. The relevant literature in addressing questions relating to the art of living is extensive, and this book can only address a limited portion of it. A substantial body of knowledge from, for example, existentialist thinkers such as Nietzsche, Sartre, Jaspers and Heidegger unfortunately cannot be discussed explicitly here. Schmid, however, takes into account existentialist thought in his concept of the art of living, which is significant for the argument in this book.

The overview of various approaches to the art of living presented in this chapter will allow us to better understand and discuss Schmid's art of living concept *Lebenskunst*, which will be argued for as a suitable philosophical concept for an educational approach to this topic. Also, some aspects of positive psychology in Chapter 4 will be discussed in light of this philosophical review.

2.1 Various interpretations of the art of living

This overview will begin with a more practical interpretation of *the art of living*, which was introduced by André Maurois and Robert Gibbings (1940), in the context of cultural similarities between the French and the British in the early 20th century. He describes in detail the nature of certain aspects of life, such as love, marriage, family life, friendship and work, as well as human behaviour and why people act in certain ways. He also voices his opinion about the way people should approach these aspects of life *to have a certain art of living*. In this way, his understanding of the concept is quite practice oriented and aims at certain cultural behaviours and norms which he deems favourable. Maurois' understanding of the art of living is, in the first place, a normative one (i.e. he defines what a good life is, in his opinion, and how people *should* live) and, therefore, will be of less importance for this study, as the aim here lies in a more holistic and descriptive concept of an (individual) art of living. However, his approach shows one possible understanding of the notion of the art of living and draws attention to the potential philosophical and ethical challenges that will be discussed later on.

A different conceptual understanding, but also prescriptive, is proposed by Paul Mackendrick (1952), who distinguishes between simply *living* and *living well*. The latter, according to Mackendrick, is in particular "to have leisure for uninterrupted intellectual activity" (p. 423). For him, the "most important product of living as an art is intellectual enjoyment; the highest intellectual pleasure lies in pushing back the frontiers of knowledge" (p. 424). This point of view can also be found in other places in philosophical history, as far back as Aristotle, who "said that the very best life is the life of contemplation" (Grayling 2006, 5). In his article, Mackendrick (1952) argues for a broader, more general education in higher education as obligatory for any tertiary student and calls this an *Education for the Art of Living*. The aspect here that will be of value for the later discussion is the emphasis on a wider knowledge base and a deeper understanding of the world, which is also important in other concepts of the art of living. However, a more individual-based concept will be proposed, which will take into account the uniqueness of every person and can only allow for limited predefined compulsory content for students.

Going further back in history, in the context of ancient Greek philosophy, Plato (and Socrates) argued for *philosophy as the art of living*. Philosophy here is mainly understood as practising Socrates' dialectical irony: to critically engage with every assumption, belief and conviction one may have or encounter and consequently live up to the insights gained from this reflection. To live a life in a philosophic way means not only to reflect and meditate, but also to follow through with all aspects one's critical thinking brings to light (Nehamas 1998).

A different approach to living a good life can be found in Epicurus' philosophy (Feldman 2004). Epicurus believed *hedonism* to be the way to human happiness and an art of living. For him, the essence and purpose of human beings are to find pleasures in life and to avoid pain. The value of a life and if it is good or not in the hedonistic understanding are determined by the amount of experienced pleasures minus the amount of pain.

Another approach, from a different angle, to a definition of the good life has been conducted by moral philosophers, such as Kant and Aristotle: the *morally* good life. For Kant a good life is a life that is led in consistency with the *categorical imperative*: "act only in accordance with that maxim through which you can at the same time will that it become a universal law" (Kant 1997, 31, AK 4:421).[1] An individual who follows this principle has, according to Kant, a *good will*, which is his definition for a moral good life. As important as his philosophy and moral considerations are, they will only be of subordinate significance for the understanding of a *good life*. However, moral aspects will be taken into account in the discussion of Schmid's art of living concept.

More recently, Foucault (1984) discussed a theory about the good life, mainly based on the philosophies of Epictetus and Seneca, in his book *The Care of the Self*. The key to a good life, for him, is to pay attention to one's own self – to care for oneself. Successful care of the self leads to true independence and allows the individual, or better *the agent's soul*,[2] to be free of influences from the external world in terms of one's well-being and happiness. Foucault's notion of the care of the self is significant for Schmid's concept, as Schmid partially builds on Foucault's work.

The primary concept of the art of living this book will focus on has been formulated by Wilhelm Schmid, a contemporary German philosopher. The main purpose of his philosophical inquiry is the development of a foundational theory[3] of the art of living. He defines it (in short) as "the wholeheartedness of the attempt, [...] to acquire one's life in good time and maybe make a 'beautiful life' out of it" (Schmid 2000b, 7, my translation).[4] His concept takes into account the philosophical history of the art of living, beginning with the ancient Greek and Roman philosophers up to recent philosophers. He also refers to developments in sociology and psychology in the mid-to-late 20th century: the topic of the art of living, according to Schmid (2000a, 38), has been neglected by philosophers in the last century but has been picked up by other disciplines.

In terms of values and norms, the question of how to live a good life and develop one's own art of living is not limited to, but is definitely touched by, religion and spirituality. I will not include a discussion of different religions and their relation to or versions of an art of living concept, but it will be shown how beliefs, mind-sets, worldviews and spirituality can influence an individual's perception, well-being and art of living. One example will be the introduction of the philosophy of Anthony de Mello, an Indian Jesuit padre, who died in 1987. De Mello emphasised that one's beliefs and mind-set can strongly influence a person's experience of his or her own life as a good and happy one, mostly independent from external circumstances. The main point of his philosophy, which is influenced by Christianity and Buddhism alike, is to be aware of one's own feelings and to know that these feelings are not *in the world* (external) but *in oneself* (internal). His intent was to make people "awake", to let them see that they have to change themselves (their beliefs and expectations) and not the world around them to improve their experience of life and happiness. De Mello's spiritual approach links also with Cziksentmihaily's psychological approach of control of consciousness, as discussed later on.

This short overview of some of the possible interpretations of an art of living has shown at least three points: (i) there is not one way, but rather many, to live a good and happy life: in fact, depending on one's viewpoint, happiness does not need to be part of a good life at all; (ii) the definition of terms and being clear about them is crucial, as a "good life" can mean many different things to different people; and (iii) the question of how to live a good life has been pursued throughout centuries and cultures, which indicates that the striving for *eudaimonia*, as Aristotle (NE 1097b19–21) claimed, is indeed the utmost goal for human beings, and the development of an art of living, therefore, is of importance for all people and cultures.

The following section will explore some of the more important philosophical concepts in this context in more detail to lay the path for Schmid's theory of an art of living, which draws on most of these concepts, among others.

2.2 Relevant philosophical concepts explored

As Socrates, through Plato (n.d./2003), is one of the earliest philosophers we have written evidence of who also explored the question of how to live a good life, this section will start with a review of his thoughts on this topic. Socrates focused mainly on the concept of *areté*, which, in the ancient Greek context is the question of *success* in life or the *right way* to live a virtuous life. Then, Epicurus and his model of *hedonism*, which focuses more on *personal happiness* in life instead of living a philosopher's life of contemplation and virtue, will be explored as well. Only a brief introduction to Aristotle's concept of *eudaimonia* will be given, as aspects of his concept will be revisited throughout the text later on. Kant (1997) – to some extent similar to Aristotle – focused on an ethical approach to the good life, which will be of relevance for the ethical considerations of the art of living concept proposed in the following chapter. This section will close with a review of Foucault's (1984) concept of *the care of the self*, which provided a starting point for Schmid (2000a; Schmid 2000b) and his theory of *Lebenskunst* [art of living], which will be discussed in detail in Chapter 5.

Many more philosophers and concepts could be reviewed in this section: Seneca, Stoicism, Montaigne, Confucius, Christianity, Buddhism and Islam, to name only a few. However, due to the introductory character of this chapter, the concepts discussed here will suffice for the purpose of this book. Chapter 5 will provide a detailed summary of Schmid's concept of the art of living, which will provide the main philosophical background for the following educational considerations.

The philosophic life – Socrates

According to Nehamas (1998), most topics and concepts in philosophy claim their roots in Socrates or at least refer to Socrates' philosophy. The art of living is no exception:

> [T]hough Socrates holds a number of extraordinary philosophical views, each one of which repays serious study, his main concern, as Plato eventually was to put it, is how to live (*Rep.* 325d6). And his major accomplishment is that he established a new way of life, a new *art of living*.
>
> (Nehamas 1998, 96, italics added)

Socrates' main concern and the focus of his study was *areté*, which is often translated as *virtue*, but, according to Nehamas (1998, 77), can also mean *perfection, excellence* or *success*. Therefore, having *areté* is not only about living a virtuous life, but also a successful life. As the ancient Greeks held bodily health in high regard, *areté* included the perfection of the body as much as the training of the mind and the care for one's soul. The last, which seemed more important for Socrates, can mainly be achieved by improving one's own character to perfection.

10 Philosophical concepts of art of living

The result of the perfection of one's self is, hence, to live a successful life. Consequently, Socrates' considerations about *areté* are mainly considerations about how to live a good and successful life. *Areté*, however, was of common concern for Greek culture at that time, and, the same as today, the interpretations of *areté* have been manifold. The exceptional part about Socrates was that he introduced an interpretation of the concept that reached beyond the common understanding of the term at his time.

The oracle of Delphi declared Socrates the wisest of all Athenians, something Socrates himself had trouble believing. In the *Apology (Ap. 21)* Socrates describes how he tested the oracle's decision and talked to the people of Athena, who were considered the wisest of all. He found out that he did not know better than these people what *areté* is, but he was aware of his lack of knowledge, whereas the "wise" men claimed to know the essence of *areté*, but obviously did not. Socrates' wisdom resulted from his *awareness of his own ignorance*. This awareness expressed itself in Socrates' way of life, which is the life of a philosopher:

> What we can at best expect from a philosophic life is that the views and the actions that make it up be in harmony with one another, not that the views will entail the actions. Both 'views' and 'actions' are equally parts of life; there is no reason one should be prior to the other.
>
> (Nehamas 1998, 96)

In this citation, Nehamas points out the distinctiveness between the philosophic life of Socrates in contrast to the way of the *Stoics*, for example, who sold their knowledge for money. Socrates highly disapproved of this practice, as he considered the Stoics mostly unwise and dangerous in their teachings. He was convinced that (purchased) knowledge directly affects one's soul and one cannot simply forget what one has learnt.[5] Therefore, it is highly important to make sure to buy only "good" knowledge. Unfortunately, as he argues, only experts in the field of *areté* can distinguish true teachings from false – not so the one in need of it. This is a dilemma which seems to be hard to solve, as wrong teachings compromise one's soul, but to recognise proper teachings one has to have the desired knowledge already. This is why Socrates (Ap. 19e-20c)[6] claims not to be a teacher at all, but only to be a student himself and a seeker of *areté*. He claimed not to teach, but only to ask questions in his own ironic way. This technique of the so-called *Socratic dialogue* will be of further interest in Section 9.2 where requirements and techniques of how to teach the art of living will be explored.

So far, it has been established that for a philosophical life, according to Socrates, the harmony of views and actions is important. But apart from that, other questions arise: What does a philosophical life look like? What else defines the life of a philosopher? Plato offers a more distinct description in his later work *Phaedo*. Among other aspects, Harold Tarrant (2003, 99–108) identifies three major points of a philosopher's life in this dialogue from Plato: *overcome pleasures of the body, desiring death* and a *philosopher's virtue*.

Tarrant explains the need to overcome the *pleasures of the body* as a release of the philosopher "from the preoccupation with the body" (p. 101). Pleasures are understood as needs and desires of the body, and pains as "the growth of these needs or the needs themselves." This link between pleasures and pains, he argues, creates a cycle that cannot be balanced through pursuing satisfaction of pleasures and aversion of pains. Rather, a "philosopher must free himself from this purposeless alternation of pain and pleasure" (p. 101) as much as possible to focus more on one's intellectual goals. In addition to the link between pleasure and pain as described by Tarrant, *pleasures* and *needs*, in Socrates' understanding, are not necessarily limited to basic needs of the body but include all sorts of *desires* in general. Socrates tried, for example, to convince people not to make money, reputation and honour their only purposes in life, but to think about "truth and understanding and the perfection of [. . . the] soul" (Ap. 29e). Thus, the life of the philosopher in this reading is to overcome one's desires and focus on the care for one's soul and on higher goals, such as the proper way of living and how to achieve *areté*.[7]

At this point, it is important to mention that the whole theory of a philosopher's life, as described in *Phaedo*, is based on Plato's philosophy of an undying soul which contains the essence of a being and will leave the body after death. The thought of an eternal afterlife increases the importance of the choices made in life and adds a whole new dimension to the care of the soul. This notion will be of even more significance for the following, second aspect of a philosophical life.

To *desire death* is a difficult concept even for Plato, as it is linked with the possibility of suicide, which he does not approve of: the basic requirement for this point is that "if somebody ought to follow a given course of action, then that course of action must be good for him" (Tarrant 2003, 102). With the description of Socrates' death and his refusal to escape it and flee, Plato shows that the "conduct leading to one's own death can be just, honourable and good" (p. 102). Tarrant also points out "that the philosopher desires to be released from this world," as this is the final release of pleasures (and pain) of the body, and, therefore, "death is good for him" (p. 102). But to prevent suicide, there needs to be a reason to stay alive, which Tarrant explains to be the case, as staying alive is also good for the philosopher in so far as it might be good for the philosopher:

> [T]o *be dead* does not entail that it is good to *become dead* by any means, even unjust or impious ones. To incur divine displeasure may challenge the very serenity which he thinks he will enjoy on death. He acts in his own interests by waiting for another means of death, just as a slave who is promised freedom tomorrow acts against his own interest if he annoys his master by running away today. So he waits for self-interested reasons, not for altruistic ones, even though his master may have the interests of the rest of his household at heart when he bans premature escape.
>
> (pp. 102–3)

The reason for Socrates to accept his death is, on the one hand, the release of pain in this world and, on the other hand, the expectation of an afterlife and "a further existence in which he will again have fine friends and fine gods for his masters" (Tarrant 2003, 103). He sees it as "the natural culmination of everything which he had been pursuing in this life [. . .]. Thus it will be only a slight step further along the path which he was already travelling" (p. 103).

The third aspect of a philosophical life, the *philosopher's virtue*, is, to a certain extent, a consequence of the former two but reaches further:

> The philosophers are actually said to be particularly brave and particularly temperate even according to popular criteria, facing death cheerfully and not being excited by physical desires. By contrast other people are brave only because they fear other things more and temperate only because they fear that profligacy will later deprive them of other pleasures for which their desire is greater. These people have neither mastered fear nor mastered desire.
>
> (p. 107)

The difference between the popular and the Socratic morality here is not the way of acting, but the motivation behind one's actions. Whereas ordinary people act to avoid pain and gain pleasure, the philosopher acts to pursue *wisdom*. But one could argue that there is no real difference, as wisdom for the philosopher is just another kind of pleasure. Further, Tarrant states that "we select our pleasures and our fears with a view to wisdom; we use our wisdom to select our pleasures and fears – to perform for us a hedonistic calculus" (p. 108). The difference is that "where wisdom controls the process [of pleasure-seeking and pain-avoiding], it will do so only in such a way as to encourage the acquisition of further wisdom" (p. 108). In this way, there is a "higher" aim (wisdom) in all this "pleasure-seeking and pain-avoiding," (p. 108), which is not necessarily true for the contrary:

> Pleasures may not have been given up, but they have become subordinated to the search for wisdom, as one would expect in the case of the philosopher (who is literally a 'wisdom-lover'). Hence it is possible for Socrates to represent true temperance, justice and courage as cleansing operations that sweep away hedonistic motivation, and wisdom as the cleansing agent.
>
> (p. 108)

The concept of the philosopher's life is not easy to grasp in the first place, and it seems to be an extraordinary hard way to lead a good life. Socrates, for example, who was relatively poor due to his preference for philosophy rather than making a living, was condemned to death in the end for irritating people on the streets and supposedly misleading the youths.

Therefore, it is necessary to ask what relevance Socrates' philosophy has for an educational approach to the art of living, apart from drawing attention to the question of how to live a good life in the first place. Various points can be noted here: he points out that a good life is not defined by money, reputation or status; instead, he emphasises *areté* – virtue and (self-) perfection, which links to Schmid's understanding of an art of living as will be discussed in Chapter 5. Additionally, the three aspects of a philosopher's life – overcome pleasures of the body, desiring death and philosopher's virtue – can provide important insights for personal well-being and happiness, and they are surprisingly similar to recommendations made by later philosophers and psychologists, as will unfold in the course of this book.

Hedonism – Epicurus

Roughly one century after Socrates, Epicurus proposed one of the most discussed theories of a good life: *hedonism*. Fred Feldman (2004), for example, argues for *pleasure* as the natural basis for a good life. His arguments about the pro and contra of hedonism and a pleasurable life will not be repeated here – this is much better done by Feldman himself – but his concluding formulation of an attitudinal hedonism, which, according to Feldman, resolves most of the criticism towards hedonism, needs to be briefly commented on. Feldman (2004) claims, in an Epicurean fashion, that human beings are mainly driven by the wish for a pleasant life and the avoidance of pain. Parallels in formulation to Aristotle's notion of *eudaimonia* (happiness) as the utmost goal for human beings are not accidental. Indeed, the interpretation of pleasures as *attitudinal pleasures*, as proposed by Feldman, seems to bridge the gap between these two concepts to some extent.

According to Feldman, one of the main reasons for objections against hedonism is a missing clarification of terms and subsequent misunderstandings. This includes the distinction between *sensational* and *attitudinal* hedonism: sensational hedonism, according to Feldman, is based on bodily (sensational) pleasures, whereas attitudinal hedonism builds on higher pleasures, which Feldman also calls attitudinal pleasures.[8]

Feldman argues that most criticism towards hedonism aims at formulations of sensational hedonism, whereas attitudinal hedonism is mostly unaffected. A review of Epicurean philosophy (see later) indicates that Epicurus himself was aware of different qualities of pleasure and indeed favoured a form of higher pleasures similar to Feldman's attitudinal pleasures. However, Epicurus' angle of pain avoidance is not necessarily a technique in line with Aristotle's ideas.

Long (2006) summarises Epicurean philosophy as follows:

> The essential message of Epicurean ethics, and indeed of Epicurus' entire philosophy, was encapsulated in the 'fourfold remedy' (*tetrapharmakos*): 'God presents no fears, death no worries. And while good is readily attainable, bad is readily endurable.' (Philodemus, *Adv. soph.* col. 4,9–14 = LS 25J) Incorporating, as it does, the first four of Epicurus' *Key doctrines (Kuriai doxai)*, the fourfold remedy is a panacea for unhappiness. Repeated and memorized by Epicurean disciples, it was intended to remind them that supreme happiness was available at any time, provided that they wholeheartedly endorse and base their life upon the practical implications of its four propositions.
>
> (p. 178)

The basic core of Epicurean philosophy is the avoidance of pain and, with it, the maximisation of pleasure. This is important, as, for him, one's own happiness is the utmost goal for human beings. "His ethics, in essence, is a system of educating people in the means by which they can secure a whole lifetime in which pleasurable experience of body and mind predominates over pain" (Long 2006, 187). To live such a life in happiness, only a few external requirements are necessary in addition to the right state of mind, which Epicurus focuses on in his ethics.[9] These requirements are generally peaceful living circumstances and the funds or income to satisfy one's bodily and necessary desires, such as food, drink, shelter and companionship.[10] Epicurus did not believe in excessive physical and sensational experiences, but in an intelligent and educated mind, which is capable of making the right choice in terms of pleasures:

> The function of ethics [for Epicurus] – and in fact of the whole of philosophy – is rather to give *everyone* a chance to morally improve; that is, a chance to understand that in order to reach true happiness, one has to learn to distinguish between pleasures conducive to that end and pleasures distracting from it; and in the course of this, to give up prejudicial and irrational beliefs which one has unthinkingly absorbed from the social surroundings one lives in.
> (Bobzien 2006, 229)

Epicurus noticed that people who fulfil the basic requirements and experience an external environment that supports a pleasurable life could still fail to reach this goal. According to Long (2006), he concludes that

> the impediment must be internal. On Epicurus' diagnosis, the internal impediments can be reduced to two factors: irrational fears and vain, and unlimited desires. Fear of death and fear of the gods, he proposes, can be dispelled by argument. As for frustrated desires, they are caused by a misunderstanding of the limited range of wants we need to satisfy in order to be happy, the failure to make proper use of the materials available to satisfy the necessary desires, and the false supposition that pleasure or happiness can be increased beyond removal of pain and anxiety.
> (p. 187)

To overcome these limiting internal factors is to cultivate the virtue of *prudence* and *practical wisdom*, which is also the key to a pleasant life. The notion of practical wisdom is also addressed in Aristotle's *Nicomachean Ethics*, and it plays a key role in Schmid's ethical considerations for an art of living in a self-regulating function, not unlike Epicurus' considerations. For Epicurus, practical wisdom together with the fourfold remedy is more important than philosophy itself, as practical wisdom directly leads to a good and pleasant life. This stands in huge contrast to Socrates, for whom the achievement of *areté* is the utmost goal for human beings, whereas Epicurus demotes virtues only to be a tool to achieve pleasure and happiness. Still, Epicurus considers an ethical life as a necessity for pleasure in life. For him, all virtues are linked and practical wisdom is the source for all other virtues. Thus, a commitment to virtues is essential for experiencing pleasures; a good life in the Epicurean understanding is always a moral one (Long 2006, 188–9).

In summary, Epicurus essentially proposed an easy life in an environment that is capable of satisfying people's basic needs and desires. His main point was to develop a satisfactory state of mind, overcome unwanted physical desires and wisely choose the right pleasures in life. All other external circumstances, for example, friendly neighbours or living in peaceful times, are just additional support to gain pleasure, but they are not essential. It is helpful, however, for one's own happiness to help one's neighbours and to lead an ethical and pleasurable life, as this supports one's own experience of pleasure in life. Epicurus also pointed out that an involvement in politics and in court influences the balance between pleasure and pain in a negative way. He did not claim that it is impossible to have a most pleasurable life while one is involved in politics and matters of state, but in his judgement it seemed most unlikely.

Hedonism today

At this point, to provide a better understanding of different hedonistic concepts, Feldman's (2004) distinction between *sensory* and *attitudinal hedonism* will be discussed in more detail. In his book *Pleasure and the Good Life*, Feldman introduces definitions for both sensory and attitudinal hedonism in quite similar ways. A slight change in wording, however, alters the focus of his theory and makes it more robust in terms of the usual critique.

The difference is that his definition of attitudinal hedonism focuses on the experience of internal pleasure towards an affair, not simply the experience of sensory pleasure. Although his formulation includes sensory experiences of pleasure and pain, as these experiences often inflict an attitudinal response, it is not limited to them. In fact, he shows that attitudinal pleasure and pain can be totally distinguished from sensational pleasure and pain.

To illustrate this, he imagines the life of a character named Stoicus, who wants to lead a life in peace without any ups and downs of sensational pleasure and pain; Feldman then assumes that Stoicus somehow manages to lead exactly this kind of life. In a pure sensational theory of hedonism, Stoicus' life would have no value at all, neither good or bad – it would be without value. But Feldman assumes that Stoicus might have experienced some internal, attitudinal pleasure through the fact that he managed to get what he wanted and lead a life without disrupting ups and downs. He further assumes that Stoicus may actually enjoy episodes of peace and quietness without any immediate sensational pleasure. Therefore, according to the theory of attitudinal hedonism, his life has a positive value. As he gets what he wants and values, he has a good life in his own opinion, and, thus, his life has value.

With *intrinsic attitudinal hedonism*, Feldman formulates a theory of hedonism that is unaffected by most, if not all, objections towards hedonism.[11] He states the basic principles of his theory as follows:

i   Every episode of intrinsic attitudinal pleasure is intrinsically good; every episode of intrinsic attitudinal pain is intrinsically bad.
ii The intrinsic value of an episode of intrinsic attitudinal pleasure is equal to the amount of pleasure contained in that episode; the intrinsic value of an

episode of intrinsic attitudinal pain is equal to the amount of pain contained in that episode.

iii The intrinsic value of a life is entirely determined by the intrinsic values of the episodes of intrinsic attitudinal pleasure and pain contained in the life, in such a way that one life is intrinsically better than another if and only if the net amount of intrinsic attitudinal pleasure in the one is greater than the net amount of that sort of pleasure in the other. (p. 66, italics removed)

To avoid misunderstandings of this definition it is important to keep in mind that the terms *good* and *bad* are always in the meaning of *good for the individual* and *bad for the individual*. They are not meant to be read in a morally or generalised way of "good or bad for everybody" or "good or bad at all". Hence, Feldman formulates

> a form of *universal* attitudinal hedonism. That is, it is a theory according to which every episode of intrinsic attitudinal pleasure is good in itself. [. . . Intrinsic attitudinal hedonism] is also a form of *pure* attitudinal hedonism, since it implies that attitudinal pleasures and pains are the only things that contribute in the most fundamental way to the value of a life.
>
> (p. 66)

However, essential for an educational art of living concept (with regard to hedonism) is that the wish to lead a pleasant life and avoid pain as much as possible is a basic drive for human beings and needs to be considered in a concept of a good life. Also, it is important to understand the differences between sensational and attitudinal pleasures and their significance for happiness. As Feldman pointed out, a good life cannot be determined by sensational pleasures, but, more importantly, it is closely related to episodes of attitudinal pleasures. And, as the definition of a good life in this context implies, attitudinal pleasures are always based on and caused by the individual's own feelings, beliefs and judgements, which resonates well with Schmid's notion of a *beautiful life* based on the personal taste and judgement of each individual, as will be discussed later on.

A distinction between various forms of emotions and the role of attitudinal (or higher) pleasures in relation to enjoyments and their impact on one's overall well-being and happiness in life can be found in Chapter 3.

Eudaimonia – *Aristotle*

In book one of the *Nicomachean Ethics* (n.d./1996; n.d./2002), Aristotle discusses the nature of "good" and the highest "good" for, and aim of, human beings. He states that *eudaimonia*, often translated as happiness or being happy, is commonly agreed on to be the aim and utmost goal of human beings (1095a15–20). However, he continues to argue that what happiness actually is, the nature of happiness, is not as easily agreed upon.

As happiness has various interpretations today (see Section 3.3), and the translation of happiness for *eudaimonia* does not reflect the concept entirely, Aristotle's original term will be used in this section to discuss his theory.

Aristotle's reasoning for *eudaimonia* being the highest good and utmost goal of human beings is based on the argument that *eudaimonia* is the only concept that is pursued for no other reason than for itself. All other aims – virtues, knowledge, wisdom, pleasures and so on – although pursued intrinsically as well, are mainly perceived as a means to achieve *eudaimonia*:

> And happiness [*eudaimonia*] seems to be of this sort most of all, since we choose this always on account of itself and never on account of anything else, while we choose honor and pleasure and intelligence and every virtue indeed on account of themselves (for even if nothing resulted from them we would choose each of them), but we choose them also for the sake of happiness, supposing that we will be happy by these means. But no one chooses happiness for the sake of these things, nor for the sake of anything else at all.
> (1097b1–8)

Similarly, Aristotle considered *eudaimonia* in terms of self-sufficiency and completeness (which was for him the highest possible form of "good") and concluded that it "appears to be something complete and self-sufficient, and is, therefore, the end of actions" (1097b20–21).

In terms of the nature of *eudaimonia* and how it comes to pass, he argues (1097b22–1098a20) it to be the innate purpose of human beings, the same as making shoes is the purpose of a cobbler and similar. To reach and experience *eudaimonia*, one has to engage in a "being-at-work of the soul" (1098b15) in accord with *areté* [virtues]. As discussed earlier, *areté* not only means virtues, but also perfection and success. An active shaping of one's own soul, one's self, towards virtuous perfection will, therefore, provide a life of *eudaimonia*. This concept of actively shaping one's own self will be revisited by later philosophers of the art of living, such as Foucault (1984) and Schmid (2000a; Schmid 2000b). Similar to Foucault and Schmid, Aristotle (1098a19–20) points out that this process of being-at-work of the soul is a lifelong process and not a goal to reach and be done with.

To be more concrete in terms of what "being-at-work of the soul" means, he refers to concepts that are claimed to be related to *eudaimonia*, partly by general consensus, partly by individuals of high regard:

> And it appears that all the things that are looked for concerning happiness are present in what was said. For to some people it seems to be virtue, to others practical judgment, and to others some sort of wisdom, while to others it seems to be all or some of these combined with pleasure, or not without pleasure, while others include external abundance alongside these.
> (1098b26–30)

Virtues, prudence (or practical judgement) and some "sort of wisdom" seem to build the core of a life in *eudaimonia*. To be able to shape one's own self in this

18 *Philosophical concepts of art of living*

way, however, Aristotle acknowledges that certain external circumstances need to be met. These are not necessarily a life in abundance, but at least a life that caters for one's basic needs in terms of shelter, food, friendship and the like.

In book ten of the *Nicomachean Ethics*, Aristotle discusses the role of pleasures. Similar to Epicurus and Feldman, Aristotle distinguishes between bodily and higher pleasures (1173a1–1174a17). The former are pleasures that are directly connected to our senses and that fill a gap or a need, such as food or contact to other people. Higher pleasures are described as enjoyments on an intellectual level, such as the enjoyment of poetry or music. However, although Aristotle concedes that human beings pursue pleasures out of instinct, similar to lower animals, pleasures are not identical to *eudaimonia*; they can be rather considered as one possible aspect of a life of happiness in Aristotle's sense. It needs to be mentioned here, however, that pleasures in themselves are neither morally good nor bad, but, as Aristotle argues (1172a19–1173a1), it depends on the morality of the action taken from which pleasure is derived. Hence, if a person takes pleasure by acting in an unethical way, the pleasure would be considered morally bad as well, whereas pleasure derived from a virtuous or morally appropriate action would be considered to be good.

So the question remains what constitutes *eudaimonia* and a life of utmost happiness for Aristotle. He argues that *eudaimonia* transcends a life of virtue, but that a life of *eudaimonia* has to be a virtuous life in the first place. He concedes that pleasures, as mentioned earlier, are pursued by human beings and play a role for a happy life, as morally good pleasures will make a life more amenable than without. However, the most relevant aspect of a life of *eudaimonia*, which also separates humans from lower animals, is *contemplation* (1176b34–1177a25). For Aristotle, the human intellect is humans' highest ability, and to pursue *eudaimonia* would mean to engage in contemplation, which also resonates with wisdom.

To summarise, according to Aristotle, human beings strive for *eudaimonia* as the utmost goal in life, which is pursued for its own sake and not for any other purpose. However, to achieve *eudaimonia*, a person's basic needs have to be met, one needs to live according to the virtues, and (morally good) pleasures, especially higher pleasures, will support a life of happiness. In addition, schooling one's intellect through the activity of contemplation to attain wisdom is necessary to reach this highest form of happiness. Again, Aristotle's contemplations here resonate significantly with the positions of other philosophers of the art of living as discussed in this book.

The morally good life – Kant

A different approach to living a good life was taken by Kant (1997), although some parallels can be found in the notion of virtue as described in Aristotle's (n.d./1996; n.d./2002) *Nicomachean Ethics*. Kant's interpretation of a good life, which he outlined in his *Groundwork of the Metaphysics of Morals*, will only be described briefly at this point, as his approach is mainly relevant for the ethical aspects of the art of living, as discussed in Section 5.3, and not so much for the concept of a good life as understood in this book.

Kant's definition of the *good life* is a life that is guided by *a good will* or *good intentions*. A crucial aspect in his philosophy is the intention one has, not the outcome of one's actions. Human beings can only influence, and are responsible for, their intentions to take action; the outcome is dependent on external circumstances one has no control over. This concept allows for human error and is liberating in a way, as it does not place sole responsibility for the outcome of one's action on the individual, but it expects human beings to have ethically right intentions and act upon these intentions. Kant's point is that a good life can only be an ethical one, and to live such a life one has to always follow the rational mind on the basis of the *categorical imperative*, which is to "act only in accordance with that maxim through which you can at the same time will that it become a universal law" (Kant 1997, 31, AK 4:421). The categorical imperative, hence, requires each individual to think through, as much as possible, all consequences of one's actions and consider a world in which every human being faced with a similar situation would act in the same way and what this would mean for the world we are living in and the interactions between human beings. If such a world would be desirable, the action would fulfil the categorical imperative and would be the ethically right one to choose. It needs to be said here that Kant's categorical imperative is different from the often referred to "golden rule", which would require each individual to act in a way as he or she would like (!) others to act in a similar situation. The golden rule is therefore guided by personal desire or personal preference; the categorical imperative is based on rational considerations.

So, to summarise, to life a good life based on Kant's *Metaphysics* means to always intend to act in line with the categorical imperative; if the outcome of one's actions is then in the end matching what one intended is not relevant, as our intent counts for Kant, not the result. However, Kant also distinguishes between actions that align with our desires and wishes and actions that we perform out of *duty*. An action that aligns with the categorical imperative but also matches our desires and wants is not considered as "morally good" in Kant's understanding; an action that follows Kant's categorical imperative but that we do not want to do out of our own motivation but because it is the *"right thing to do"* is to act out of duty, which Kant would consider morally good. Hence, if one's intentions are morally right, as defined by Kant's categorical imperative, if they are morally "good", depends on one's desires. According to Kant, a decision or action is only morally good if it is in line with the categorical imperative *and* if one acts in this way out of "duty", not on the grounds of one's own desires.

Kant's position that only a life of duty can be a good one seems to be an extreme one, and it partly contradicts earlier concepts of the good life. It is also based on an interpretation of "good" from a purely ethical point of view and could be considered impractical as human beings in real-life situations have hardly the time or capacity to think through every action and test their intentions in significant depth in line with the categorical imperative. The approach to the art of living by Schmid (2000a; Schmid 2000b), which is favoured here, seems more practical and appropriate. The concept does engage with ethical considerations, and Schmid takes into account Kant's categorical imperative; the understanding of how to lead a good life, on the other hand, is quite different. However, developing an art of living based on Schmid's concept will entail the development of an ethics model and an understanding of right and wrong that builds on Aristotle's notion of *phronesis* [prudence and practical wisdom].

The care of the self – Foucault

In recent philosophic history, Foucault (1984) approaches the topic of the good life in volume three of his late work, *The History of Sexuality*, which is titled *The Care of the Self*. In his contemplations about the aspects of human life that are part of our sexuality, he includes an investigation about attitudes towards pleasures and a philosophical approach to the "cultivation of the self" and the "care of oneself" (p. 44). Foucault focuses his approach towards aspects of living a good life on ancient Greek and Roman philosophy, as does Schmid (2000a), who continues Foucault's work in this area. For Foucault (1984), the care of the self is the starting point of an art of living, as can be seen in his passage about the "development of the art of living under the theme of the care of oneself" (p. 45).

Foucault distinguishes between four aspects of the care of the self: social practice, time and labour, care for the body and self-knowledge. The first one, *social practice*, is the care of the self supported by contact with people who share the same aim of cultivating themselves. Foucault notes that a habit of talking, writing or other ways of exchange with kindred spirits is an essential element for the care of the self, as stated by neo-Pythagorean or Epicurean philosophers.

The second aspect, *time and labour*, is required "to [. . . turn] one's thoughts to oneself" (p. 50) and to develop a habit of permanent care for one's self. The notion of the care of the self has a literal and a figurative meaning, as will become apparent later. It also is an active process and has to be pursued deliberately by each individual. Moreover, time is needed for this process to develop, which makes it, in an ideal case, a lifelong process. This aspect of the care of the self is of significant importance for Schmid's concept *Lebenskunst*, as will be discussed in Chapter 5.

The third aspect, to *care for the body*, is mainly described as a "turning [of] one's thoughts to oneself" (p. 50), and it covers the elements of eating and drinking habits, medicine and general health-related behaviours.

The last dimension is *self-knowledge*. As an individual, one has to practise self-awareness by observing and monitoring oneself, to find out what has a positive or a negative influence on oneself and consequently to choose the better one, if possible. This awareness should also reveal false addictions to worldly goods and external circumstances and help the individual to let go of these addictions and expectations. It also includes observing one's own thoughts and choosing the ones that have a positive quality for one's own self, instead of thoughts with a negative impact. For Foucault, successful care of the self leads to real independence and makes the agent, or better the agent's soul and its mental self and happiness, untouchable by external influences.

Foucault's work is significant for this topic as it has been quite influential on Schmid's theory of the art of living, as stated earlier. He also focuses, more than some of the earlier thinkers considered, on the distinctiveness of the individual. Foucault points out that standards for the judgement of good or bad have to be found within the individual, not without:

> It [, the conversion to self,] is to be understood first of all as a change of activity: not that one must cease all other forms of occupation and devote oneself entirely and exclusively to oneself; but in the activities that one ought to engage in, one had best keep in mind that the chief objective one should set for oneself is *to be sought within oneself, in the relation of oneself to oneself.*
> (pp. 64–5, italics added)

This focus on the individual is a development that Schmid took even further. His whole concept of the art of living takes into account the uniqueness of each individual, as will be discussed in Chapter 5 in more detail.

Summary

In this chapter, an overview of various approaches to an art of living has been given, and it has been shown that different interpretations of living a good life have been proposed in philosophical history. All of these approaches and interpretations have their own validity; however, none of these provides an encompassing theory that is suitable for a holistic education for life concept, as will be argued for later on. Schmid's art of living concept *Lebenskunst*, on the other hand, draws on the major ideas presented in this chapter (among others) and is well suited to provide the philosophical background for such an educational theory. To understand the holistic character of Schmid's philosophy, it is important to have an understanding of the underlying philosophical concepts presented in this chapter.

Further, a first indication for the importance of living a "good life" for human beings has been given. It will be shown at various points later on that Aristotle's notion of *eudaimonia* (happiness) as the utmost goal of human striving might be a phenomenon that is consistent over time and a cross-cultural human quality.

In contrast to Kant's definition of a morally good life that emphasises rationality, the approach taken in this book strives to be more holistic. Therefore, the next chapter will provide a discussion of various emotions and their relation to developing an art of living and living a good life.

Notes

1. For the citation of Kant, references to the standardised citations based on Kant's original text are given in addition to the page references of the translation used in this book.
2. Foucault uses Seneca's vocabulary here.
3. *Foundational theory*, as a translation of the German term *Grundlegung*, is understood here as a theoretical discussion that explores the underlying ideas of a concept and provides a solid basis for all further discussion in this area.

22 Philosophical concepts of art of living

4 "Lebenskunst ist die Ernsthaftigkeit des Versuchs, [...] sich das Leben beizeiten selbst anzueignen und vielleicht sogar ein 'schönes Leben' daraus zu machen." This and all further quotes from Schmid are my translations.
5 According to Nehamas, this is discussed in "the *Protagoras* where Socrates warns the young Hippocrates, who can't wait to run to the sophist's side, not to rush to Protagoras for instruction in *areté* (313a1–314c2)" (Nehamas 1998, 79).
6 Standard referencing to Socrates' *Apology* is used here and elsewhere in this book.
7 Similar ideas will be presented later on, for example, in the philosophy of de Mello in Section 9.1.
8 The distinctions between sensational and attitudinal pleasures will be discussed in more detail in Section 3.3.
9 It will become apparent later on that Epicurus' notion of 'the right state of mind' links closely to Csikszentmihalyi's findings of 'control over consciousness' in his concept of flow.
10 Links to Maslow's pyramid of needs can be found here.
11 Due to the scope and purpose of this book, it is not feasible to repeat all objections and arguments for and against hedonism at this point. For further reading on this topic please refer to Feldman (2004).

3 Emotions and the good life

As outlined in Chapter 1, *happiness* and *well-being* are popular terms in current discussions, and both are in the focus of positive psychology research, as will be discussed in Chapter 4. The understanding of these and other emotions, however, and their relevance for concepts of a good life are quite different in philosophical and psychological contexts. This chapter will establish a general understanding of emotions and affects and explain how certain emotions, such as happiness, pleasure, enjoyment and so on, are used in this book. Additionally, some differences in interpretation of terms between concepts will be discussed to allow for a better comparison and discussion of these concepts.

3.1 Defining feelings, emotions and affects

The field of feelings, emotions and affects is a widely researched area with various definitions, depending on research discipline and focus. Differences in definition exist not only between the humanities, the social and the behavioural sciences, but also *within* these fields (Loewenstein 2007; Scherer 2005). Scherer, as one example from a psychological tradition, defines emotion as "an episode of interrelated, synchronized changes in the states of all or most of the five organismic subsystems in response to the evaluation of an external or internal stimulus event as relevant to major concerns of the organism" (p. 697, italics removed). The five emotional components, according to Scherer, are a cognitive component (appraisal), a neurophysiological component (bodily symptoms), a motivational component (action tendencies), a motor expression component (facial and vocal expression) and a subjective feeling component (emotional experience) (p. 698).

Scherer also explicitly distinguishes between the terms *feeling* and *emotion*, with feelings being only a part of emotions and not identical to emotions (p. 699). However, both terms have been used interchangeably in public and academic discussions, which has led to some confusion and misunderstandings in the debate about emotions and feelings (p. 699). Additionally, Scherer defines five further "affective phenomena", which are distinct from emotions: preferences, attitudes, moods, affect dispositions and interpersonal stances (pp. 703–6).

Preferences are "relatively stable evaluative judgments in the sense of liking or disliking a stimulus" (Scherer 2005, 703). They should "generate intrinsic appraisal" (p. 703) when one is confronted with a stimulus (object, statement, situation) one has a preference for. Scherer defines *attitudes* as "relatively enduring beliefs and predispositions towards specific objects or persons" (p. 703). Attitudes have a cognitive, an affective and a "motivational or behavioral component" (p. 703), where especially the latter one distinguishes them from preferences. *Moods* are generally "considered as diffuse affect states, characterized by a relative enduring predominance of certain types of subjective feelings that affect the experience and behavior of a person" (p. 705). They distinguish themselves by emerging often "without apparent cause that could be clearly linked to an event or specific appraisals" (p. 705). *Affect dispositions*, however, are internal "stable personality traits and behavior tendencies [. . . that promote] certain moods more frequently" and which can lead a person "to react with certain types of emotions, even upon slight provocation" (p. 705). Finally, *interpersonal stances* are characterised by "an *affective style* that spontaneously develops or is strategically employed in the interactions with a person or a group" (p. 705). Examples would be to employ a polite, distant or supportive manner of interaction in a conversation or other social situation.

Loewenstein (2007, 405), however, argues against Scherer's component definition of emotion and especially against feelings being a necessary component of them. He claims the component definition is somewhat "diffuse" (p. 406), as Scherer does not clarify if all components are necessary to qualify an experience as emotion, or if a combination of, for example, three or four of them can already be called an emotion. Moreover, Loewenstein claims that it is possible to be influenced by an unconscious emotion while one's attention is focused intensely on something else (an object, person or situation). Hence, Scherer's assumed definition of an emotion requiring a conscious feeling state would not apply here. Loewenstein (2007) argues for a more evolutionary psychological approach to emotions as stated, for example, by Cosmides and Tooby (2000):

> According to this definition, emotions constitute "superordinate programs" that orchestrate a concerted psycho-physiological response to recurrent situations of adaptive significance in our evolutionary past, such as fighting, falling in love, escaping predators and experiencing a loss in status. Emotions, according to this perspective, are not reducible to effects occurring in specific parts of the brain, specific feelings, motivations or appraisals, but can and typically do involve a wide array of physiological and psychological changes, including effects on perception, attention, inference, learning, motivation and physiology.
>
> (Loewenstein 2007, 406)

Loewenstein states that "a definition of emotion should *imply* . . . [Scherer's proposed] components . . . as common features of emotions" (p. 406) instead of being seen as an exclusive definition. He also advocates for a differential approach for a definition of emotions in a historical tradition that distinguishes emotions from reason or interests. The major reason for Loewenstein's tendency to favour the evolutionary approach is that it "provides a framework for understanding how emotions can, at once, support and undermine rational decision making" (p. 407). He seems to emphasise the purpose of emotions rather than the physical, neurological and psychological effects they can have, which is the focus of Scherer's component theory.

This account shows some of the theoretical difficulties of defining emotion as a concept, which reflects on the understanding, evaluation and discussion of specific emotions in academic literature in general and for the argument in this book in particular. However, noteworthy in Scherer's and Loewenstein's argument are both the distinction between feelings and emotions, and the idea that, although emotions are distinct from reason, they are still in a reciprocal relationship to each other. Emotions do have a cognitive, qualifying component as well as an impact on rational thinking and decision-making. They can also be conscious or unconscious, according to Loewenstein, which makes their impact on a decision harder to predict and measure. All these factors play a significant role in evaluating one's own life in terms of being a good and/or beautiful one.

3.2 A classification of emotions – past, present, future

At this point, a further classification of emotions is in order to better understand judgements about the good life.[1] A sensible approach has been offered by Seligman (2010, 62), who distinguishes between (positive) emotions towards the past, the present and the future. These three areas of emotions are indeed different from each other and, according to Seligman, "not necessarily tightly linked" (p. 62). As examples, he lists as emotions about the future "optimism, hope, faith, and trust"; emotions about the present include "joy, ecstasy, calm, zest, ebullience, pleasure and flow"; and, finally, "satisfaction, contentment, fulfilment, pride, and serenity" (p. 62) are examples for emotions about the past. Seligman claims that in terms of overall life happiness all three perspectives are important, but it is quite common to make different judgements about how one's life has played out so far (past), how things are at the moment (present) and what one expects the future to hold.

Although (enduring)[2] happiness is often part of people's judgement about their own life – especially if asked what they *think* a good life for them would be – it does not necessarily play a major role when looking back on one's life and judging it from the outside perspective. The latter, however, is the more important angle for considerations of the good life in the way Schmid understands the term in his art of living concept.

It seems not far-fetched to assume that one's past experiences, which colour one's judgement about one's past and the point in life one has reached – one's personal development – influence quite strongly the view one has about one's future in general terms. Where, for example, current uncertain job prospects and possible changes in life might lead to a negative judgement in expectation of one's future happiness level, long-term past experiences of "things in life generally working out" can produce much more positive emotions towards the future than if one was always struggling to make ends meet. Also, if one is able to step back and take a look at the bigger picture of one's life, one's judgement about the quality of this life might be quite different from a judgement that is made while one is preoccupied by immediate emotions and thoughts about oneself.

This is one point where the art of living deviates from positive psychology views on happiness and well-being: one has to step back not only from the current moment, but also from oneself – one needs to be self-reflective. It might be enough to consider one's current situation with a glance back and forth to decide if one has a happy life or not, but one needs to also take into account the bigger picture of one's life in total, the people one interacts with, the society one lives in and maybe even humanity on a global scale to judge whether one has lived a good and beautiful life or not. The terms and emotional concepts that are most relevant in this regard will be discussed in the following section in more detail.

3.3 Defining relevant emotional concepts

As outlined earlier, considerations about the quality of one's life can focus on three dimensions – past, present, future – and will ideally include all three perspectives. To be able to "take a step back" and look at one's own life from a distance, certain skills, including self-reflection and distancing oneself from the current moment, are needed. A judgement made by an individual about the quality of his or her own life will always be based on the norms, values and expectations this individual has. These should be, in the best case, one's own (i.e. reflected and accepted for good reason) norms, values and expectations, and these can, and will be, quite different for each individual, not only inter-culturally but also intra-culturally. However, the underlying emotions, such as satisfaction, joy, pleasure, sadness, fear and others, seem to be consistent cross-culturally and a universal part of human nature (Plutchik 2002, 127–8, 153–6). Nevertheless, depending on the context, these terms are used with different interpretations and sometimes interchangeably, which can lead to further confusion and misunderstandings. This is not surprising, as emotions seem to be situated in a continuum that spans from negative (pain, suffering) to positive (joy, happiness), and from passive (contentment, hopelessness) to active (anger, excitement), with overlaps between various emotional states (Plutchik 2002, 6–8; Solomon and Stone 2002). The terms *negative* and *positive* are here understood as the experience of an immediate emotion for an individual. If the consequence (action, personal development) of an emotion has a positive or negative impact on an individual's life in the long term is not taken into account here. As will be discussed in Section 3.5, experiences of suffering and despair can be beneficial for the personal development of an individual, and certain forms of joy and happiness can sometimes inhibit this development.

Scherer (2005) distinguishes between *utilitarian emotions*, which are "facilitating our adaption to events that have important consequences for our wellbeing", and *aesthetic emotions*, which "are produced by the appreciation of the intrinsic qualities of the beauty of nature, or the qualities of a work of art or an artistic performance" (pp. 707–8). Although Scherer's classification does not completely match the dichotomy of active and passive emotions, significant parallels indicate that his distinction is similar to Solomon and Stone's model in the dimension of an active–passive continuum. Due to the lack of consistency in philosophical and psychological literature, definitions (or descriptions) of how relevant emotional concepts are understood for the argument in this book will follow.

Sensational and attitudinal pleasures

The focus on *pleasure* in life and the concept of living a pleasurable life have been confronted with substantial objections in the past and have led to controversial discussions in philosophical history, especially in the context of *hedonism*. As discussed in Section 2.2, Feldman (2004) distinguishes between *sensational* and *attitudinal* pleasures.

Sensational pleasure, according to Feldman, means pleasure that is directly caused by sensational experiences of the body (pp. 55–6). This can, for example, be the pleasure one experiences from the sweet taste of an ice cream or the relaxed feeling after a massage. Obviously, there are major problems in the definition of a concept which proposes this kind of pleasure as the "purpose of life". Objections are also often based on exaggerated examples related to sexual pleasure and orgies, but even when keeping to a more reasonable range of everyday experiences, a concept defining the good life based on sensational pleasure is still lacking.

Attitudinal pleasure, on the other hand, as Feldman continues, is defined as the pleasure someone experiences through having favourable attitudes to a "state of affairs": to take pleasure or joy out of a fact, a situation or an episode (p. 56). This includes being pleased or delighted about something happening or coming to pass. Hence, attitudinal pleasure includes sensational pleasure, as one can experience pleasure through eating ice cream, for example, but it is not limited to it. One can, for instance, think about the last time one enjoyed ice cream and take pleasure of the recollection of this situation, or, the other way round, take pleasure in imagining, while sitting in a stuffy office on a hot day, buying a delicious ice cream later and enjoying it sitting in the garden. Thus, one can take pleasure in an affair that is not directly triggered by sensational experiences. Another example, provided by Feldman (p. 56), is to imagine being a peace-loving person. If one then becomes aware of the fact, assumed here it were true, that there are no wars in the world, one could feel pleased about this fact and draw pleasure from it. Additionally, Feldman (p. 56) points out that attitudinal pleasure can even be totally distinct from sensational pleasure: after a busy day, running around in the city and doing errands, one might, for example, enjoy sitting down in a quiet room without any noise or stimulation at all. Therefore, one can take pleasure in the absence of sensational experience or pleasure.

This distinction between sensational and attitudinal pleasure is especially important in the context of hedonism, but also in the wider context of this book. In everyday language, happiness and living a happy life is often equated with experiencing as many pleasures and amenities as possible. However, as will be discussed in Chapter 4, despite common belief, (sensational) pleasures do not have any significant lasting effect on one's enduring happiness level (i.e. overall happiness and contentment with life, in contrast to the currently experienced level of happiness).

Due to differences in terminology, it is not clear if attitudinal pleasures (Feldman 2004) are related to enjoyments in Csikszentmihalyi's (2008) interpretation (which have a significant lasting effect on enduring happiness), but they might at least bridge the gap between these two emotional concepts as they seem to have overlaps on both ends. Feldman (2004, 55–6) links attitudinal pleasure with joy and aims to defend "the claim that attitudinal pleasure is the chief good for man" (p. 57), which indicates the same direction as Csikszentmihalyi argues for with enjoyments through flow experiences. However, Seligman (2010, 104–5, 111–21) distinguishes between bodily pleasures (the same as Feldman's sensational pleasures), higher pleasures and enjoyments (or gratifications). Having said that, Seligman's examples for distinguishing between pleasures and enjoyments are similar to the ones Feldman uses to show the difference between sensational and attitudinal pleasures. The main difference seems to be that all forms of pleasure have an immediate feeling component, whereas enjoyments, according to Seligman, "are not necessarily accompanied by any raw feelings at all" (p. 102).

However, for the argument in this book the term "pleasures" will be mainly used to refer to sensational pleasures without lasting effect on one's enduring happiness level and overall well-being. Exceptions to this rule will be pointed out where they occur.

Happiness and eudaimonia

The expressions *being happy* and *happiness* are not unproblematic either, as they are increasingly used in public and academic discussions in different contexts and as labels for different emotional phenomena. This often misleads people to give happiness a much more important role in their lives than would be necessary or realistic. At least in academia, happiness itself, as well as its value, is contested. However, in a study about the art of living and the good life, one has to engage with happiness, as it is certainly one important aspect of human life.

Two of the phenomena that are often labelled as happiness are *momentary happiness* and *enduring happiness*.[3] Momentary happiness is understood as the emotion one experiences, for example, after a great and successful day; after one received very positive news and the initial feelings of joy and excitement subside and make space for a more serene feeling; or in the company of good friends in a safe and pleasant environment. Momentary happiness is related to contentment, but is not the same. People often describe this emotion as "feeling happy" or "being happy": "I am very happy right now." Momentary happiness can be distinguished from joy, as indicated earlier, through a more serene quality, less excitement and the reflection on a certain period of time – which can be a couple of hours, a day or a few weeks. Emotions like joy and enjoyment, as will be discussed later, are more immediately experienced emotions. However, momentary happiness is also relatively short lived and can be ended quickly by various events, such as bad news or by focusing one's attention on a different task.

The second phenomenon, enduring happiness, is an emotion that can be described as having a higher cognitive component and a reduced feeling component[4] compared with momentary happiness. It is based on an evaluation of one's life as a whole – past, present and expected future taken into account – which explains the stronger rational aspect and a certain detachment from actual feelings, as one has to take a mental step back from oneself and one's life to reflect on the big picture. Interestingly, in the German language a more explicit distinction is made between these two forms of happiness: momentary happiness would similarly be expressed as *glücklich sein* [being happy]; however, enduring happiness would be described as a *glückliches (und zufriedenes) Leben* [happy (and content) life]. The latter could also be called *Glück* [happiness], although it is less commonly used in this context and has a slightly different connotation.

Seligman (2010, 102, 112) argues, from a positive psychology perspective, that enduring happiness is increased through enjoyments (or gratifications, as he calls them), which he claims are similar to Aristotle's idea of *eudaimonia*. Even so, as will be discussed in Chapter 4, enjoyments have indeed a positive influence on one's enduring happiness level, but they are quite different from the concept of *eudaimonia*. Wolfgang Müller-Commichau (2007), for example, translates *eudaimonia* as *Glückseligkeit* [felicitousness]: a person who has reached a state of *eudaimonia* can be identified through a general mental state of *gelassene Heiterkeit* [serene happiness] (p. 7). According to Aristotle (n.d./1996, 1095a15–20), *eudaimonia* is the utmost goal of human beings and the driving factor for all our striving, as has been discussed in Chapter 2. However, which decisions and actions actually lead to the experience of *eudaimonia* is not so easy to determine, and, according to Schwartz (2004),[5] people are surprisingly poor at predicting the impact of an action on their own well-being and happiness.

This third form of happiness, *eudaimonia*, is related to enduring happiness, as higher levels of enduring happiness are certainly beneficial for entering a general mental state of serene happiness. High levels of enduring happiness might even be a necessary condition for reaching a state of *eudaimonia*, although a reversed direction of causality can be imagined as well. However, these concepts are not synonymous with each other, as experiencing enduring happiness requires a cognitive effort of self-reflection, whereas serene happiness describes a more permanent attitude to life in general.

Joy and enjoyments

As indicated earlier, *joy* is an immediate feeling that is caused mostly by an object, a person or a situation. It can last longer than the actual cause is present, which distinguishes joy from pleasure (especially sensational pleasure); however, it is more immediate and reflexive, instead of reflective, than momentary happiness. It is likely that joy describes the same feeling that Feldman (2004) attributes to attitudinal pleasure, although some uncertainty remains due to differences in terminology. However, although the feeling of joy is related to the experience of enjoyment, as defined later, there are subtle differences: joy can be experienced during and shortly after a joyful episode; enjoyment, on the other hand, is an experience that occurs *after an episode of flow* (see Section 4.5).

The understanding of *enjoyments* in this book will follow Csikszentmihalyi's definition: "Enjoyable events occur when a person has not only met some prior expectation or satisfied a need or a desire but also achieved something unexpected, perhaps something even unimagined before" (Csikszentmihalyi 2008, 46). For Csikszentmihalyi, enjoyments are characterised "by a sense of novelty, of accomplishment" (p. 46), which is created mainly through the experience of flow. According to Seligman (2010), enjoyments can occur without any "raw feelings" at all, or even be accompanied by feelings of exhaustion and tiredness due to the intense engagement with a task during the episode of flow (p. 102). Nevertheless, enjoyments, as will be discussed in Chapter 4, have a lasting positive effect on one's enduring happiness level, in contrast to mere pleasures, as noted before.

Satisfaction and contentment

Satisfaction and contentment are both emotions about the past, but they are distinguished by the scope of meaning. *Satisfaction*, as understood here, is an emotion that occurs as a consequence of fulfilled expectations or desires, mainly in a short-term context. One can, for example, have the expectation to do a good job on a task at hand and feel satisfied when one finishes this task successfully. Or one expects to get a certain item or to buy something for a certain price and experience satisfaction once these expectations are met. Satisfaction is a rather short-term emotion, similar to pleasure, and connected to expectations and desires at hand.

Contentment, on the other hand, is more closely related to enduring happiness and describes an emotion one has towards one's life as a whole. It is not triggered by fulfilment of immediate desires and expectations, but by an emotion one experiences when one is reflecting upon one's own life and is content with one's overall achievements and the direction of it. In the context of the art of living, contentment is the more significant emotion, as it relates to one's life in general.

However, this distinction is not a universal one, and other authors and disciplines use these two terms interchangeably. In positive psychology, for example, it is quite common to use phrases such as "satisfaction with life" or "life satisfaction" to refer to what I define as contentment here.

Well-being and subjective well-being

Well-being is, similarly to happiness, used more and more in current public and academic discussions; its meaning, however, is as diverse as happiness or the notion of a good life itself. According to Soutter, Gilmore and O'Steen (2011), well-being research has been conducted in areas "including economics, sociology, psychology, the health sciences and education" (p. 592), which each have their own – at least one if not many – definitions of well-being.

In the philosophical domain, well-being has been interpreted either in the tradition of hedonism (pleasures) or *eudaimonia* (happiness), and sometimes even as a mix of both. Soutter et al. refer to Nussbaum and Sen's (1993) capability approach as one example of an interpretation of well-being in the *eudaimonic* tradition:

> Nussbaum (2000) draws upon the Aristotelian notion of the good life to specify ten universal elements of well-being: life; bodily health; bodily integrity; senses, imagination and thought; emotions; practical reason; affiliation; other species; play; control over one's environment (political and material).
> (Soutter, Gilmore, and O'Steen 2011, 593);
> cf. (Nussbaum 2000, 78–80)

Positive psychology, on the other hand, often uses the term *subjective well-being*, which is based on philosophical considerations of well-being, but is also defined through what is actually measurable with quantitative research methods. Such an approach is not unproblematic as this practical limitation affects the definition of this term and makes it appear as if this is all there is to well-being. In this context, according to Soutter et al., "well-being is often interpreted in terms of life satisfaction, quality of life, happiness and subjective well-being" (p. 594, italics removed).

In education, the term well-being "appears in curriculum documents and frames mission statements of education associations worldwide" (p. 599). Among these are, for example, the New Zealand Health curriculum (Ministry of Education 2007), the Curriculum for Excellence Scotland (Education Scotland n.d./2013), and the UK Qualifications and Curriculum Development Authority (2012). However, due to the diverse interpretations of well-being, "it remains unclear how, to what extent, or even if, high school students' educational experiences relate to it [well-being] in today's schools" (Soutter, Gilmore, and O'Steen 2011, 599).

For the discussion in this book, (subjective) well-being will mainly be used in the discussion of psychological concepts and will therefore follow a positive psychological interpretation of this term. It needs to be noted that well-being, as understood here, is *not* synonymous with happiness, *eudaimonia* or notions of the good life (see later).

3.4 Positive and negative emotions

So far, the focus has been on emotions that could be categorised as "positive". Reasons for this focus are that (a) discussions about the good life, the art of living and enduring happiness are mainly concerned with the terms noted earlier; (b) immediate "negative" emotions are less likely to increase one's quality of life; and (c) most emotions are situated on a continuum with two extremes, which means that a definition of one end of the continuum – pleasure, for example – is sufficient to define the other extreme – pain – as the opposite.

The antonyms to the emotions discussed so far are sensational pleasure–pain; attitudinal pleasure–displeasure; joy–sadness; satisfaction–dissatisfaction or disappointment; contentment–discontentment; and happiness–unhappiness. Well-being, although spanning a continuum as well with different levels of well-being, seems to have no appropriate antonym – at least none that would be used in public or academic discussions.[6] The concept of *eudaimonia* as it is understood here neither has an antonym, nor is it part of a continuum – either one is in a state of *eudaimonia* and has an overall attitude of serene happiness towards life, or one does not. In this sense, *eudaimonia* is not an emotion as much as an attitude. However, as one can change one's attitudes, similarly one can lose or exit the state of *eudaimonia* if one does not take proper care of one's self (see Sections 2.2 and 5.4).

In this context, it is also necessary to reflect upon what is meant by "positive" and "negative" emotions. According to Solomon and Stone (2002), emotions in philosophical literature have been discussed in terms of "good and bad, right and wrong, and virtue and vice [, which] are by no means on the same moral scale" (p. 419). Solomon and Stone summarise the first dimension (good and bad) to be about "satisfaction of needs and desires;" the second (right and wrong) to "have to do with obeying certain impersonal (universal) rules or principles[;] while virtue and vice [, the third dimension,] are attributes of personal character" (p. 419). Although the ethical dimension of right and wrong is an important consideration in the concept of the art of living, the distinction between positive and negative emotions in this context is based on the first dimension: *whether an emotion has a positive or negative impact on one's overall happiness and contentment with life*. The other two dimensions, ethics and character, might be of more significance in the context of the good life and the art of living, but this is up to each individual to decide for himself or herself. On the other hand, distinctions between positive and negative emotions are generally less important in Schmid's art of living concept than they are for positive psychology research and the pursuit of happiness.

Judgements about which emotions might be "good" or "bad" for oneself are not straightforward. Fear, for example, can be quite negative for one's happiness level – especially when one lives a life of constant fears; however, if this emotion prevents us from getting harmed in a certain situation, it might have a quite positive impact on our health and well-being. Also, which emotions are experienced as positive and enhancing for one's level of happiness is subject to the culture one is socialised in (Solomon and Stone 2002). Nevertheless, some emotions – for example, enjoyment – seem to be universal in contributing positively to one's level of enduring happiness (Csikszentmihalyi 2008, 48–9). Enjoyments that derive from flow experiences would be considered positive emotions in this context, although they might be accompanied by immediate feelings of exhaustion and tiredness.

Also, as indicated earlier, it must be said that happiness – especially in the common understanding of being in a joyful state of mind – is not central for living a good life. On the contrary, a life without much happiness can still be a good life in the judgement of the individual living it (see Section 3.6 for more details). In the same way, a high level of enduring happiness and achieving a state of *eudaimonia* does not prevent one from experiencing the full scale of emotions, positive and negative. As Mello (1992) points out, being "awake" and having reached happiness (in the meaning of *eudaimonia*) in life does not mean one does not experience short-lived emotions, such as sadness, suffering, anger and so on. However, the overall quality of one's life is different, which will change the way one is able to cope with these emotional episodes. Still, even the happiest person will encounter negative emotions and even experience suffering and despair, which can have a positive impact as well in terms of living a good life. The next section will argue this point in more detail.

3.5 Suffering and despair

There are at least two reasons why suffering and despair are important in the context of living a good life and education: both are part of human life and human experience as such, and, according to Peter Roberts (2013), education can also lead to, and enhance, despair and suffering for students.

Suffering, like despair, is mainly understood here as emotional suffering instead of suffering bodily pain. Although suffering pain clearly affects one's level of wellbeing, these episodes are often short lived and less influential on one's overall enduring happiness level and quality of life. An exception is chronic pain, which can have a similar impact on one's overall level of happiness and well-being as does persistent mental-emotional suffering. The latter form refers to emotional states of dissatisfaction and suffering due to existing or perceived injustice towards oneself or someone or something one cares about, perceived personal deficiency or similar causes. Some examples in a schooling context could be receiving bad marks, rejection from teachers or fellow pupils or being a victim of bullying in any kind of way. Continuing suffering in this sense can lead to despair with all its consequences.

Roberts (2013) argues that despair is commonly "seen as the very anti-thesis of happiness, and education [. . . is] regarded as a means to lift us from this profound form of unhappiness to a more desirable state of mind" (p. 2). Despair is perceived, especially in the current time where happiness is taking a predominant position, as an illness that is temporary and needs to be fixed. The aim is to be "happy" again. However, Roberts (p. 2) argues further that, "contrary to the spirit of our age, [. . .] apparent happiness can be dehumanising. To be educated is, in part, to be aware of one's despair, accepting of it, and able to work productively with it." The function of education is, according to Roberts, not to rid oneself of despair, but to accept it to a certain extent and to work with it. Roberts shows, based on examples from Dostoevsky, Kierkegaard, Unamuno and others, "that to be human is to suffer – to experience despair" (p. 9).

This notion of suffering and despair being part of human life, and the necessity to accept and work with it, is closely related to de Mello's (1992) notion of *awakening*. De Mello claims, as will be discussed in Section 9.1, that there are only two ways to "wake up", as he calls it: the one is awareness paired with (self-)reflection, and the other is suffering enough to finally cross the line where "enough is enough" – the line of despair, where one finally develops and shapes one's own life and thinking in a healthier, more refined direction. In this reading, suffering and despair have an educational function, as they provide the need and motivation for personal change and development. A person being completely happy has no motivation to change anything; intentional change and development in human beings only happen through need.

An education for the art of living, as will be developed in the course of this book, can provide some support for this change and development to happen. It can also help in utilising one's suffering and despair and shaping one's own life to be a good one – despite, or rather because of, suffering and despair in one's own life. Along these lines and beyond, Roberts (2013) argues "that despair need not be seen [as] an aberrant state from which we should seek to escape; rather, it is a key element of any well lived human life. Education [. . .] is meant to create a state of discomfort, and to this extent may also make us unhappy, but is all the more important for that" (p. 2). Some knowledge and insights about the world we are living in, gained through educational processes and reflection, can make us aware of misconceptions and injustice in a way that leads to personal unhappiness, suffering and despair. Therefore, educationists have, and always have had, a responsibility for their students, as their actions affect their students' well-being.

Is this reason enough to *not* educate people? The answer to this question must clearly be "no", as education (in the wider sense of the world) is not ever on its own responsible for "the wrong" in the world, but only opens one's eye and one's mind to recognise it. It does, however, create a necessity for each individual to take responsibility for his or her actions and to take steps towards the betterment of humankind and the world (see Section 8). In addition, as argued earlier, despair can lead to personal growth and development and be a motivational factor for change. The important part for educationists is to be aware of these interconnections and to help the student not only to see the difficulties, but also develop the skills needed for change and development – to become more fully human. The role of education and suffering will be addressed again in Section 9.1.

3.6 The good life

Emotions in general play a significant role in the art of living and most concepts of a good life. However, although people often assume that especially happiness and/or pleasures are an important part of it, this is not necessarily the case. Feldman (2004, 8–9), for example, identifies at least five different approaches to a definition of a good life: a *morally*, a *beneficially*, a *biologically*, an *aesthetically*, and an *individually* good life. Beyond Feldman's classification, Gadamer (1978) explores the question of *the idea of the good* in a broader philosophical context. Gadamer analyses the works of Plato, Aristotle and Kant to shed some light on what "the good" might mean for human beings. He indicates that what is truly good cannot be learned, but needs to be discovered in each situation by the individuals involved. However, drawing on Plato, he suggests that *the good* has to be seen in the context of being good for an individual's life. For a person to be able to unravel what is good, however, Gadamer points to *phronesis* (practical wisdom) as the most important faculty. As will be seen later on, practical wisdom is also an integral part for Schmid's concept of the art of living and for developing one's own good and beautiful life. Unfortunately, the scope of this book does not allow me to explore Gadamer's considerations about *the idea of the good* to their full extent. Therefore, the more tangible interpretations of *a good life* as proposed by Feldman will be discussed later, which will be sufficient to point out the difficulties of employing the term *a good life* in the first place and to indicate the range of different interpretations that are possible.

The moral approach to a good life is defined as a life that is lived according to the law and in concordance with the norms and values of the present culture and society. It is a life that is guided by the ethical question of *right or wrong* and commonly considered "good", when the amount of "right" decisions and actions significantly outweigh the "wrong" ones. One could also call this a *virtuous life*. Feldman (pp. 8–9) proposes Mother Teresa as a possible example for a morally good life, and in philosophical literature, this line of interpretation is mainly represented in the Kantian and Aristotelian tradition.

The outcome-based interpretation of a good life focuses on the question if the life being considered has been *beneficial*, taking into account all actions and consequences of these actions. Beneficial can hereby mean either for the individual himself or herself, for the people and society the person in question is affiliated with or both – it depends on who is making the judgement on this basis. Feldman (2004, 9) proposes the outside position of this approach: a life is a good one when it is beneficial for other people or society as a whole.

Feldman's third interpretation, the biological view, basically judges a life by a predefined "human nature" on the basis of our biological condition (p. 9). A good life is, therefore, one where one lives in harmony with one's biological human nature. Especially in light of post-humanistic critique, this approach would be not unproblematic. However, for the argument in this book, this view is of little relevance and will not be discussed in further detail.

An *aesthetically* good life can be, for example, a life with an exceptional biography. Feldman refers to the literary figure of "King Lear, [who] we might think [. . .] had an aesthetically outstanding life [. . .,] but a life that was less than ideal for him" (p. 9). It would be a life that, from an outside perspective, could be seen as a work of art – a *beautiful life*. I will show later on that Schmid (2000a; Schmid 2000b) refers to the term "beautiful life" in his concept of the art of living; however, his interpretation is based on the *inside perspective of the individual* living the life in question. Schmid proposes a combination of an aesthetic and an individual approach to the good life.

The individual perspective is Feldman's (2004) fifth interpretation, and he defines a good life in this reading as "the concept of a life that is good in itself for the one who lives it" (p. 9). Feldman's interpretation, however, borders on what

36 *Emotions and the good life*

has been introduced earlier as a beneficially good life, only that it is beneficial for the individual living this life. Coming from a hedonistic perspective, his argument is in so far understandable as he argues for attitudinal pleasures to make a good life. In this, his position is related to current prominent positions about happiness and subjective well-being, although different in terminology and argument. Schmid, on the other hand, as will be discussed in Chapter 5, argues for an individualistic approach to the good life based on one's personal norms, values and beliefs. His argument in this context is that outside opinions do not matter, as one's life is not lived by other people, but only by oneself. Each individual can only judge his or her own life on the basis of what one believes to be important in life – one's own norms and values. This does not mean, however, that one can chose to do whatever one likes: Schmid establishes an ethics of the art of living, originating in each individual and based on the faculties of prudence and practical wisdom (Section 5.3).

As shown in this section, there is no single interpretation of the good life. On the contrary, in Schmid's reading it is likely that there are as many definitions of what a good life is as there are living human beings. For some of the definitions in this section, especially for Schmid's interpretation, many of the emotions described earlier in this chapter play a role in deciding whether one's life is seen as a good and beautiful one or not. Therefore, the considerations in this chapter are important to be kept in mind for the following discussions of concepts of the art of living – of Schmid's approach, *Lebenskunst*, and of positive psychology research.

Summary

It has been mentioned before that clarity of terms is important for a philosophical concept of the art of living. Also, discussing the notion of the good life is hardly possible without a clear understanding of a range of emotions, such as pleasures, happiness and suffering – especially if this discussion involves positions from different disciplines. In this chapter, an understanding of the concept of emotions has been presented, which draws strongly on psychological considerations, a classification of emotions in relation to time has been given and definitions of relevant emotions have been offered. Although there are tensions between psychological definitions of emotions and philosophical ideas about this topic, the approach taken here is best suited for the purpose of better understanding the value positive psychology might add to philosophical considerations about living a good life. These clarifications are necessary to compare not only various philosophical concepts with each other, but also to discuss concepts of the art of living in relation to positive psychology research, which, to a large extent, focuses on emotions like happiness, satisfaction and pleasure.

Further, it has been shown again that the term "a good life" can be interpreted in various ways. The understanding in this book will follow Schmid's individualistic notion of the "beautiful life", as will be discussed in Chapter 5. On the basis of the analysis of emotions in this chapter and the previously considered concepts of the art of living, the next chapter will explore the relevance of positive psychology research for an education for life concept based on the art of living.

Notes

1 The term "good life" in this section is used in Schmid's understanding of the beautiful life of the individual. Judgement is made on a subjective basis of what the person living this life values and considers good and beautiful. See Chapter 5 for more details.
2 See the next section and Chapter 4 for details about enduring happiness.
3 The terminology used here is based on Seligman (2010, 45–7); the interpretation of momentary and enduring happiness used in this text, however, differs to some extent from Seligman's definition.
4 See Scherer's component definition of emotions earlier.
5 See also Section 5.2.
6 WordNet (http://wordnet.princeton.edu/) offers ill-being as an antonym to well-being.

4 Positive psychology and the art of living

As mentioned earlier, positive psychology research is concerned with questions of happiness, well-being and how to live a good life. The approach taken, however, is quite different from philosophical considerations in regard to a good life. Although this study is mainly of an educational philosophical nature, relevant findings from other disciplines cannot be ignored. On the contrary, a discussion of these findings against the background of philosophical and educational considerations can enrich concepts of the art of living and contribute positively to the development of a good and beautiful life. Parallels between quantitative psychological research and qualitative philosophical concepts can strengthen the argument and provide further insights for educational practice. This chapter will provide an overview of relevant positive psychology research to allow for a more detailed comparison with philosophical concepts of the art of living, which will be conducted in Chapter 6. However, it also needs to be kept in mind, especially in light of the current popularity of positive psychology research and the notion of happiness, that positive psychology only provides a limited understanding of the idea of a good life. Schmid's philosophical concept of the art of living, as discussed in Chapter 5, can broaden this understanding and provide a more holistic view on the topic.

4.1 The relevance of positive psychology for an art of living

Psychology is traditionally a science concerned with the question of *what is wrong* with people. The art of living, on the other hand, is more concerned about *how to get it right*. Therefore, it seems necessary to give a short introduction about how these two areas are connected and why this connection is important for an educational approach.

Beginning in the middle of the 20th century an increasing number of psychologists shifted their focus of research from the pathological question of "What is wrong with humans?" to the more positive research question of "What is right?". This new focus became known later as the field of *positive psychology*, which was introduced under this name around the year 2000 by Martin Seligman and Mihaly Csikszentmihalyi, who have since been known as the founders of this new area of psychological research. The term positive psychology subsumes a range of areas, including *flow, positive emotions, wisdom and knowledge, happiness and well-being, creativity, strengths and values, (life) goals, positive coping strategies, humour* and many more (Boniwell 2008, 1–6). As this area of research has grown significantly in the last 15 years, the focus in this chapter lies on Martin Seligman's (2010) book *Authentic Happiness*, which provides a good overview of positive psychology, and the book *Flow* from Michael Csikszentmihalyi (2008), which offers insights in one of the main theories for happiness and well-being. Csikszentmihalyi also includes some thoughts about the history and development of happiness in humanity.

The contribution positive psychology can make to an educational approach to the art of living is manifold and singular at the same time. The main focus of positive psychology lies in explaining and increasing happiness and positive emotions, which appears to be a singular topic. On the other hand, research shows that such an increase has a positive effect on health, performance, creativity and coping with negative emotions, and it also prolongs life[1]; all these outcomes can contribute significantly to an individual art of living. Further, the scientific knowledge and evidence-based results provide a solid basis for educational teaching strategies and contents.

Still, it is important to point out that happiness in itself does not make a good life alone. On the contrary, someone might consider one's life a good one, although he or she does not experience much happiness at all. However, for many human beings in many cultures, happiness and positive emotions are an essential part of their expectations for a good life; therefore, it is of significant relevance for this study, as argued before.

4.2 The usage of terms

One common objection against the research and measurement of happiness is an assumed lack of definition of happiness to meet philosophical standards. Another is that when a definition is given, it is only based on what can be measured and does not include all aspects of what happiness actually might be. Although the first part of this objection might have been true in the early stages of positive psychology, various definitions for happiness have been given since (Csikszentmihalyi 2008; Seligman 2010; Seligman 2011). This leaves the second objection about the quality of these definitions themselves; an answer here is not that easy to give.

Seligman (2010, 45, 112), for example, does take philosophical considerations into account for his definition, in which he distinguishes between *momentary* and *enduring* happiness. The first is closely related to immediate pleasures and does not have any lasting impact on our overall and enduring level of happiness. The latter is related to experiences, which Seligman calls *gratifications*, and which he compares with Aristotle's *concept of eudaimonia*. In line with this distinction, Csikszentmihalyi (2008)'s terminology distinguishes between pleasures versus *enjoyments* (see Section 2.3).

40 Positive psychology and the art of living

The working formula Seligman uses to explain enduring happiness is H = S + C + V, where H stands for *enduring happiness*, S for a *set range* in which one's happiness level resides, C for one's *life circumstances* and V – as the single most important factor – for one's *voluntary control* over one's own level of happiness. The question at hand is if this formula and the results which are based on it are in line with the concept of *eudaimonia* and Seligman's philosophical definition of enduring happiness. As has been discussed in Section 3.3, this is not the case. The claim made by Seligman is that enjoyments are the utmost goal of human beings and, similar to *eudaimonia*, cannot be supported, as enjoyments are defined as an experience following flow, whereas *eudaimonia* seems to reflect a more comprehensive feeling of serene happiness in life. However, as previously indicated, the notion of enduring happiness is significantly closer to Aristotle's concept of *eudaimonia*. Still, due to differences in terminology and methods, it cannot be assumed to be the same.

One argument to support the parallels between enduring happiness and *eudaimonia* is that what is regarded as enduring happiness – and hereby is meant not that what leads to it, but the perception of enjoyments themselves – has been tested in many countries with both Eastern and Western orientation and with many different cultures and has been found inter-culturally valid for human beings in general.[2]

To take into account the more recent research and development in the field of positive psychology, it is also necessary to introduce the term *subjective well-being* (SWB). This term has recently been used as a substitute for enduring happiness, as the term happiness itself (often used without the adjective) is likely to lead to misinterpretation. In this chapter, subjective well-being and (enduring) happiness will be used interchangeably but with a preference for the earlier one.

Further, Seligman (2010, 62) mentions some other terms, which are not only relevant for happiness and positive psychology, but for an art of living as well. He distinguishes between several forms of positive emotions on the basis of their orientation in time, as discussed previously. Positive psychology has also identified techniques and factors that influence these emotions in all three time layers. For the art of living, however, emotions towards the past seem to be of more relevance to judge about one's own art of living, and emotions towards the future are important to actively shape one's self and one's life to make it a good and beautiful one.

4.3 Subjective well-being and positive emotions

The research areas of subjective well-being and positive emotions are key fields of positive psychology. The main objective is to identify influencing factors and to develop techniques to increase one's level of SWB and the experience of positive emotions. Questions to raise at this point might be: *Why should one at all seek to increase positive emotions and one's SWB? How relevant are these concepts to a good and beautiful life?* The second question will be answered later on in Chapter 6;

an answer to the first question is best given by research results that make a strong argument for positive emotions.

The first point to make is that higher levels of positive emotions and SWB lead to better health and prolong life. Strong evidence has been found to support a causative relationship of this point and not only a correlative one (Danner, Snowdon, and Friesen 2001; Redelheimer and Singh 2001). To show the causation, researchers needed to find a group of people with very similar living circumstances to limit other influencing factors on the health situation of participants. Such a group could be found among nuns, whose life in a convent controlled most other factors such as sleeping and eating habits, workload and social interaction and limited or no consumption of alcohol and cigarettes (Seligman 2010, 3–4, 9–10). According to Seligman, a research study investigating general positive emotions and attitude among these nuns has shown that nuns who seemed to display a more positive attitude and more positive emotions throughout their lives lived longer on average than other nuns.

Another argument that can be made is that when someone is in a better mood, which is not the same as but goes in line with the experience of positive emotions, one is liked better by other people, "and friendship, love, and coalitions are more likely to cement. [Further,] in contrast to the constrictions of negative emotion, our mental set is expansive, tolerant, and creative. We are open to new ideas and new experience" (p. 35).

Additionally, positive emotions lead to enhanced intellectual processing, such as mental performance and creativity. Seligman (2010, 36), for example, refers to an experiment done by Alice Isen (2000) with a group of physicians who were challenged with a hard-to-diagnose case of liver disease. The doctors in the positive emotions group were more creative and had a significantly higher success rate then participants in the control groups. Consequently, one should make sure that one's doctor is in a good mood when one is seriously ill.

Moreover, people with higher SWB in summary make better life choices, although their perception tends to be over-optimistic rather than realistic. In addition, a correlation with increased productivity at work has been identified (Seligman 2010, 37–41). Finally, positive emotions undo the mental effects of negative emotions; hence, people who experience more positive emotions can cope better with misadventures in life, and they can even endure more physical pain.

All these factors are good arguments for people to be interested in raising their level of subjective well-being. Even if the measured concept of SWB is not identical with Aristotle's concept of *eudaimonia* per se, the benefits outlined earlier can clearly contribute to living a good and beautiful life.

The relationship between subjective well-being, positive emotions and the art of living calls for a closer examination of various aspects of these emotions. The distinction made here follows Seligman (2010), who groups positive emotions by their relation to time (as outlined in Section 3.2): emotions about the past, present and future.

Emotions about the past

The main factor, according to Seligman (2010, 65–6), of how someone feels about the past lies in one's thoughts and beliefs. Other than the present, where emotions can be immediate, emotions about the past can only be experienced through cognitive reflection. An important discovery in this context is the connection between *beliefs* and *choice*. It is not new to state that one's beliefs limit one's possibilities and choices. Richard William Pearse, as well as the Wright brothers, was only able to invent an aeroplane because he *believed* that it was possible for humans to fly. Similarly, research shows (Seligman refers to Beck 1999) that beliefs about the past influence our potential choices in the present: people who believe that the past (e.g. childhood experiences, upbringing) determines our future are more passive and less able to change than people who do not share this belief. Moreover, twin studies show that effects of early childhood experiences and events on an adult personality are overrated; children seem to have a higher resilience than so far assumed (Rutter 1980). Therefore, Seligman (2010, 66–8) concludes that one's distant past and experiences are not responsible for one's problems and situation today. This knowledge can enable students of the art of living to live up to their potential instead of limiting themselves in their choices to change and shape their own selves and their own lives.

Another interesting finding is the impact of anger on our health. According to Seligman, a common belief in America has been that the expression of anger is better for one's health than not to follow its urge (pp. 69–70). Positive psychology, on the other hand, showed that the dwelling on or expression of anger is unhealthier than not to give in to it. This proves the psychodynamic theory of anger, which is the belief that suppressing one's anger and rage will lead to an even more destructive outburst later on, to be wrong – especially as the expression of hostility appears to be a strong link to having a heart attack. Friendliness, in contrast, lowers blood pressure, whereas anger raises it. As indicated earlier, emotions also trigger a change of mood. Therefore, dwelling on anger, which is a multiplication of negative emotions, consequently leads to a negative mood, whereas, if the feeling is left alone, one soon goes back to normal. The recommendation based on these results is to practise *gratitude* and *forgiveness*, as these techniques enhance positive feelings and lessen negative feelings about the past (see Section 4.4 for more details). This also leads to an increased *life satisfaction*, which again is an important aspect for one's view about one's own life in the context of the art of living (see Section 5.3).

Emotions about the future

In accordance with Seligman, emotional aspects about the future will be discussed first before moving on to the more important part of emotions in the present.

Emotions towards the future are mainly influenced by someone's view of the world: either one is more *optimistic* oriented and possesses *hope*, or one is rather *pessimistic* and holds negative expectations towards the future. This worldview and one's tendency towards optimism or pessimism is dependent on one's beliefs about *permanence* and *pervasiveness* of positive and negative events, experiences and personal qualities.

Permanence in this context describes whether one believes that an occurrence, or something that happened, is of a temporary or a permanent nature. Seligman (2010) provides examples, such as "You never talk to me" (permanent, pessimistic) versus "You haven't talked to me lately" (temporary, optimistic), or "I try hard" (temporary, pessimistic) versus "I'm talented" (permanent, optimistic) (pp. 88–9). The more someone attributes positive occurrences to be permanent and negative occurrences to be temporary, the more optimistic is his or her attitude; the contrary applies for pessimism. *Pervasiveness* is the belief whether something is specific or universal: "Books are useless" (universal, pessimistic) versus "This book is useless" (specific, optimistic), and "I'm smart at math" (specific, pessimistic) versus "I'm smart" (universal, optimistic) (pp. 90–1). Therefore, a person tends to be more optimistic if he or she believes positive events to be universal and negative events to be specific and limited; this, again, applies vice versa for pessimism. The level of hope one experiences in life, according to Seligman (2010), is directly related to the sum of one's belief in permanent, universal good and temporary, specific bad (pp. 92–5).

Seligman suggests that the benefit of an optimistic worldview lies in the increase of one's work performance and health, and in the decrease of one's likelihood to experience depression (p. 83). Additionally, the concept of the self-fulfilling prophecy (Merton 1957) proposes that optimistic people will have a better outcome and more positive encounters than pessimistic ones, as their subconsciousness will do its best to make the expectations of each person come true.

The interesting point for an educational approach to the art of living is that optimism can be learned. A raised awareness and monitoring of one's train of thoughts helps to identify pessimistic thoughts and confront them with a healthy dispute. A technique of how to identify pessimistic beliefs and how to argue their validity with oneself will be discussed in Section 4.4. In general it is important to realise that beliefs are *only* beliefs; they can be right, they can be wrong. Seligman (2010, 95) states that especially beliefs about oneself are more often false than true.

Emotions about the present

After paying attention to the past and the future, it is worthwhile to focus on the present and to identify the factors that influence our emotions and our subjective well-being in the present moment. First of all, it is important to distinguish between two major categories of emotions: *pleasures* and *gratifications* (Seligman 2010, 102). As previously indicated (Section 3.3), Seligman's term "gratifications" is similar to Csikszentmihalyi's notion of "enjoyments". Although the term enjoyment is favoured in this book, this section will use Seligman's terminology. Seligman characterises pleasures as mostly sensory emotions with less thinking involved and as immediate, but only short lasting. Additionally, he divides pleasures into *bodily* and *higher* pleasures, whereas higher pleasures have a more cognitive component, in contrast to the pure bodily sensations, such as the feeling of a touch or the taste of ice cream. Still, he subsumes both as "delights that have clear sensory and strong emotional components" (p. 102) and refers to them as so-called "raw feels". An example of higher pleasures might be the emotional response one has while listening to a favourite classical concert or an opera; it is clearly an immediate sensational experience of listening, but demands a higher cognitive interaction than having a bath or eating chocolate. Gratifications, on the other hand, are less emotional; they demand more thinking and involve challenges; they occur when one is doing something one likes; they have the tendency to absorb oneself, which means that one loses one's self-consciousness while being engaged in the task at hand (compare the phenomenon of flow in Section 4.5); and gratifications are also longer lasting than pleasures. Therefore, Seligman points out that the currently popular question of "How can I be happy?" is the wrong one to ask, as it often aims to increase pleasures in life; the right one would be to ask "What is the good life?", as this would, in his opinion, lead to an increase of gratifications in life (pp. 120–1). The answer to the latter question, however, might not be that simple, which probably has become apparent in this book already.

Increasing pleasure in someone's life is, generally speaking, not a bad idea; however, it does have only a very limited impact on one's enduring happiness and subjective well-being, and if it contributes to a good and beautiful life at all is a different question altogether. Therefore, this topic will only be touched on briefly here, and the following section will be focused more on longer-lasting techniques. For short-term positive emotions, Seligman advises, on the one hand, to arrange for regular pleasures but, on the other hand, to be careful and prolong the time between pleasures of the same kind, as frequent, similar pleasures can lead to addiction through the effects of habituation and craving (pp. 105–10). It is important to identify the latter and stop following these needs.[3] He also recommends surprising oneself and the people around oneself with daily pleasures. This will provide positive feedback and additional pleasures for oneself. Doing good to people one loves can have a gratifying effect.

Further research (Bryant 2003) in positive psychology has shown that to stop living in the future and to start *savouring* the present – paying attention to one's surroundings right now and taking pleasure from it, as a sunset on the ocean, for example – can provide pleasure and increase positive emotions. Similar is the technique of *mindfulness*: slowing down one's mind and taking time to see actively what is hidden normally. One method to do this is meditation, which also helps to dampen anxiety. The research on savouring and mindfulness itself draws from Buddhism, but is valid for people from Eastern and Western societies alike (see also Sections 9.1). This indicates again that there are transcultural techniques and global human mechanisms for increasing happiness and well-being, and maybe even for developing an art of living and a good life.

4.4 Enhancing positive emotions and enduring happiness

Positive emotions

How to enhance positive emotions in the present has been touched on in the previous section and is best answered by each individual. According to Seligman (2010, 104), most people are genuinely experts in how to provide themselves pleasures in everyday life. That these pleasures are often highly overrated and do not have much, if any, significant influence on one's overall level of happiness and well-being is a different matter.

Less obvious, and less known, might be how to improve one's satisfaction about and emotions towards the past. As mentioned earlier, the techniques to employ here are gratitude and forgiveness. A way proposed by Seligman to practise gratitude and to become more grateful in life is to recapitulate each day before going to bed and write down up to five things one is grateful for that day (p. 75). This can be simple and obvious things, such as "being healthy", "having good friends", "waking up this morning" and so on. Experiments have shown that continuing this exercise increases happiness and life satisfaction (Emmons and McCullough 2003). The second technique is forgiveness, which often turns out to be more difficult to accomplish. Seligman (2010, 70–81) describes a five-step process conducted by Worthington (2006), which is called "REACH", and which supposedly can help to forgive and let go of wrongs against oneself. REACH stands for: *Recall* the hurt as objectively as possible; *Empathise* and try to understand the other person's point of view; remember an *Altruistic* gift of forgiveness you once received and pass it on; *Commit* to this forgiveness by making it public; and *Hold* onto this forgiveness whenever the episode crosses your mind again. On the question why one should forgive at all, Seligman (2010) provides a simple answer: "You can't hurt the perpetrator by not forgiving, but you can set yourself free by forgiving" (p. 77). Another reason is one's health, which is likely better in people who practise forgiving than in those who do not.

Positive emotions about the future can be increased through optimism and hope. Seligman states that "[t]here is a well-documented method for building optimism that consists of recognizing and then disputing pessimistic thoughts" (p. 93). The skill of disputing is inherent in everybody and is mostly used "when an external person – a rival for our job, or our lover – accuses us falsely of some dereliction" (p. 93). Unfortunately, one normally does not use this skill at all when one accuses oneself of anything. The false conclusion responsible for this lack of criticism is that, as one is the person stating this accusation and one apparently knows oneself, this accusation must be true and there is no need to verify this statement. Unfortunately, this belief is mostly wrong. The remedy is the so-called ABCDE model, which should be used when one recognises a pessimistic thought about oneself:

> A stands for adversity, B for the beliefs you automatically have when it occurs, C for the usual consequences of the belief, D for your disputation of your

routine belief, and E for the energization that occurs when you dispute it successfully. By effectively disputing the beliefs that follow an adversity, you can change your reaction from dejection and giving up to activity and good cheer.

(p. 93)

It needs to be admitted here that the concepts introduced in this section have a slight "self-help" character, which does not necessarily sit comfortably with a philosophical discourse. However, it cannot be denied that knowledge about certain mechanisms of our brain and emotional response systems can lead to a better understanding of one's self and to more self-knowledge. Being able to anticipate how certain behaviours can influence one's emotions positively or negatively can be helpful on the way to a state of serene happiness and *eudaimonia*. The techniques introduced here and elsewhere in this book in the context of positive psychology cannot be taken as a prescription of what to do to live a happy and beautiful life, but they should certainly not be disregarded out of hand either. A prudent way would be to take these techniques and other psychological research findings under critical consideration for shaping one's own self and one's own life.

Enduring happiness

For a better understanding of increasing enduring happiness through gratifications, it is necessary to take a closer look at Seligman's definition of this term. He claims that there is usually no difference in everyday English between pleasures and gratifications, which is quite unfortunate, as they describe two different sets of feelings (p. 111). He refers the lack of this distinction back to the mutual use of the verb "like" in this context: "we casually say that we like caviar, a back rub, or the sound of rain on a tin roof (all pleasures) as well as saying that we like playing volleyball, reading Dylan Thomas, and helping the homeless (all gratifications)" (p. 111). The distinction between gratifications and pleasures for him is as follows:

> *Eudaimonia*, what I call gratification, is part and parcel of right action. It cannot be derived from bodily pleasure, nor is it a state that can be chemically induced or attained by any shortcuts. It can only be had by activity consonant with noble purpose. [. . .] The pleasures are about the senses and the emotions. The gratifications, in contrast, are about enacting personal strengths and virtues.
>
> (p. 112)

Therefore, Seligman identifies his understanding of gratifications with Aristotle's idea of *eudaimonia* and the idea of taking the "right action". Indeed there seem to be parallels between these two theories, especially taking into account Seligman's theory about signature strength (see later), which could be seen as a basis for Aristotle's virtues and are necessary for gratifications to come to pass. However, as discussed in Section 3.3, it is arguable if gratifications in Seligman's understanding describe the same idea as *eudaimonia*. They are more likely only a part of the concept proposed by Aristotle. Considering Stoic philosophy (see Kraut 2010) and their definition of *eudaimonia*, one might find more consensus here. Still, according to Kraut (2010), the term *eudaimonia* plays a more "evaluative role" rather than being simply a description of "someone's state of mind". In any case, there seem to be enough parallels with ancient philosophical concepts of a good life to underpin the importance of this recent research for modern concepts of the art of living. However, it needs to be pointed out that the consistency of theoretical terms and philosophical background in actual positive psychology research is arguable to some degree.

Gratifications occur after activities which are marked by a state of mind and experience of challenge, concentration, clear goals, immediate feedback, deep involvement, sense of control, loss of self-consciousness and unawareness of time (Seligman 2010, 116). This state of mind has been named *flow* by Csikszentmihalyi (2008), which he describes in detail in his book of this name (see Section 4.5 for more details). Seligman assumes that it marks *psychological growth* and that this growth and improvement of one's self and one's own abilities are part of the gratification we experience *afterwards*. Hobbies and taking part in (extreme) sports are not necessarily pleasurable at the moment of engagement, but they build up a *psychological capital* on which one's SWB and enduring state of happiness can grow (Seligman 2010, 116–17).

Signature strengths and the six core virtues

The key, according to Seligman (2010, 121), to increasing the frequency of flow and gratifications is to identify and use one's *signature strength*s. Strengths, in Seligman's terminology, are not talents; they are distinguished by a component of moral value (p. 134). Talents, such as being a good sprinter or a good writer, are non-moral. One can only slightly improve an existing talent, and there is hardly anything one can do when the talent for something is not existent; talents are innate. On the other hand, "strengths, such as integrity, valor, originality, and kindness, can be built on even frail foundations, and [. . .] with enough practice, persistence, good teaching, and dedication, they can take root and flourish" (p. 134). A strength also always involves an active will and decision: for example, one can always decide for or against being generous towards a beggar in the street or being kind to someone who feels miserable.

One of Seligman's objectives for positive psychology was to create a "backbone" to permit reliability and comparable results in this new scientific discipline. To accomplish this, he gathered a research team to develop a DSM[4]-like classification of sanities (in opposition to mental health issues) in a three-year process. Interestingly, they not only identified 24 main character strengths,[5] which are mostly shared throughout cultures and time, but also identified six core virtues that are equally ubiquitous. His claim is that these virtues – namely wisdom and knowledge, courage, love and humanity, justice, temperance and spirituality and transcendence – can be gained by building and acting on one's signature strengths of character (pp. 129–33, 137–40). This process of building one's strengths and character is an aspect of *self-bildung* in Schmid's concept of the care of the self.

The aspect of forming one's self and one's own character is what makes these findings highly relevant for this research. The fact that Seligman considers strengths to be developable, even from "frail foundations", by practice and good teaching is particularly promising for this educational approach. This will be discussed further in Chapter 6, but first it is necessary to discuss the concept of *flow*, which is the underlying experience to provide gratifications and enjoyments.

4.5 Flow

Why flow?

Csikszentmihalyi (2008, 1–22) argues that the modern technical, materialistic and capitalistic developments in the last centuries did not improve the experience of happiness and contentment in (Western) societies at all; despite all achievements, the contentment through experiences did not grow by much. His explanation for this phenomenon is, on the one hand, that most cultural achievements enhance only pleasures in life but not longer-lasting enjoyments and, on the other hand, the existence of a general false belief of human beings in a panacea for happiness. A formula found once, working at a certain time and for a certain people, or even only for an individual, is often proposed and believed as *the* way for enduring happiness (or equally for any other human problem or desire), but, in fact, it is only *one* way and only valid for a limited amount of people. Contentment needs to be built through experiences and cannot be learned through teaching alone, but experiences and ways of learning need to be adjusted to one's actual cultural context. This observation obviously causes some trouble for a scientific approach, as a common solution cannot be found. But, according to Csikszentmihalyi, there is an indirect way – as happiness cannot be reached by searching for it directly – to take us as close to enduring happiness as possible: *the control of inner experiences.* He states that "the way is through control over consciousness, which in turn leads to control over the quality of experiences" (p. 22). Therefore, a person can make himself or herself happy or miserable independent of external circumstances; the event itself is just information, the value of the incident is given by the individual.

A conclusion Csikszentmihalyi draws in this context is that, as cultural and social developments cannot enhance enjoyments and enduring happiness and individuals can only raise their level of subjective well-being internally, people need to become independent of social and cultural punishment and reward systems as "civilisation is built on the repression of individual desires" (p. 17). People need to learn to enjoy every day in their ongoing life. Csikszentmihalyi (2008) offers two main strategies for improving one's quality of life: *to change one's living circumstances* – which is not working so well, as shown earlier; and *to change one's own expectations and inner experiences*, which is more likely to lead to a "better life" (p. 43). For the latter option, to improve the quality of life "the flow theory can point the way" (p. 5).

What is flow?

As mentioned previously, Csikszentmihalyi's terminology distinguishes between pleasures as sensational experiences and *enjoyments*, which are characterised by "forward movement: by a sense of novelty, of accomplishment" (p. 46). The latter can involve a struggle and a not necessarily pleasurable exercise, but afterwards enjoyments leave a feeling of happiness and of having had "fun". *Flow* is the experience one has when exercising control in a challenging situation that is just on the brink of one's skill level necessary for the task, and it ends with the experience of enjoyment. The conditions (1–4) and characteristics (5–8) of flow, which Csikszentmihalyi also calls *optimal experience*, are the same for all human beings independent of their cultural heritage:

1   a chance of success/of completing the task,
2   able to concentrate,
3   clear goals,
4   immediate feedback,
5   deep but effortless involvement,
6   enjoyable experience (exercise sense of control),
7   concern for self disappears, but sense of self emerges stronger,
8   experience of time is altered (time often seems to run by, but sometimes it seems to be prolonged). (pp. 48–9)

"The key element of an optimal experience is that it is an end in itself" (p. 67); a flow experience has, therefore, an *autotelic* (end-in-itself) nature. This is important, as most activities one does are of a mixed nature, or initially even mostly exotelic (means-to-an-end). Still, with growing skills and the right preliminaries (see earlier) many experiences can become flow experiences and are worth doing for internal reasons only. People regularly spend vast amounts of money and time to engage in activities such as sailing, rock climbing or other sports, as the enjoyment they take from these is worth all their efforts (pp. 67–70).

An important point of Csikszentmihalyi's theory for the argument in this book is the possibility to increase flow experiences. Although Csikszentmihalyi is not deliberately discussing techniques of increasing their frequency (Seligman is more detailed in this regard), he indicates the way one can reach this goal. The key is the stated control over one's consciousness, which is achievable through *attention*. Attention is the ability to focus one's mind on an affair and to process the information one perceives. Psychological research (Marois and Ivanoff 2005; Luck and Vecera 2002) determined that one's consciousness is limited in the amount of information one can process at any given moment: not surprisingly, the amount of knowledge one can gather and the experiences one can make are limited by the lifetime from which one has subtracted the time one sleeps and needs for daily routine tasks, multiplied by the limited capability of one's consciousness. This adds up to quite an impressive amount of information we can process; however, there seems to be a tendency (Csikszentmihalyi 2008, 83) – especially in Western cultures – to waste much of this capacity through excessive use of short-lasting, immediate pleasures, such as watching TV (sometimes several hours per day) to divide one's attention. Some people even have never learned properly how to focus their attention on tasks at hand and get easily distracted. This again limits their quality of experience, as undivided attention and concentration are necessary for an optimal experience. But

> when a person is able to organize his or her consciousness so as to experience flow as often as possible, the quality of life is inevitably going to improve, because [. . .] even the usually boring routines of work become purposeful and enjoyable.
>
> (p. 40)

The organisation of one's consciousness is the ability to alter the task at hand in a way that the activity meets the preliminaries for optimal experience and to enable oneself to experience flow as often as possible. This leads to more enjoyment and to growth of one's self and one's own strength through an increase of one's psychic energy.

As an example to alter a repetitive and boring task, Csikszentmihalyi introduces the case of a factory worker called Rico, who had a rather monotonous position in an assembly line where he was supposed to do the same operation about 600 times a day, which most people would experience as a rather boring environment. Rico, however, has managed to still enjoy his task even after five years of work:

> The reason is that he approaches his task in the same way an Olympic athlete approaches his event: How can I beat my record? Like the runner who trains for years to shave a few seconds off his best performance on the track, Rico has trained himself to better his time on the assembly line. With the painstaking care of a surgeon, he has worked out a private routine for how to use his tools, how to do his moves.
>
> (p. 39)

Csikszentmihalyi states that Rico's motivation has been partly to impress his superiors and earn a bonus, but often he kept his achievement to himself, as he was satisfied with the positive experience of his performance alone. He created his own optimal experiences in this unlikely environment; this is an example for Csikszentmihalyi's notion of the organisation of one's consciousness (pp. 30–3, 39–41).

Social and cultural perspectives

An interesting aspect with regard to flow is the social and cultural perspective: Csikszentmihalyi (2008, 77–83) claims that probably "no social system has ever survived long unless its people had some hope that their government would help them achieve happiness" (p. 77). Therefore, every government and cultural setting has to have the happiness and contentment of its citizens as a goal if it is intended to be a lasting one. But Csikszentmihalyi also points out that this goal, similar to the flow experience itself, does not make a government or culture an ethical "good" one. He just emphasises that happiness, through flow and optimal experiences, needs to be supported in modern societies. Although there seems to be no valid method yet to classify to what extent different governments are on track with this objective, Csikszentmihalyi proposes two possible factors for evaluation: the amount of people who can make experiences in accordance with their goals and if the experiences people make contribute to the growth of their selves. One reason for Csikszentmihalyi's claim that societies with higher levels of flow for their citizens are not automatically "better" societies is derived from the fact that flow in itself is neither good nor bad; it is simply *energy* or *power*. The value is determined by the purpose and intention by which this power is utilised. A criminal – a professional burglar or thief, for example – can equally experience flow when engaged in unethical activity. Flow "is good only in that it has the potential to make life more rich, intense, and meaningful; it is good because it increases the strength and complexity of the self" (p. 70). However, according to Csikszentmihalyi, violence and crime are outcomes of unsatisfied needs in life and could be reduced through increased flow experiences in positive rather than in destructive settings (p. 69).

Another social factor is the influence of parents and family on the likelihood of flow experiences in one's life. Research has shown that a so-called "autotelic family context" (p. 89) is most beneficial to have an increased amount of optimal experiences in life (Rathunde 1988). A family context that can be called autotelic provides an ideal environment for the child, especially in the teenager stage, to learn how to enjoy life. Csikszentmihalyi (2008) identifies five core aspects of these settings: the first is *clarity*, which means that the teenager is given clear rules and expectations and knows the consequences of failing these rules (pp. 88–9). The second is *centring*, which is the focus on the here and now in parenting instead of focusing mainly on the future outcome of the child. Third, these families offer a multitude of possibilities for the teenager to choose from: *choice*. The fourth aspect is *commitment* of the parents, which helps the child to trust in them. The fifth and last differencing factor is *challenge*, where parents provide new and increasingly complex opportunities and activities. These five points have a strong positive influence on the growth of the teenager and his or her ability for optimal experiences in life.

Limitations of optimal experience

According to Csikszentmihalyi, most impediments to flow are located in the individual: the inability to concentrate, "attentional disorders and stimulus overinclusion prevent flow because psychic energy is too fluid and erratic. Excessive self-consciousness and self-centredness prevent it for the opposite reason: attention is too rigid and tight" (Csikszentmihalyi 2008, 85). Other examples are mental illnesses and behavioural disorders, for instance, attention deficit hyperactivity disorder (ADHD), which also often prevent focusing attention on the task at hand. Other obstacles can be of natural origin and can be determined by one's surroundings: living a hard life in a desert or, as the Inuit, in the constantly cold and icy north, can limit the opportunities for optimal experiences. But, on the other hand, according to Csikszentmihalyi (p. 85), cultural achievements and settings, such as singing and dancing in the case of the Inuit, can overcome these natural limits and provide possibilities for flow experiences.

A much bigger impact on one's chance for optimal experiences are cultural obstacles. Csikszentmihalyi (2008) names three settings in this context: *suppression* and *slavery, alienation,* and *anomie* (pp. 85–6). As an example of *suppression*, he refers to the now-extinct natives of the Caribbean islands, who had to work under conditions that made their lives so "painful and meaningless that they lost interest in survival, and eventually ceased reproducing." Another cultural factor is *alienation*, which happens in an existence with so many boring and meaningless tasks that they prevent the individual from spending his or her energy on desired activities. This can come to pass in constraining social systems, where people have to do tasks for survival that prevent them from following their goals in life. An example can be Rico's colleagues at the assembly line, who have to do the same meaningless task hundreds of times a day and often fail, due to lack of education and knowledge, among others, to change these tasks into optimal experiences. Finally, Csikszentmihalyi names *anomie*, which means literally "lack of rules" and is a state where "it is uncertain what public opinion values, [and] behavior becomes erratic and meaningless. People who depend on the rules of society to give order to their consciousness become anxious" (p. 86). This can happen in disastrous situations such as economic crises or cultural destruction – in times of war for example – but also "when prosperity increases rapidly, and old values of thrift and hard work are no longer as relevant as they had been" (p. 86).

These limitations through social and cultural circumstances indicate the importance for families and societies to support settings in which individuals can grow to fill their lives with optimal experiences. The last point particularly underpins the previously mentioned significance of the art of living for today's societies and provides another link between flow and the philosophical concept of the art of living itself. Implicitly, Csikszentmihalyi, like Seligman, provides more points for and connections with an educational approach to this topic, as both call attention to the cultural and familial significance for developing an autotelic lifestyle, flow experiences and subjective well-being.

4.6 Meaning in life and harmony

Both Seligman (2010, 250–60) and Csikszentmihalyi (2008, 214–40) point out the importance of an overall goal and meaning in life:

> If a person sets out to achieve a difficult enough goal, from which all other goals logically follow, and if he or she invests all energy in developing skills

to reach that goal, then actions and feelings will be in harmony, and the separate parts of life will fit together – and each activity will "make sense" in the present, as well as in view of the past and of the future. In such a way, it is possible to give meaning to one's entire life.

(Csikszentmihalyi 2008, 214–15)

To give one's whole life meaning, one needs to find at least one overall goal or vision, which connects all other goals or aims in life. This will enable the individual to experience as much flow as possible and subsequently provides the highest amount of enjoyments. This maximum of positive energy can help the individual to cope much better with obstacles and external negative influences on one's own life than without. In Seligman's terms, a good life is a life of gratifications (flow experiences); a meaningful life is a good life with a set purpose to increase the greater good. This notion of the greater good and the inclusion of the good for others and/or mankind in one's purpose can also be found in Csikszentmihalyi's contemplations, described later on in this section. This is also the connecting link between the care for others (compare Schmid's theory in Chapter 5) and positive psychology.

In an attempt to grasp the dimensions of *meaning*, Csikszentmihalyi first concludes that "the meaning of life *is* meaning: whatever it is, wherever it comes from, a unified purpose is what gives meaning to life" (p. 217). To get a better understanding of what meaning entails, he identifies and describes three dimensions: *purpose*, as the overall goal for life itself; *resolution*, which is the intentionally carrying through of this goal; and *harmony*, which is the contentment of the mind that follows the earlier two.

Purpose

Every culture has purposes to offer as each culture contains a meaning system by definition, which provides a multitude of possible goals for a "good" and meaningful life (Csikszentmihalyi 2008, 218–23). If one or more of these goals and purposes are fitting for each individual is a different question altogether. However, Csikszentmihalyi follows the theory of Pitrim Sorokin (1962) who identified three major types of cultural settings (at least in Western history): *sensate* cultures, which emphasise the experience of pleasure, have practical principles and define "good" as what feels good; *ideational* settings, which strive for non-material and supernatural goals, have abstract and transcendent principles and aim for reaching inner clarity and conviction; and *idealistic* cultures, which cultivate both of these dialectical tendencies – sensation and ideation – by preserving their positive aspects and neutralising their worst ones. Nevertheless, according to Csikszentmihalyi, both tendencies are existent in every culture as much as in every individual, and it is not hard to accept that a balanced idealistic setting and life are often the most desirable. A balancing act needs to be done in any case, and the outcome determines, or at least strongly influences, the way an individual arranges his or her actions.

As another way to describe people's actions, Csikszentmihalyi refers to complexity models, as proposed by Maslow, for example, where the order and nature of one's actions is ordained by the needs that are most present at a time. A recent example would be the state many people in Christchurch, New Zealand, were in after the earthquakes in September 2010 and February 2011. With houses partly or fully destroyed, lack of power and water and a general feeling of unsafety and uncertainty, people were preoccupied with managing basic daily routines such as having enough drinking water, having a shower somewhere or where to cook food. The higher goals of self-fulfilment and self-actualisation were not priorities for many people in the initial time after the earthquakes.

Resolve

Csikszentmihalyi's (2008, p. 223) argues that, despite having purpose and goals, without resolve these goals hardly come to pass, which would be necessary for any goal to become meaningful. A problem of current modern times is the flexibility and the amount of opportunities one has in life, and especially the number of "shortcuts" to pleasures and distractions.[6] It has become easier to live a comfortable life, but this also endangers commitment and resolve and, therefore, makes it easier to live a meaningless life at the same time. This is one reason why, despite all cultural and technical progress, the overall level of happiness for people today has not grown significantly at all.

The main question at this point is how to find or determine an overall purpose for one's life. The answer Csikszentmihalyi (2008) suggests is as old as it is simple: know yourself (pp. 225–7). "*Self-knowledge* [. . .] is the process through which one may organize conflicting options" (p. 225, italics added). The difficulty of this claim is *how to* achieve self-knowledge, which needs to be rediscovered in every generation and defined for every individual anew. Not only language but also experiences people have and, therefore, their understanding and interpretation of the world change significantly over time and with increasing speed in the last centuries. Csikszentmihalyi argues for a current approach towards self-knowledge through awareness of the sheer number of competing desires, goals and claims on one's attention and to select purposefully the essential claims from the non-essential once. To achieve this, he suggests two possible ways: "what the ancients called the *vita activa*, a life of action, and the *vita contemplativa*, or the path of reflection" (p. 225). According to one's personality and disposition one might follow more the first or the second of these two paths. A life of contemplation and reflection is, therefore, according to Csikszentmihalyi, historically considered the "best approach to a good life" (p. 226): repeated reflection of one's self, one's own goals and one's approach to reach these goals leads to more self-knowledge than a life that is led by action and a dedication to achieving pragmatic ends. The latter one "might eliminate internal conflict, but often at the price of excessively restricting options" (p. 226). The ideal case would be a life in which reflection and activity complement and support each other, which provides

Harmony

Harmony is the contentment of one's mind that comes to pass when an individual chooses an overall purpose and follows the process of resolution. In this case one's own life can become a nearly unified experience of seamless flow. According to Csikszentmihalyi (2008, 227–9), animals supposedly experience this state of mind most of the time, when they are undisturbed by external negative influences such as threats or primal needs, including hunger, thirst or other urges. Humans, according to Csikszentmihalyi, are the only species who are able to make themselves miserable through the power of their own mind. The increased range of possibilities and choices in modern cultures often inspires a human mind to imagine what *could* be, and, thus, it provides a diversion of the mind that makes focusing of one's attention more difficult and the experience of flow and harmony less likely. Limited choices and simple desires provide less complex choices and help recover harmony in life.

The way to create meaning and harmony in life leads through reasoning and making one's own reflected choices. In this context, Csikszentmihalyi (2008) follows the tradition of existentialist philosophy and distinguishes between so-called *authentic* projects or *discovered* life themes, which are freely chosen by the individual out of conviction and internal motivation, and *inauthentic* or *accepted* ones, which are taken up because of an individual's conviction that this is what should be done or is expected of him or her (pp. 230–1). Both types can add meaning to life, but both have different drawbacks. The earlier kind often appears novel and incomprehensible to other people, as its origin lies in a self-reflective struggle of the individual, which is hardly apparent for others and, therefore, often has less social support and legitimacy. Accepted life goals, on the other hand, can be fine in a sound society, but can also lead to abstruse actions if the cultural moral system is adrift. As an example, Csikszentmihalyi describes the case of a Nazi official, whose belief in bureaucracy and obedience let him calmly ship thousands of humans into the gas chambers. The social system of that time perverted his life theme, which could have been appropriate in many other circumstances or settings.

Discovered life themes, on the other hand, come to pass through interpretation and reflection of the individual and are often triggered through an episode or event of suffering, which is often perceived by the person to be a challenge. This interpretation encourages the development of appropriate skills to meet this challenge. These skills, and the development and growth of the individual in the pointed direction, often lead to a life goal that aims to dissolve the cause of the challenge not only for oneself but for other people or the whole of mankind as well. In the best case, a life theme of this kind can spread and bring meaning and harmony to the life of many (pp. 233–4).

Csikszentmihalyi's exploration of supporting structures and strategies for lives with successfully established meaning concludes with a simple and often-overlooked answer: to learn from the knowledge and information of past generations, which, he claims, is encoded in music, art, drama and other recordings of cultural achievement (p. 235). The problem with this strategy of finding meaning by learning from existing cultural knowledge is that many people ignore the past or distance themselves and try to "create meaning in their lives by their own devices" (p. 235). According to Csikszentmihalyi, this is like rebuilding a whole cultural material from scratch. The consequence for an educational approach must be not only to provide cultural knowledge and tradition, but also to enable pupils to understand the importance and significance of this knowledge for their own lives and to teach them the necessary skills to reflect on and interpret this knowledge to extract meaning for their own lives from it. The approach to hermeneutics (Section 5.5) in Schmid's theory of *Lebenskunst* and the discussion in Section 9.1 are especially relevant for this objective.

Summary

In this chapter, relevant aspects of positive psychology in relation to the art of living have been discussed, including the positive impact of various emotions on one's health and one's satisfaction with life, as well as the concept of flow, which leads to enjoyment and a long-lasting increase of one's overall level of happiness in life. However, it has also been pointed out that happiness does not necessarily lead to a good life but that, in fact, a life can be a good one despite the absence of happiness. Still, as has been argued before, happiness is an important aspect of living a good life for many people and hardly prevents a life from being a good one in the eyes of the one living it. However, this cannot be said for pleasures, as has been pointed out before in this and the previous chapters.

The contributions of this chapter to the main argument of this book are, first, the discussion of significant knowledge about human psychology that can prove valuable for each individual to develop his or her own art of living and a good life. This knowledge is even more important for educationists in the context of an education for life, as a teacher's influence on students' positive emotions and experiences of flow goes beyond teaching *about* these aspects – it is relevant to *how* one teaches at all. Second, the quantitative research findings presented in this chapter support various philosophical arguments and conclusions made in this book. Especially the mentioned cross-cultural studies by Csikszentmihalyi indicate some qualities of human life that seem to be persistent over time and between cultures. These findings can support a universal education for life concept, provided this concept is open enough to cater for the differences of human beings as well as to what they have in common – especially in relation to Aristotle's notion of *eudaimonia*.

After this excursus into possible positive psychology contributions to living a good and beautiful life, the next chapter will discuss Schmid's concept *Lebenskunst* as a more holistic philosophical approach to the art of living.

Notes

1 Seligman (2010, 272, 276) refers, for example, to the study from Danner, D., D. Snowdon and W. Friesen. 2001. "Positive Emotions in Early Life and Longevity: Findings From the Nun Study." *Journal of Personality and Social Psychology* 80: 804–13. For further positive influences through positive emotions, see Fredrickson, B. 2001. "The Role of Positive Emotions in Positive Psychology: The Broaden-and-Build Theory of Positive Emotion." *American Psychologist* 56: 218–26.
2 Csikszentmihalyi (2008, 48) mentions interviews conducted in America, Europe, Korea, Japan, Thailand and Australia. He refers to previous research: Csikszentmihalyi, M. 1975. *Beyond Boredom and Anxiety.* San Francisco, CA: Jossey-Bass Publishers;and Csikszentmihalyi, M., and I. S. Csikszentmihalyi. 1988. *Optimal Experience: Psychological Studies of Flow in Consciousness.* New York, NY: Cambridge University Press. He also refers to studies by Professor Fausto Massimini and colleagues.
3 This recommendation is in line with Epicure's hedonistic approach of distinguishing between positive and negative pleasures and choosing wisely. Compare Section 2.2 for more details.
4 DSM stands for the *Diagnostic and Statistical Manual of Mental Disorders*, which is one of the standard tools to diagnose mental and psychological disorders.
5 A detailed description of all 24 strengths and how to determine which are one's signature strengths and which are not cannot be given here. Please refer to Seligman (2010, 140–61) to find a suitable survey and descriptions.
6 See also Barry Schwartz (2004), *The Paradox of Choice*.

5 "*Lebenskunst*" – Schmid's concept of the art of living

As mentioned before, beyond the contribution positive psychology can have to one's enduring happiness and well-being, Schmid's work on an art of living concept *Lebenskunst*, which unfortunately has not been translated into English language yet, provides a more holistic approach to living a good and beautiful life. Schmid's ideas will be presented here as a suitable concept for an educational approach to this topic and will be used as an underlying philosophical concept for the further argument in this book. As will be shown later, Schmid proposes a holistic philosophical theory about the art of living, including social, ethical, individual and educational considerations.

It needs to be pointed out again that Schmid's approach is focused on the development of an individual art of living, which means that a judgement about one's life as a good or beautiful one is only relevant for a person if done by himself or herself. Society cannot and must not prescribe how a good life and an art of living should look like, as no single way of living can suit everyone. If society were to prescribe how people should live a good life, applying this idea to education would be highly dangerous and potentially destructive, as will be discussed in Section 7.2. However, society certainly provides the background and experiences on which each individual can build his or her own understanding of a good and beautiful life. Likewise, it provides the framework for people to live and grow in, which can be liberating and limiting at the same time.

An example would be the current neo-liberal climate, as can be found in New Zealand and elsewhere (Peters and Marshall 1996; Roberts and Peters 2008). Despite some (or many) people's dislike of the implications of this environment on their daily lives, one cannot escape its consequences if one is living in a country with a strong neo-liberal setting. Beyond external influences such as a strongly competitive job market, a political environment that focuses on economic growth in disregard of, for example, environmental costs and an ill-founded belief in meritocracy (McNamee and Miller 2004; Snook and O'Neill 2010), the influence of such an environment reaches to the core of a society's belief and value system. This influence affects significantly the shaping of a person's self-concept, as one is raised in a neo-liberal context with the belief of individuals to be self-interested, consuming and perpetually choosing (Roberts and Codd 2010). These socio-cultural conditions limit, as indicated earlier, a person's ability to shape his or her own self based on his or her own reasoning and choosing. Further, limitations emerge also for the education system of a neo-liberally driven country: Roberts (2004), for example, introduces the term "market knowledge" (p. 357) in this context, which has been given preference over other forms of knowledge in recent New Zealand educational policy developments.

Coming back to the focus of this chapter, after summarising and discussing Schmid's theory, his concept will be put into dialogue with positive psychology research in Chapter 6 to inform the further development of an educational approach to the art of living. I need to mention here that it is not my intent to present a comprehensive philosophical critique of Schmid's work at this point, as this would go beyond the scope of this book and would probably warrant a book of its own. However, Schmid's theory is implicitly and explicitly compared and contrasted with other relevant philosophical theories, as discussed in earlier chapters, as well as discussed in relation to positive psychology and education. A critique of Schmid's work from an educational perspective is presented later on in Section 7.4.

5.1 Schmid's approach

In his work, Schmid focuses on the nature of the good life, or better: the *beautiful life*. In his considerations, he not only takes into account earlier theories about the art of living, but also develops a new philosophical approach to this topic with reference to the conditions of current modern and postmodern societies.

At this point a clarification of Schmid's use of the terms *modern* and *postmodern* and their understanding in this book is necessary. According to Burke (2000), modernity started with the enlightenment and could be characterised by "the power of reason over ignorance [. . .], the power of order over disorder, [and] the power of science over superstition" (Modernism, §1).[1] Modernity also brought forth "capitalism as a new mode of production and a transformation of the social order" (§2). Postmodernism and postmodernity, on the other hand, are harder to define: Aylesworth (2005) claims postmodernism to be "indefinable" (Postmodernism, §1). However, to better understand postmodern developments, Burke distinguishes between three dimensions of (post-)modernity: *art, philosophy* and *new times* (the social world). He lists, as examples, various characteristics in art, media and architecture that can be attributed to postmodernity; that many philosophical concepts and thinkers are referred to as postmodern (although many of them would not like to be categorised in this way themselves); and that various social and cultural changes have taken place that can be seen as part of postmodernity, such as a postindustrial society, disorganised capitalism and unregulated markets.

Burke's distinction between these three dimensions is significant for the understanding of *modernity* and *postmodernity* in Schmid's context and for the way they are employed in this discussion: there seems to be a slightly different emphasis in meaning when using these terms in the English versus the German discourse. Whereas the terms *modern* and *postmodern* in English academic writing seem to be mainly interpreted as reference to various philosophical concepts and ideas, the emphasis in the German context seems to be on changes in social and real-world settings. Hence, Schmid's use of *modern* and *postmodern* refers more to the changed experienced life reality of human beings than to particular philosophical positions. However, the meaning intended when he uses these terms includes philosophical notions, such as external social influences on the construction of one's self and the shifted emphasis of science and knowledge "from the ends of human action to its means" (Aylesworth 2005, 2, §3). Similar to others (Postmodernism, §2), Schmid's take on postmodernity is not a turning away from modernity, but an intensification of modernity: faster growth of technological achievements; faster and more scientific developments; higher demands on people; time seems to run faster; not having enough time is a more frequent experience; and changes in people's everyday lives come about faster than before.

The terms *modern* and *postmodern* are used here, likewise, with an emphasis on social circumstances and the *Lebenswirklichkeit* [experienced life-reality] of human beings in today's societies. A relation to the notion of postindustrialism is intended, as well as an escalating notion from modernity to postmodernity. Similar to Bauman's (2000) theory of *Liquid modernity*, neither modernity nor postmodernity are assumed to be fixed stages, but rather in fluid motion. The terms are employed to describe certain characteristics of current, mostly Western, societies. However, relevant aspects from an art of living point of view can be found at other points in time in global history as well: Schmid (2000a) states that

> the interest in an art of living seems to be a matter of time: it flares up and loses itself again. [. . .] People who are looking for an art of living are these for whom life does not go without saying anymore, in whichever culture or time this might be.
>
> (p. 9, my translation)[2]

Bauman (2000), like Schwartz (2004), acknowledges that too much choice limits freedom and calls for "*more, not less, of the 'public sphere' and 'public power'*" (p. 51) for "*true liberation*" (p. 51, cf. Gane 2001). Schmid (2000a, 9) and Bauman (2000, 7–8) both point out that in current (post-)modern societies a loss of traditional values, rules and patterns as points of orientation has led to uncertainty and a lack of guidance: "individuals now face a range of conflicting life-choices on their own, meaning that they face them in increasing isolation and with little prospect of assistance from any collective body or system" (Gane 2001, 269). This is one reason for Schmid to emphasise the individual-based approach to an art of living today.

However, as Rizvi (2012) points out, current developments in (post-)modern Western societies affect through globalisation the living circumstances of so-called second and third world societies even more strongly: a village in India that 30 years ago had no paved roads, no petrol vehicles, no electricity and nearly only wood and mud houses has now mostly brick houses, paved roads, electricity, televisions in nearly every house, scooters and some cars and tractors. Many people even have cell phones and access to the Internet. These cultures and societies face different living circumstances than people in central Europe or North America. However, the amount of changes and challenges people of these cultures have to deal with in their lifetime might prove to be similar to those of people in "modern" and "postmodern" societies – at least with regard to the art of living and how to live a good and beautiful life.

However, coming back to Schmid's concept of the art of living, he does not claim to develop a finished philosophy of the art of living; his aim is rather to explore the field, discover the boundaries of this topic and open it up for a new philosophic and public discussion. In the course of this exploration, he also raises the question of a new modernity in light of the art of living, which would reverse some of the developments of postmodernity, decelerate people's lives and develop a consciousness for what it means to live a good and beautiful life. On the background of Schmid's philosophical theory, Chapter 7 will explore the consequences that arise from his ideas for education.

One definition Schmid offers as his understanding of the art of living is "the wholeheartedness of the attempt, [. . .] to acquire one's life in good time and maybe make a 'beautiful life' out of it" (Schmid 2000b, 7). For him, the term "beautiful life" is more than the often-used term of a "successful" or "good" life. Being successful in life is too narrow in its meaning and too focused on accomplishments in life, whereas the term "good life" is used too widely in its interpretations and meanings. A beautiful life, for Schmid, is a life that can be seen as a work of art. He refers back to the ancient Greek term *kalos zen* (living beautifully) and aims to renew this original meaning through his concept of the art of living. As with every work of art, a beautiful life is unique and not determined by a set of rules and norms, but created by the individual out of opportunities and possibilities – thus a philosophy of the art of living can only be "optative", not "normative" (p. 8).

But why should one strive for an art of living? What are the reason and motivation to follow this path? Schmid answers this question with death as the *final argument*. According to Schmid (2000a, 88–9), only the finality of life gives reason to shape it into something good, something beautiful. However, for Schmid death here means not necessarily the ultimate end of one's life – this depends on the cultural and religious beliefs one has – but it certainly is a boundary, an end for this instance of one's life. He assumes that every human being wishes to live a beautiful life, similar to Aristotle's idea of *eudaimonia* as the utmost goal for human beings. This statement, however, could be questioned in its absolutism. To clarify this point, one has to consider that "beautiful" is a subjective quality. It might be safe to assume that every individual tries to achieve a beautiful life according to his or her *own point of view*. This point of view might include considerations of a subsequent life or an afterlife, or it might not. Whether this individual interpretation of a beautiful life is shared by others is not relevant for the individual or for Schmid's concept at this stage.

Beyond the final argument, Schmid names the amount of *freedom* in modern and postmodern societies, and the resulting demands, as reasons for pursuing an art of living. He also criticises some modern interpretations of freedom and claims that an excessive urge for liberation neglects to consider possible forms of freedom. This is one reason for him to express the need for "a new modernity, which is concerned with the elaboration of a practice of freedom"[3] (2000b, 27). The tragedy of the notion of freedom in modernity, for Schmid (2000a, 115–16), is the impossibility of living and experiencing absolute freedom, whereas every realisation of freedom has to be limited to be practical. Therefore, the pursuit of absolute freedom can only lead to continuous disappointments, "as its demands always go beyond of what its realisation is able to provide" (p. 116). See Section 5.2 for more details about Schmid's understanding of *freedom*.

In the light of death, as the final argument, and a practice of freedom, the main question for the subject[4] of the art of living is: "*How can I lead my life?*"[5] (Schmid 2000b, 26). An exploration of this and other questions of the art of living will be conducted in Section 5.3.

The underlying idea of Schmid's art of living concept is the "*labour of care*"[6] (p. 32, italics added). With this term, he expresses two fundamental factors of the art of living. The first one is the care of the self (cf. Foucault 1984) and to care for one's own life. The individual of the art of living has to take responsibility and actively develop his or her own art of living. The premise for this care and development is *choice*.[7] The second factor is "labour". A beautiful life does not come easily; as with every work of art, it takes effort to shape one's self and to shape one's own life. Schmid distinguishes four areas of the labour of care: *to form habits, to enjoy pleasures, the purpose of pain* and *to live with death*. These aspects will be discussed in more detail in Section 5.4.

However, Schmid proposes not only a theory *about the art of living*; he also offers ideas and techniques for *a practical development of one's own art of living*. He describes five techniques, which will be expanded on in Section 5.5: *to make conscious use of time, to live experimentally, the art of rage, the art of irony* and *negative thinking*. He also offers some thoughts in terms of the role of education in this context and emphasises the importance of *hermeneutics* – as a basic skill and central point – for an educational approach.

5.2 Choice and freedom

One of the underlying ideas for developing an art of living is the ability to make choices and to have a certain *freedom of choice*. These terms and their use, however, are quite controversial. This section will, therefore, clarify Schmid's understanding of these terms and their interpretation in this book.

Freedom of choice is important for the art of living, as an active shaping of one's own life requires available options one can choose from in the first place. *Choice* and *freedom*[8] are in general important factors of modern human self-conception and fundamental for many social constructs and ideas, such as state constitutions or the universal human rights movement.[9] The idea of freedom in a general understanding is that human beings can make decisions with regard to their person, their actions and their location based on their own judgement and desires, without oppression or unreasonable limitations. Hence, freedom is largely understood as a freedom of choice. Therefore, the existence of choice in the first place is a preliminary for freedom as well as for the development of an art of living.

The terms *choice*, *freedom* and *freedom of choice*, however, have been shaped by political agendas, especially by neo-liberal streams, in recent years; therefore, it seems necessary to clarify their meaning in the context of this discussion. The neo-liberal movement, and very strongly so here in New Zealand, used *choice* and *freedom of choice* as slogans to advocate for less governmental influence and more liberal market structures in all possible areas of former welfare state agendas. The idea was, and still is, that market rules are far more efficient than governmental management, and that market rules can be applied not only for commerce, but also for social policy areas such as healthcare and education.[10] Recent global developments and international research (Wilkinson and Pickett 2010) indicate that this "ideology" (Codd 1993, 32) does not work out as well as believed. However, in this discussion these terms do not align with neo-liberal interpretations, but they are understood as follows: *choice* describes the process of choosing, which everyone has to go through hundreds of times per day (see later); *freedom* refers to a literal freedom and the ability to do something (in the least of all in terms of governmental restrictions, but in any other way – mental, physical or emotional); finally, *freedom of choice* describes the freedom that *evolves through or is limited by* choice, and it means only in a second instance the freedom *to* choose.

Problems of choice

There are various problems concerning the concept of choice on theoretical and practical levels. The question, for example, of whether human beings are capable of having a freedom of choice at all is contested. Deterministic ideas and neurobiological science question the existence of humans' free will and even proclaim that there is no such thing as "free will". Gerhard Roth (2001), for example, a German neurobiologist, argues that free will cannot exist, as neurons in an area of our brain related to decision-making are activated significantly *before* one is aware of the decision one is making. So, he concludes, neural areas in our brain are making decisions for us without our conscious mind knowing it. We merely get informed about the decisions our brains make, which we perceive as our own independent decision. This argument, however, is contestable in at least two regards: first, the human brain is a network of interconnected areas, and it is very likely that one's choice-making area has been influenced by conscious considerations before triggering a decision; and, second, the idea of a free will, which is totally independent from all neurological determents (as it is often the underlying assumption in deterministic arguments) is a too extreme interpretation of this concept. Human consciousness, thinking and decision-making are functions of the human brain; therefore, they are dependent on physical neurological processes. However, concluding that a physical representation of human decision-making alone negates the existence of free will is a flawed argument. Roth subsequently qualified his statement in later works and moved closer to an interpretation of free will in line with the philosophy of Peter Bieri (2006), who himself is strongly influenced by the ideas of Daniel C. Dennett (2003).

Dennett's argument builds on a deterministic background, but opens the possibility for the existence, or better evolvement, of free will through evolution:

> To say that if determinism is true, your *future* is fixed, is to say . . . nothing interesting. To say that if determinism is true, your *nature* is fixed, is to say something false. Our natures aren't fixed because we have evolved to be entities *designed* to change their natures in response to interactions with the rest of the world. It is confusion between having a fixed *nature* and having a fixed *future* that mismotivates the anguish over determinism.
>
> (p. 93)

His main argument for free will is that our future is determined by everything that happened before: we make judgements on the basis of causality in the world – through earlier experiences and the events that have happened to us, but we are not fixed in our nature. We can change *our nature, our self* and even adjust our choices when circumstances change. If, for example, someone could predict how we will decide and lets us know, this information alone will enable us to change our decision – or not, if we so chose. Therefore, the idea of free will is compatible with a deterministic worldview. The philosophical debate about the existence of free will is by far too extensive for the scope of this discussion. However, Dennett (2003) proposes a good argument for the evolution of free will, and Bieri (2006) discusses different forms and experiences of freedom and dependence in more depth than can be done here. It will be assumed, based on the arguments outlined earlier, that the experience of one's own freedom through one's own decision-making is a resemblance of reality and no illusion. Otherwise, all human undertaking and striving would be an illusion and not only devastating for an art of living, but for humankind in general.

Following the assumption of the existence of "free will," and having determined that choice is necessary for freedom to exist, a new problem arises: in some, especially modern, societies an underlying, widespread belief has evolved, which assumes that *more choice leads to more freedom*. Unfortunately, this belief has proven to be false, as Barry Schwartz (2004) argues in his book *The Paradox of Choice*. His main point is that if we, as human beings, are presented with too many choices, as, for example, over a hundred different salad dressings in the supermarket or hundreds of different models of mobile phones, we tend to avoid making choices and, therefore, *limit our freedom through not choosing*. Moreover, if we spend the time to categorise all available choices, limit down the numbers, assess the remaining items and finally come to a conclusion and choose, for example, a particular mobile phone, we will be less satisfied and draw less pleasure from our choice, as we will experience a nagging feeling that with so many options available we most likely would have been able to make a better choice. *Hence, a* key problem for developed, modern societies is the limitation of freedom and a reduction of pleasure and satisfaction through an oversupply of choices.

Another problem in this context, according to Schwartz, is our poor ability to make the right choices. He points out that people are often overly positive about the pleasure and outcome they expect to gain from a particular choice and fail to anticipate the reduction of experienced pleasure and happiness through adaptation. Further, it often happens that people make a less beneficial choice due to false judgement or expectations. Seligman (2010) and Csikszentmihalyi (2008) found out that this phenomenon is especially true for the amount of happiness one predicts. People seem to be drawn to making wrong judgements about what will increase their overall happiness and life satisfaction. This lack of ability alone would be reason enough to explore choice and prudent decision-making from an educational viewpoint, but choice, as pointed out earlier, is also an important aspect for a good life and the development of one's own art of living.

Choice and the art of living

Schmid (2000a, 188–93) approaches the question of choice from a different perspective than deterministic or neuroscience researchers. He states that today people often have the *impression* of not having a choice, despite their constitutional guaranteed freedom of choice and an increased number of opportunities available in modern developed societies. This perceived lack of choice, according to Schmid, is based on three dilemmas: the *necessity to choose*, *not being able to choose* and the *loss of opportunities* through every choice made.

Schmid's first dilemma for people in modern societies is the *necessity to choose*, which is required by the sheer number of possibilities and offers one experiences every day (p. 189). The range of choices one is confronted with forces the individual to make decisions in a split second, even if it is only a half-conscious "not interested", which is a real limitation to one's freedom of choice. Schwartz (2004) states further that the number of opportunities and choices experienced in developed (Western) societies has reached an unprecedented level, which the human mind is simply unprepared for. Hence, we limit our freedom through avoiding choices.

Schmid's (2000a, 189) second dilemma, *not being able to choose*, results partly from the mentioned increased pressure to make choices, often on the basis of uncertain or unexplored criteria, and from the inability to make right choices due to a lack of preparation. This, again, is in line with Schwartz's (2004) observation that people are ill prepared to make beneficial choices and misjudge their experience of positive emotions significantly.

Schmid (2000a, 189–90) claims, similar to Schwartz (2004, 117–46), that the third dilemma, *loss of opportunities*, is not new but much more obvious and significant today. Every decision made potentially renders a pile of opportunities impossible – for the near future or in general. Schwarz (pp. 117–46) explains how this loss of opportunity not only adds to the "cost" of a decision, but also reduces the satisfaction one experiences afterwards. In sum, these three dilemmas can lead to the false perception that one has no choice at all.

Schmid (2000a, 190–1) also points out that our freedom of choice is not completely independent, but determined to some extent by internal and external conditions. Internal conditions are, for example, one's aims, values and norms, and also one's current emotional state and the level of mental energy at one's disposal. External conditions or circumstances can be anything external to the choosing individual, such as time frame, situation or resources. Schmid proclaims that it is important to reveal these dependencies to identify the actual scope of opportunities one has in a certain situation. Only when one is aware of these limiting factors can one determine the actual options at hand or work to change these factors, if possible, to open up more or different opportunities. In any case, for Schmid, choice is the core of "self-mastery" [*Selbstmächtigkeit*], and reflective decision-making is fundamental for practising an art of living (p. 192).

Further, Schmid (2000a) explores the role of perception for choice and decision-making (pp. 194–200). He distinguishes between three types of perception: our common *sensual perception*; a *medial perception*, which mainly developed in the last century through radio, TV and computer; and a so-called *virtual perception*, which has been developing more and more in the last 10 to 20 years through, for example, virtual realities and social media in the Internet. The link between perception and choice is *attention*. To make a decision, according to Schmid, we need to focus our attention on what lies in front of us, on the choice at hand. If there is no immediate choice to make, our attention releases or broadens the focus to put ourselves into relation to our surroundings and to find our place in our experienced living reality. A point Schmid does not discuss, but which might be interesting to follow up on, would be the impact an increasing number of choices and attention-demanding situations have on our ability to find our place in the wider context of our living environment and reality. What he comments on, however, is the necessity to consciously limit one's focus of attention and point it on one's own self. Focusing on one's own self is important to find a coherent way through the multitude of opportunities, and it pays credit to the limits of our perceptional abilities. Developing sensitivity or "*a feel*"[11] for what is relevant, combined with reflecting upon one's experiences, is necessary for an individual to finally make good choices.

Schwartz (2004, 222–36) concludes, similarly, that a focus on one's own happiness and meaning in life is helpful to mediate not only the number of opportunities, but also the effects of social comparison, which are often part of the evaluation of one's decision. He states that one needs to choose when to choose, to rely on heuristics to make decisions that are of limited importance and to appreciate the freedom that comes from constraints one is subjected to – or subjects oneself to. Schwartz also proposes that an attitude of "*satisficing*" – being satisfied with a "good enough", a sufficient outcome – is by far more helpful to cope with the dilemmas outlined earlier than a strategy of "maximising" – always searching for the best possible option (pp. 225–6).

In terms of *types of choices*, Schmid (2000a, 205–15) distinguishes on various levels, which are not all important in an educational context. However, his distinction between what he calls "*Einzelwahl*" [particular choice] and "*Fundamentalwahl*" [fundamental choice] is of relevance: to comprehend these two types of choices can help the choosing individual make better choices and to develop habits and heuristics to make quicker choices without risking being incoherent or random. A *particular choice* is, according to Schmid, a choice with immediate consequences: "Do I go to work now or should I do some shopping first?" or "Shall I buy this shirt or the blue one?" It describes the type of everyday choices one has to make countless times a day. *Fundamental choices*, on the other hand, are choices that determine future developments and bias upcoming particular choices. These are choices about one's own character, one's own self: "Is the way we treat animals important enough for me to become a vegetarian?" or "Shall I rather buy fair trade products, as they guarantee that the people who produce these products can at least make a living?" Once a fundamental choice is made, it becomes part of one's self-concept and belief system and, therefore, influences upcoming particular choices as, for example, which products to buy in the supermarket or which clothing store to go to.

The central point for the art of living is the *sensitive choice*, in contrast to the often-emphasised rational choice. It depends on having a feel (see earlier) for what is right in a certain situation, and it allows mediating between conflicting demands (p. 203). Through this notion of sensitivity, Schmid links choice with the concept of practical wisdom (*phronesis*) (p. 221). He uses this term, as defined by Aristotle, as "being" in the middle between the upper (rational) and lower (sensual) faculties; thus, it combines rationality with sensitivity. Practical wisdom, according to Schmid, is the key to keeping the right balance between too much and not enough; between the I and the Other; between new and old, to name only some examples.

Education and choice

What consequences follow for education from these deliberations? First of all, the topic of choice and how to choose must not be ignored in the educational upbringing of pupils. Our inherited choice-making faculties, the way our brain makes assumptions and uses heuristics to make choices, are not sufficient anymore to cope properly with today's reality of life. Education needs to supplement not only the background knowledge on which to base one's choices on, but also the knowledge about our choosing ability itself. Only this added knowledge can help the individual understand why certain choices might not be in one's best interest, although they might seem this way, or which pitfalls might lead to decisions that are possibly contrary to one's own best interest.

One might argue that even without this knowledge, people are doing quite well, and even additional knowledge about our limitations cannot prevent bad decisions. However, this view has two significant flaws. As mentioned earlier, this is the first time in human history with such an amount of options, opportunities and the demand to make more and more choices every day. Additionally, the knowledge about our limitations is not only available, but it is used in advertising and in political speeches, for example, to influence one's decisions often not in one's own best interest, but in the interest of a third party. Therefore, to prepare our young people for the world they are living in, they need to be aware of conditions that can and will be exploited by other people.

Beyond the obligation to prepare and protect one's pupils, it will be argued in Section 7.2 that education should help the individual to develop his or her own art of living. Choosing well, especially in terms of fundamental choices, which influence one's own beliefs and one's own self, is significant for this charge. Therefore, being aware not only of the practical implications of how our brain works in regard to choosing, but also of the philosophical and ethical implications related to particular and fundamental choices is an important outcome of educational processes. Further, Schmid's notion of sensitive choice and its grounding on practical wisdom emphasise the importance to incorporate appropriate learning domains and settings in educational concepts.

The following sections will now introduce Schmid's art of living concept *Lebenskunst*, including individual, social, ethical and educational considerations. As mentioned earlier, the interpretation of *choice* and *freedom* as has been outlined in this section is significant for a proper understanding of Schmid's theory and the subsequent use of these terms throughout this book.

5.3 The quest for a new art of living

According to Schmid (2000a, 9), the question of the art of living arises – and has done so repeatedly in history – when traditions, conventions and norms are no longer convincing. People feel a loss of belonging, a loss of safety, and they start asking questions about life itself, the purpose of life, how they should live and how they *want* to live. The modern and especially the postmodern age is one such time: relationships are unstable, rapid developments and changes demand high flexibility in professional and personal life settings and people are often confronted with new and alien situations. Traditional norms and values to base decisions on are losing their validity (Schmid 2000a, 101–3).

It needs to be pointed out here that Schmid seems to focus on Western (post-)modern social and cultural settings. He does not expand on how an implementation of an art of living might be possible in other (e.g. traditional, pre-modern or collectivistic) cultural settings. These points need further discussion, which exceeds the scope of this discussion and should be part of future research in this area.

The question of the good life and the art of living – referred to by different terms over time – has been discussed repeatedly in philosophical history. However, Schmid (2000a, 27) claims that this topic has been nearly lost in modern academic philosophy and only started to make its way back again into the philosophical discussion in the middle of the 20th century, although other philosophical and psychological research topics explored related areas. He refers, for example, to philosophers of the 19th and 20th century, such as Dilthey, Freud, Heidegger, Adorno, Sartre and Foucault, among others, who contributed ideas that are relevant to the discourse of the art of living. Foucault (1984), especially, made progress on this topic with his concept of "the care of the self", which strongly influenced Schmid's approach.

In his reflections about the philosophy of the art of living, Schmid distinguishes two different relational viewpoints. The first is "philosophy *as* the art of living", which is, for example, Socrates' approach: the art of living is practised through living a philosophical life. The second perspective is "philosophy *of* the art of living", which is a theoretical reflection of how life might be lived in a mindful way. This latter relation is the starting point for Schmid's work. The general understanding of an art of living, according to Schmid (2000a), is "the opportunity and effort [. . .] to live life in a reflected way and not simply to let it flow unmindfully" (p. 10). This is the point where philosophy can play a part for an art of living: it can help to increase awareness and "work out the material and the methods to help an individual in different situations to understand his or her own life and to make his or her own choice" (p. 10). Schmid's aim is to (re-)introduce the art of living to the philosophical and public discourse – not to present a finished concept, but to explore the topic, identify its boundaries, define the horizon and main issues and open it up for discussion again.

Philosophy of the art of living

When discussing the art of living, one needs to be aware of the fact that this term has multiple dimensions and can be understood in different ways. Schmid distinguishes in general between the popular and the philosophical spheres. The popular interpretation of the art of living has its place in knowing how to deal with the problems of everyday life and how to enjoy the immediate pleasures of life. The philosophical art of living, however, adds the following aspects: "the knowledge of interrelations [in life], their origin, their "reasons" and their possible future developments, to set one's own way of living in relation to these"[12] (p. 50). This *reflective element* is necessary to enable the subject of the art of living to cope with the freedom and challenges of current (post-)modern societies. The nearly unlimited opportunities and choices, not to speak of the influences one is exposed to, demand for a more reflective art of living to enable individuals to make their *own* decisions. Unfortunately, Schmid provides limited consideration of the influence of social and cultural settings on the general ability for developing one's own art of living. Some aspects, in this context, are discussed in Sections 9.1 and 6.4.

The starting point of a *reflective art of living*[13] is the care of the self. Schmid explains that this care can initially be of a frightened nature, but it should evolve to a sensible and prudent care under philosophical guidance. This development shifts the individual care from an egoistical to a more prudent and wiser perspective, which not only includes one's self but also the relationships between oneself, others and society. It also provides the foundation for an ethics of the art of living, which can be followed voluntarily and out of conviction by the individual, as one is aware of one's relationship with and part of society. The development of this care of the self enables individuals to consider themselves and matters of life from a distant perspective. In doing so, they can reassess their orientation to life and acquire new criteria for defining their own version of a beautiful life, which is not based on superficial pleasures. This *Socratic-Platonic* element, as Schmid calls it, along with the *Aristotelian* elements of prudence and practical wisdom, in the meaning of being able to make sensible choices, is essential for a reflected art of living (pp. 50–1).

Schmid introduces, further, the *Cynic* and the *Epicurean* elements of the art of living. The Cynic element features an autonomous self – a self that has mostly authority over itself – and the necessary labour of the self to change and consolidate itself. Schmid calls this latter part *askesis*, not in the sense of a lonely retreat, but as the active work on oneself to learn how to let go of addictions (to all sorts of things in life); shape one's newly gained freedom; develop habits of attitudes and behaviour; and especially gain an openness of mind. The Epicurean element, on the other hand, is both a *condition* for an autonomous self and a *goal* for the subject of the art of living: only through "training of the sensible handling of affect and a calculated, open [*freimütig*] use of pleasures" (p. 52) can autarky of the self be gained. In addition, through these learned skills of how to use and deal with emotions properly and how to make sensible choices, an individual will be able to maintain a balanced and joyful life (p. 52).

In addition to these fundamental elements of the art of living, Schmid explores some other components based on the history of the art of living. Among these is one more essential factor for an art of living: the *Stoic* element. According to Schmid, the development of one's self and one's life "is a matter of [. . .] self-acquisition through which it [, the self,] is able to escape occupation through both others and fateful circumstances even if it is not able to avoid them"[14] (p. 52). This stoic element focuses mainly on these parts of life that are not controllable by the individual, but which are a matter of fate. To accept the given circumstances, to guide one's own thinking and to choose wisely are the challenges of individual growth in this context. On the other hand, Schmid cautions that an excessive stoicism can lead to extreme acceptance and to neglect the question of what can be changed.

Finally, with a reference to Montaigne, Schmid subsumes three more factors under the category of the "*modern elements*"[15]: the *essayistic*, the *sceptical* and the *critical* element (pp. 53–5). All these elements are of increasing importance in the modern and postmodern age. For Schmid, the term *essayistic* means, in this context, to live experimentally: in a world of change and loss of orientation, the subject of the art of living has to choose between increasing numbers of possible ways of living without knowing where they might lead. The *sceptical element* describes a questioning approach to knowledge. Knowledge claims are often tentative and fallible; they need to be open to revision. This shows that the right way of life cannot be derived from an inappropriate belief in knowledge. The

Schmid's concept of the art of living 71

second dimension of this element is scepticism about the present: the point is to live in the actual present, but also to keep a healthy distance and an open mind about what could be different. The *critical element* finally is directed towards definitions of life and life itself. It cautions to be critical and not to easily accept definitions and opinions about how life supposedly is or how it should be lived. It also demands to keep a critical perspective of the art of living itself. In light of this factor, an explicit definition of rules and formulae for the art of living is not possible; only a description of potential aspects and the foundation of an art of living concept can be accomplished. The philosophy of the art of living cannot determine the content, but only make suggestions of what might be possible for an individual to shape his or her own life.

Ethical considerations

The ethical perspective for an individual art of living in a postmodern culture, where traditional justifications for moral standards are not valid anymore, has its difficulties. Schmid (2000a, 60–71) explores this issue in his contemplations and offers a conceptual answer. He states that the foundation for an ethics of the art of living *evolves from a reflective art of living*.

To avoid misunderstandings, a clarification of Schmid's definition of the terms *moralism, morality* and *ethic*[16] is needed. *Moralism* is used here as a validity and an obeying of heteronomous duties that are imposed by religion, politics or nature. The implied norms are usually unquestioned and define good and evil, or nice and awful, for example, and are phrased like "you should. . . " or "you should not . . . act in a certain way". The purpose of *morality*, on the other hand, is historically to question those norms and morals; therefore, it adds a reflective element to the discussion. It approaches moralisms with a critical attitude, but does not rebut them completely. From the second half of the 20th century on, the critique of moralisms has become a common problem for people in current societies, due to the erosion of traditional forms of justification for moralities (religion, higher authorities). Consequently, the questions of "*What should I do? What should we do?*"[17] (p. 61) span the field of *ethics*, which affects "the whole individual and social behaviour in the space of freedom" (p. 61). Previous heteronomous norms (cultural and religious conventions) need to be redefined through the power of persuasion [*Überzeugungskraft*], which can only derive from the free and good judgement of the individual.

Schmid refers back to Kant as the first philosopher who identified this problem. He develops a hierarchy model that spans between moralism, on the one end, and Kant's *meta-ethics*, which Schmid calls ethic I, on the other end (see Figure 5.1). Between the practical norms and Kant's abstract categorical imperative, which is a formula to judge the quality of a particular norm if it is wishable or not, Schmid places an ethic II (*practical ethics*), which is more applicable in everyday life than Kant's ethic I. This practical ethic II contains principles that have a wide consensus, mostly based on commonly accepted fundamental and human rights, without having an ultimate foundation. This is, according to Schmid, the layer mostly

> **Moralism** (norms, "you should . . .", "you should not . . .")
> **Ethic_II** (practical ethics, social layer)
>   **Ethic_III** (Individual layer, ethics of practical wisdom)
> **Ethic_I** (meta-ethics, categorical imperative)

Figure 5.1 Hierarchy of ethics as proposed by Schmid.

used in modern ethical discussions to find common rules and ethical standards for general science, economy, medicine, biology and genetic science, for example. These principles come to pass through discussions and a common understanding. Therefore, this ethic II is applicable for groups and societies only.

The challenge for the art of living, however, is to define an ethic that is mainly based on the individual, but still suitable for a social setting. Schmid calls this ethic III *individual ethics*, or *ethics of practical wisdom*. The ethic III could be seen as a sublayer of ethic II (see Figure 5.1), as it has its focus not on questions of social living, but, as the name implies, on the form and organisation of an individual's life. It is an ethics of choice, which is the foundation for an individual and self-responsible lifestyle. The faculties of prudence and practical wisdom of the individual are the basis for this ethic, and it also ensures, "based on the self-interest of the individual [. . .], the consideration of the interests of others and the general public, as this again is of importance for the individual's own interests" (p. 67). Schmid describes further the art of living itself as a form of individual ethics:

> The individual ethics that is understood as an art of living finally occurs in the artful realisation of existence, which is based on reflection of the conditions and possibilities that are of importance for this realisation; instead of presuming the self and its capability for life, the reflected art of living aims at the development of one's self and on learning how to shape one's own life.[18]
>
> (p. 67)

He gives four reasons for the importance of the development of this individual ethics: (a) the *motive* for morality in current (post-)modern societies can only be well understood self-interest. Other points of orientation imposed through religion, politics or nature are not commonly accepted anymore, and a universal altruism cannot be counted on. Only Socratic self-care and Kant's duties towards the self can be a foundation for acknowledging duties towards others and caring for others. (b) The *ability* for morality is based on an active and strong self that is capable of realising moral principles. To develop this self is an exercise of the art of living. Further, (c) the *realisation* of morality takes place mostly in a private space. This is the reason for Schmid's claim for an ethical discourse which is only concerned with general norms for everyone to be fatal. To expect individuals to conform to rules and norms that are formulated in a theoretical discourse is to rely on wrong assumptions. Finally, he identifies (d) a *limited importance* of morality in everyday life: most actions and decisions of individuals in their daily routines are not relevant in any moralistic way other than the question of personal responsibility for one's own life. A philosophical discourse cannot provide categorical norms for these situations, but can only offer help in the form of advice (pp. 67–8).

Descriptions of the art of living

As argued earlier, there can be no final definition about the content of the art of living, but there can be a philosophical evaluation and description[19] of an art of living concept. Schmid's (2000a, 71–3) approach begins with the perspective of art: life as a work of art. Each art needs a material that is shaped by the artist; in the art of living, *life* itself is the material to be formed. His interpretation of life is neither a biological nor a mystical one; he simply regards life as it is lived by the individual. Hence, Schmid's first description (I) of the art of living is "the continuous work of forming one's life and one's self" (p. 72). This shows that there is no end to the art of living until it is forced to end with the death of the individual; it is an ongoing process. As the subject of the art of living forms his or her own life and self, he or she becomes also the object of the art of living – in contrast to other arts, the subject (artist) is the object. Moreover, Schmid wonders if there might always be an art of living involved in practising any kind of art. He refers back to the ancient Latin saying *fabricando fabricamur*, which means "through forming something, we form ourselves".

However, approaching it from an art perspective, Schmid (p. 72) identifies three skills that are necessary for practising any art, including the art of living: first, a creative evaluation and identification of *possibilities* of how to form an object. This can be done through ideas, imagination, research or liberation of narrowing circumstances. Second, to *realise* these possibilities of forming, he describes the practical layer of "know-how," which includes the competence and the skill of performance. Finally, he names the mastery of *artful* realisation of possibilities. This requires insight, familiarity of and reflection on all aspects and details of the matter at hand.

Based on these contemplations, the art of living can be interpreted as an "art applied to living" performed through an *art of choice* – an aware and reflected choice between various options. Therefore, an individual art of living is flexible, as it is full of opportunities to shape one's life in different ways. Life has to be considered a "work in progress" (p. 73) that takes a whole lifespan.

As mentioned earlier, art in general and the art of living in particular are strongly connected. Thus, topics and questions of the art of living are often the theme of works of art, literature and movies. As is the norm with works of art, they reveal their topics not through bold lecturing, but through the interpretation of the individual. Schmid calls this interpretation the "*hermeneutics of existence*"[20] (p. 78), which enables the recipient to decode the work of art, identify the question and apply it to his or her own life. This hermeneutic skill not only applied to art but to life itself is of crucial importance for the subject of the art of living. To read and interpret life settings and situations and to reflect about them enable the individual to make sensible choices, include art in his or her own life and, finally, to make it a work of art. Schmid calls this the individual's "*aesthetic of existence*"[21] (p. 78).

In addition to this approach from the origin and realisation of the art of living, Schmid offers another description (II) that includes an aim and purpose:

> The art of living is the wholeheartedness of the attempt, out of [. . . the responsibility for one's own life] to take charge of one's life in good time and to maybe even make a "beautiful life" out of it.[22]
>
> (Schmid 2000b, 7)

In this second description, Schmid sums up three important aspects of the art of living. Beginning with the "wholeheartedness of the attempt", he points out that the art of living is not a process that can be done half-heartedly or that happens on its own. Far from being simple, the art of living, as shown earlier, is a lifelong labour on one's own self and one's autonomy. The second part of the quote shows, on the one hand, an obligation for one's own life: nobody else will – and nobody can – take up the responsibility for one's own self and one's life. On the other hand, this part demands timely action, as has been pointed out by Epicurus: it is never too late but also never too early to care for one's own life. After the premises in the first and the demand in the second part, the third part finally specifies the direction of the art of living and aims for the beautiful life. However, Schmid includes a "maybe" in this sentence, which indicates that a practised art of living does not necessarily result in a beautiful life, but it increases the probability of it.

As could be seen earlier, Schmid attaches importance to the art factor in his concept; therefore, the term "beautiful" has an artful connotation, *but the individual defines the actual content of "beautiful" and gives the answer to the question of what is beautiful and what is not for him or herself. Beautiful in this reading means that it is something the individual can approve of, can say "yes"*[23] *to*. This leads finally to the invitation or description (III) of the art of living, which Schmid (2000b) calls the "*existential imperative*": "Shape your life in a way that it is worth being wished for" (p. 178).

Fundamental questions

On the way to a reflected art of living, Schmid (2000a) identifies a number of fundamental questions that span the field between "Why at all?" to "What shall I do?" The initial question is whether the art of living has a right and a purpose to exist at all: "*Why shape my own life?*" One answer for this question can be found in ancient philosophy: it is the shortness of life itself. Schmid calls this the "*final argument*"[24] (p. 88). One's own death, which is not the end of life in general but only of a form of life, gives reason to add purpose to one's life; to live a good and fulfilled life. Without this boundary, life would be endless, and, therefore, one would lose any reason to shape it at all, as there would be always an eternity left to do so.

It should be noted that the argument of death as the *only* reason to care for one's life is quite questionable. However, the limitedness of one's own life is certainly *one* important factor for human beings to feel an urge and a purpose to "do something with their life". But whatever an individual's motivation might be to take responsibility for his or her life and to shape it in a way that might make it a good one, to be a valid reason in light of the art of living, it needs to be an intrinsic motivational factor (i.e. it needs to be pursued for one's own sake, not to satisfy anybody else's desires or demands).

As soon as the matter of shaping one's own life is taken seriously, the succeeding fundamental question for the individual is, according to Schmid: "*How can I lead my life?*"[25] (p. 89). For Schmid, this question is an expression of the underlying ethical question of the art of living (ethic III), "What should I do?" and, therefore, the first step to actively take possession of one's own life. As the possibility for shaping an individual lifestyle is an idea and the result of the concept of freedom in modernity, Schmid sees the difficulties in answering the previous question in the conditions of life and the multitude of possible interpretations of *life* in a modern and postmodern age.

This problematic comes to pass through an extensive demand for liberation and the neglect of developing strategies to cope with this new level of freedom. Schmid claims that this is one reason for the existing contradictions and inconsistencies for lifestyles in modern and postmodern societies. Therefore, he calls for the development of a new modernity with an understanding of a "practice of freedom"[26] (p. 90). It would be a modernity in which the subject of the art of living tries to develop one's own lifestyle and to shape one's own life in and through the challenges of modern freedom, as much as through media, IT and the Internet, for example.

Turning back to the topic at hand, Schmid's next fundamental question is: "*In which circumstances do I live? How is it possible to produce circumstances that are suitable to live in?*"[27] (p. 90). An important part of the art of living is to consider one's own life in a broader context. Schmid focuses here especially on social and community settings, which are mainly dominated through structures of power[28] – mainly the power *over* the individual, but also the power *of* the individual. The aim is, on the one hand, not to become subjected to the power of others and, on the other hand, to carefully use one's own power in a society to take part in the structures of power and politics in a responsible and prudent way (p. 90).

A further question is the question of choice: "*What choice do I have?*"[29] (p. 90). Presuming that there is a choice at all, the problem in modern societies seems to be an exponential increase of choices (see Section 5.2). Unfortunately, one could argue that most people are not properly prepared to face the flood of choices in their life, which means they do not have sufficient coping strategies to make good choices at the right time. As every decision opens and closes a whole horizon of opportunities at the same time, it changes the direction of an individual's general and social life. The basic components of a sensible choice, according to Schmid,

76 Schmid's concept of the art of living

are intuition, sensibility, prudence and practical wisdom (pp. 90–1). How to develop these faculties and how educationists can support their development will be discussed in later chapters.

To find answers to these questions, one needs to have an idea and a concept of oneself. The question to answer in this context is "*Who am I?*"[30] (p. 91). To develop a concept of one's self and to shape one's own self is mainly a matter of the care of the self (see Section 5.4). However, it also involves the care for others (see Section 6.4) as a formation of one's self can only be done in connection and exchange with others. A self-concept is not only shaped by itself, but through others one is in contact with as well. Therefore, it is important for the individual to care for his or her relationships with others and for the society he or she is living in (p. 91).

Together with an understanding of one's self, according to Schmid, a conceptual understanding of life itself is necessary as well: "*Which understanding of life do I have?*"[31] (p. 91). This hermeneutic question and the interpretation of one's own life and one's life circumstances enable the individual to lead his or her life in the desired direction. "It will be clarified through the labour of interpretation, what has meaning for one's self, what does not, what appears to be significant or insignificant, and in which way the realisation of one's life has to be aligned respectively"[32] (p. 91). Also helpful, according to Schmid, is to know and to understand life's various phenomena and circumstances: for both, hermeneutics is not only meant to be the interpretation of an implied meaning, but also to construct one's own meaning based on one's own self and to identify and give significance in terms of one's own life. This technique is the basis to acquire "*Lebenwissen*" [life-knowledge] (p. 92), which is important for the development of one's own art of living. This life-knowledge is different from scientific or facts knowledge, as it entails a personal and conscious perspective. In terms of supporting the learning of life-knowledge in educational settings, Schmid (2000a) points out that it is mainly the skill of hermeneutics, as the ability to interpret and unravel life-knowledge on one's own has to be taught (pp. 91–2). This will be discussed in Section 5.5 in more detail.

Finally, the last fundamental question Schmid names is of a practical nature: "*What can I do concretely?*"[33] (p. 92). This question concerns, on the one hand, the underlying attitude of an individual towards life and, on the other hand, everyday life itself. The answer can only be given by each individual. However, Schmid suggests some exercises and techniques that are supposed to be exemplary and can support the shaping of one's own life. These are, for example, the formation of habits to experience relief from recurring choices; to develop coping strategies to handle pleasures and pain; and to learn how to live with death, which is of high priority, according to Schmid. Various other techniques include dealing with effects such as anger and rage; making proper use of time; practising to live experimentally; and, finally, to practise one's own ability for irony and negative thinking. These techniques will be discussed in Section 5.5 in more detail.

As a final remark, Schmid (2000a) points out that these questions are not to be asked in a sequential order, but that they require each other in a reciprocal way (p. 93). Raising these questions does not provide a final answer of how to live a good and beautiful life, but they are operable and possibly helpful for the individual to develop his or her own art of living. As a result, Schmid chooses not to discuss the concrete matter of how to live a successful, happy or good life, as these questions can only be answered on the basis of individual norms, values and beliefs. Therefore, these fundamental questions have to be left for each individual to resolve while developing his or her own art of living. This does not mean that these questions, as outlined in this section, are insignificant; on the contrary, they just cannot be answered categorically in a philosophic discussion about the art of living. They find their place in each individual's practical approach to the art of living.

Having approached the art of living from a philosophical perspective, the next two sections will move the theoretical discussion towards practical implementations of the art of living. This will include considerations and suggestions for developing one's own art of living and how to support this development from an educational point of view.

5.4 The care of the self

The subject of the care of the self

At this point, a further clarification of terms seems to be indicated. The term *subject of the art of living*, which is used by Schmid for an individual who practices the art of living and tries to lead a good and beautiful life, might have a slightly different meaning in English as it has in the original German. A subject, in Schmid's reading, has an active and a passive connotation: the individual actively practises the art of living, and this practice of the art of living, again, influences the individual and makes him or her into the subject (passive) of the art of living. Therefore, the self has a relation to itself as object in a shaping manner (see also Section 5.3). The same applies for the use of "subject" in relation to the care of the self.

One of the main qualities of an individual who practices the art of living is the *care of the self*,[34] or to care for oneself. To emphasise the importance of care in this context, Schmid (2000a, 244) refers to Heidegger who stated that the terms "care" and "self" are describing one and the same concept. Although this extreme position is questionable, it highlights the connection between "care" and "self" and, further, the importance of the care of the self. Initially this care can be of a frightened, anxious nature: one worries about oneself and one's own life. This worry often leads to a growing self-interest, which, again, triggers the process of self-acquisition (see Section 5.3). The individual no longer lets his or her own life be mainly determined by others and external circumstances. This is the starting point of a development that leads to an enlightened and "*klugen Selbstsorge*" [*prudent self-care*] (p. 245), which combines self-awareness and self-formation. According to Schmid (p. 245), as the subject of the art of living creates a distance to himself or herself, one obtains an outside perspective to look upon oneself and to make one's own self the object of one's care. The self of an individual becomes the object of the individual's self-care. This is related to what Foucault (1984) had in mind with his concept of *the care of the self*, and this is also Schmid's starting point for a concept of an individual art of living.

To offer a clearer understanding of the concept of *self-care*, as proposed earlier, Schmid (2000a) refers to three aspects of this concept, which together provide a foundation to living a good life: a *"selbstrezeptive"* [*self-receptive*], a *"selbstrelexive"*[*self-reflective*] and a *"selbstproduktiv"* [*self-productive*] aspect (p. 246). The *self-receptive* aspect, according to Schmid, defines the moment of the awakening of one's self-interest and one's self-consciousness. An individual experiences himself or herself as an autonomous, self-governed being and not as the property of and under the governance of others. The *self-reflective* aspect marks the transition from self-consciousness to self-awareness. It enables the individual to look and reflect upon himself or herself, the circumstances of his or her life and current and future opportunities from an outside perspective. Finally, the *self-productive* aspect of the care of the self is the progression towards an active shaping of one's own self and one's own life.

Other factors that are important for Schmid as well are the ability to understand oneself in a hermeneutical way (see Section 5.5), to take a frank and honest stand towards oneself and to develop a foreseeing and anticipating habitus that keeps future developments and opportunities in mind while making decisions in the present (p. 247).

The labour of care

In line with Foucault, Schmid emphasises that the care of the self is not an effortless process, but involves labour. Accordingly, he introduces the term *"Arbeit der Sorge"* [*labour of care*] (Schmid 2000b, 32, italics added), which describes the effort taken by the individual to achieve self-mastery, to create new opportunities for oneself and to make oneself less dependent on external circumstances. The two major factors of the labour of care are, first, *self-nursing*, in the meaning of looking after oneself – not in a healing but in a caring way, which takes care of one's needs – and, second, *self-development*, which is, in Schmid's reading, the improvement of one's self in relation to what one can wish for. Schmid claims that the prudent self-care also demands an altruistic perspective, which he describes as *reciprocal care for others*: each individual needs to give others the same care and attention he or she receives from them in terms of his or her own development.

Further aspects evolving from the demands of prudence and the care for others are a *pedagogical* and a *political* perspective. The pedagogical or educational consequences in this context are that "others [are] not solely to be used as resources for own means, but they [are] to be empowered to their own care of the self"[35] (Schmid 2000a, 248). Schmid's more in-depth discussion of this aspect will be taken into account in Chapter 7. Care for others also expands in circles, which, in their widest form, reach the realm of the care for one's society as a whole. Schmid refers to this circle as the political aspect of the care for others (pp. 247–8).

Schmid summarises all these aspects of an active labour of care under the term "*Asketik*" [askesis] (p. 325), which includes the four practices of the labour of care, as described next, as well as five additional techniques for practising an art of living, which will be discussed in Section 5.5.

Development of habits

The first practice of the labour of care is the *development of habits:* to engage in the art of living implies taking up responsibility for one's own life and actively making one's own choices. According to Schmid (2000b, 32–41), habits are important for one's self as they help to provide quietness and relief from continuous choice making. A choice made once that has proven to be a good one has the potential to become a habit for similar situations. Schmid uses the German word "*Gewohnheit*" [habit], which is related to the German word for home: "*Wohnung*" (in English one could probably employ the word "habitat" here, which comes from Latin *habitare* and means "to dwell" or "to live" somewhere), to make a connection between habits and home: a habit is not a special place, but a repeated action that feels familiar and allows the self to be at rest.

Further, Schmid (2000b) points out that one has to distinguish between two forms of habits: *heteronomous* habits are unreflected habits, adopted from the cultural and social environment one is living in, and *autonomous* habits, which are self-reflected habits based on one's own norms, values and choices (pp. 34–5). Heteronomous habits mostly occur in dealing with issues of everyday life, but they can also contain strange and abnormal beliefs and routines that become "normal" through repetition. Examples of this form of habits are fashion, facial expressions, ways of speaking (e.g. dialects), but also relationships of power, predominance and oppression. More important in the context of the art of living are autonomous habits, due to their self-reflected nature. Formal heteronomous habits can become autonomous habits through critical reflection and the acknowledgment of their value based on one's own norms, instead of blind adoption. The challenge and the aspect of labour for the subject of the art of living are to transfer heteronomous habits into autonomous ones.

Most important in this context, according to Schmid, is that habits can shape one's self and one's character; therefore, one needs to choose and cultivate habits wisely in line with the direction one wants one's own character and self to develop. Although it is necessary to accept some culturally conformed heteronomous habits to fit into the social setting one is living in, a modern society should allow and emphasise the development of a self-defining *habitus* that is the core factor of individuality in general. Schmid calls these self-defining habits *existential* habits, as opposed to *functional* habits, which are a set of habits for different standard situations. Especially in fast-changing environments, as in our current modern times with its myriad choices every day (see Section 5.2), it is prudent to develop a set of functional habits for recurring situations.

The danger of habits, on the other hand, is to grow too comfortable with keeping them and becoming inflexible in one's ability to adopt and change. To counter this, Schmid (2000b) suggests that one should habitually reflect upon one's own habits – adopt a habit of self-reflection, so to speak, and critically revisit one's habits (pp. 39–40). He also points out that *awareness, spontaneity* and *flexibility* are useful personal traits one should cultivate to counter the trap of getting caught in one's habits.

Enjoying pleasures

As the second practice of the labour of care, Schmid (2000b, 42–50) proposes, similarly to Epicurean philosophy, to abandon (unhealthy) worrying – especially in terms of pleasures and enjoyments – and to make the enjoyment of pleasures part of one's own art of living. Pleasures in life should not only be accepted when presenting themselves, but they should be actively increased when it is possible to do so. This said, he also points out that it is important to be aware that not all pleasures are good at all times and one should choose wisely which pleasures, when, with whom and how long to enjoy them. He proposes to develop a *selective habitus* towards pleasures, but nevertheless to make pleasures a part of one's life, and, once decided after prudent reflection that now is the time and place for certain pleasures to enjoy, then to enjoy them properly without worrying and the burden of a bad consciousness.

Schmid's considerations on this topic are influenced by Foucault's thoughts about pleasures, and he tries to advocate for a balance between a positivistic view on pleasures as part of life and a prudent approach to pleasures that does include knowledge when to follow one's desires and when to restrain oneself. He also seems to express an alignment with Epicurean ideas in terms of taking pleasure from small things in life and not necessarily to indulge in pleasures that can have a negative impact on oneself or others. He refers to the care for others and the ethical implications deriving from prudence and practical wisdom, as discussed earlier, to take into account the effect on other people and to see the Other as an end in his or her own right and not just as a means to an end.

It needs to be pointed out here that Schmid does not distinguish between pleasures and enjoyments, as discussed in Chapter 3. However, his reference to Epicurus and his proposal to be selective with regard to pleasures indicate that he would most likely be in favour of what has been discussed earlier as higher pleasures and enjoyments.

The meaning of pain

The meaning of pain is, according to Schmid (2000b, 51–61), to provide a cause or incentive to care for oneself and to engage in the labour of care. Similar to physical pain, which urges us to remove the cause for this pain or to tend to an injury, psychical or mental pain and suffering indicate areas of our self that are not well or negative circumstances that influence our well-being and provide an incentive for change and development. The sweetness of life and the value of happiness and well-being need pain, suffering and death to come to the fore and have value.

Schmid (2000b) claims that a proper way of dealing with pain is not to suppress or annihilate it, but to heed it, to pay attention to it and to become aware of the cause – the external trigger and the wound itself. Causes for bodily pain are often straightforward; in terms of mental pain and suffering, the cause can be multifaceted and elusive: a word, a look, a slap or a lack of love and attention are only some examples of external triggers. The internal wound, however, can only be caused if one is perceptive to such a trigger. A critical statement might not affect one person at all – it might even encourage this individual to use the critique offered in a constructive way; the same statement might cause severe mental pain and distress for another individual. Therefore, every mentally hurtful experience has more to say about the person who got hurt than about the person or circumstance that triggered this pain. It offers the opportunity to become aware of a sore spot in one's self-concept, one's personality. It offers the opportunity to become aware of this point, to engage it, to shape one's self accordingly and finally to leave this weak spot behind (pp. 53–4).

However, Schmid (2000b) acknowledges that pain and suffering can take effect in two different ways: destructive and constructive, and both are often intertwined (p. 58). The destructive effect can lead to illness and prolonged suffering, the constructive effect to personal growths and development. Illness and pain, where they cannot be overcome, need to be accepted and integrated into one's life. The artistic skill of an art of living is not only to accept these impediments, but finally to transform them into a state of "serenity and happiness, for which Epicurus once gave an example, where he understood how to gain happiness in life from the experience of pain" (p. 59).

Finally, pain and illness are reminders of one's own limits and one's limitedness in life, which can become the strongest motivation for change, taking up responsibility and actively developing one's own art of living. Schmid argues in similar lines for the role of the fourth aspect of the labour of care: death.

To live with death

Similar to modern ways of pain avoidance, such as medication, drugs, television and so on, Schmid (2000b, 62) claims that "death" has been tuned out of many people's lives. To experience death, to deal with people's dying and to reflect upon one's own mortality, is rarely part of modern people's experiences. This is a fact that needs to change in the context of an art of living. According to Schmid (2000b), death is the natural boundary of life; it creates a limitation that provides value for life. If one would never die, what reason would one have to live a good life, to put effort into life and actively shape one's own life and one's own self? If there was infinite time to live a good life, it would be quite possible that people would wait indefinitely for the good life to start, as there was no need to start working on it at any given moment. Therefore, to live with death means to be

82 Schmid's concept of the art of living

mindful of the limitedness of one's life and become aware of the need to actually "do something" with the rest of one's remaining lifetime (pp. 62–70).

A technique often used in an art of living context is to "think about death" (p. 65). Seneca advised Lucilius in his letters to exercise daily his ability to leave this world in tranquillity, and Montaigne proclaimed to picture death each day, "not to fret, but to take pleasure in life more than ever" (as cited in Schmid 2000b, 66). This technique cannot only open one's mind for real pleasure and happiness in life, but it can also reduce one's fear of death and dying. It can also show the real meaning in life, which "is not the modern trias [threefold] of money, power and sex, but the fundamental trias of *birth, death and the erotic which lies in between*" (p. 68): the experience of every moment of life with all its possibilities and beauties.

Having established the fundamental concept of the labour of care and the care for the self, the next section will discuss some of Schmid's educational considerations in terms of the art of living, including further techniques for developing one's own art of living and living a good and beautiful life.

5.5 An educational perspective

Hermeneutics

A fundamental skill for practising the art of living is the ability to interpret and make sense of life and life surroundings. Schmid (2000a, 286) employs here the tradition of "*hermeneutics*", based on Gadamer's (1975) broader interpretation of this term. For Gadamer, hermeneutics is not so much a skill as a phenomenon: it is a circular self-shaping process that not only lets a person understand the world he or she is living in, but also gives meaning to the world through interpretation and, therefore, creates meaning for the individual (Weinsheimer 1985). This process, which will be explained in more detail here and also later on in Section 9.1, is important for the concept of learning as it is understood in this book, as well as for acquiring *Bildung* and the development of one's own self in the context of the art of living. Despite hermeneutics being a larger phenomenon, the term *hermeneutical skill* will be employed here to describe the aspects of the hermeneutic circle (see later) that can be influenced and strengthened through educational intervention: one's ability to make interpretations of the world that are significant and sensible, that is, interpretations that reflect "reality"[36] as much as possible. This aspect of hermeneutics, which includes to sharpen one's perception, is meant when the term hermeneutical skills is used here and later on.

In the context of Schmid's concept of the art of living, hermeneutics is important for individuals to determine their way through the world and give their life the intended direction, the right orientation. However, hermeneutics in the art of living does not only refer to the interpretation of life circumstances, but gives meaning to objects, events and situations surrounding us, as indicated earlier. Individuals, therefore, become the originators of meaning: they add meaning to the world, identify the interrelations of their surroundings and thus give their own life meaning. Central for Schmid are interrelations in life, as items or events do not have meaning on their own, but receive it in connection with other appearances or situations (pp. 286, 294).

Hermeneutics, or interpretation, is based on signs; language is the most commonly used form of signs today. Therefore, a prerequisite for hermeneutics in the art of living is language, which contains meta-signs to describe our perception of the world. According to Schmid, the last or final interpretation of the world is done by each individual himself or herself. Individuals construct their own reality based on their perception and interpretation of the world. We are living in what Schmid calls "interpretation-worlds"[37] (p. 288), and, at the same time, each individual is influenced and formed by his or her experienced reality [*Lebenswirklichkeit*], which again influences his or her perception and interpretation. Consequently, *the self shapes itself through this hermeneutic circle*. This, then, is the foundation for the art of living: to be able to shape one's own self. Hence, good language and hermeneutic skills are important for an individual art of living and central for an education for the art of living. This is one of the key areas Schmid identifies for the development of *Bildung* (see next section), which needs to be supported through education and teaching practices.

Schmid also states some demands for hermeneutics in the art of living. Each interpretation needs to be *plausible* and *understandable*. This is mainly a demand of the principle of prudence, as an uncritical interpretation could lead the subject astray and cannot serve as a reliable point of orientation for one's own life. Thus, it is important to keep an open mind, consider other possible interpretations and train one's own *critical faculties*. But despite these demands, an interpretation does not necessarily have to conform to the public view. On the contrary, each individual has his or her own hermeneutic competence to make interpretations that are plausible on the basis of *his or her own* reflected reasoning and experience. Schmid calls this "*autonomic hermeneutics*"[38] (pp. 289–90). Beyond that, to learn how to take a *change of perspective* and contemplate other interpretations is important to prevent egoism and egocentricity. To reason through and comprehend other viewpoints or to try experiencing the other's living environment and perspective opens up different interpretations and ways of life. This furthers tolerance for others and is the condition for doing justice to other people, circumstances and creatures (pp. 296–7).

Further, hermeneutics can be divided into two elements: "*fundamental hermeneutics*" and "*practical hermeneutics*".[39] The first element, according to Schmid (2000a), consists of the individual's underlying beliefs, norms, values and aims (p. 291). It is the origin of one's existence and everyday life. The second element applies these underlying principles to actual, immediate choices in concrete situations. The experiences one has through these choices, again, influence the fundamental hermeneutics of the individual. The significance of hermeneutics lies in the familiarity with the constructed reality and in the construction of *a sense of life* – in the literal meaning of *life and its settings making sense to the individual*.

Humans in general do not feel comfortable in alien situations and surroundings, which they do not understand properly. Individuals interpret their perceptions of the world and the situations surrounding them, and by identifying the interrelations they make themselves familiar with their living environment and determine meaning and sense. A change to this environment disturbs this constructed familiarity and irritates the individual, who has to use his or her hermeneutic skills to adjust his or her perceived reality and recover the experience of familiarity. The postmodern age, with all its short-lived and quickly changing settings, is a constant disturbance to this experience and, therefore, a challenge for people in today's societies. This again underlines the importance of hermeneutics and an individual art of living (pp. 292–3).

The result of using hermeneutics is the accumulation of "*life-knowledge*"[40] (p. 298). For Schmid this is the knowledge acquired through and for life: "through" because it is mainly acquired through experience and reflection, and, hence, of a subjective and practical nature; "for" as it is concerned with the *know-how* of life and how to live: the context and interrelations of life. Life-knowledge is not identical with scientific or theoretical knowledge. But this kind of knowledge can lead to life-knowledge when it is transferred through reflection and hermeneutics to be applicable to the individual's life in a useful way. And, although it is based on experience, life-knowledge can be taught, or at least supported, in learning processes. This is possible not only through the experiences of the individual, but, for example, through educational stories and narratives that help the pupil make imaginary experiences. In this context, Schmid points out that life-knowledge also enables one to reach autonomy, which is an important aspect of the art of living, as described previously.

Techniques for an art of living

In terms of practical methods that can support the development of an art of living and working towards a general *habitus* of serene happiness, as discussed by Schmid, Aristotle and others, Schmid (2000b, 71–110) proposes five basic techniques: *to make conscious use of time, to live experimentally, the art of rage, the art of irony and negative thinking*.[41] This section will introduce Schmid's techniques with an educational perspective in mind.

To make conscious use of time

It goes without saying that the lifetime each individual is limited. As discussed earlier, this is a strong argument to make use of one's time as much as possible. According to Schmid (2000b, 71–8), to develop an art of living, it is necessary to take responsibility for one's time in life, the same as taking responsibility for one's life itself. Time is passing on its own account; one cannot influence it in any feasible way. However, one can (mostly) control the way one makes use of one's time – or not for that matter. To use one's time consciously instead of letting it pass by is part of living an artful life, according to Schmid.

Schmid (2000b) acknowledges, on the other hand, the difficulties of dealing with time, what he calls the "gap of time" (p. 72). For most people and most of their lives, their future seems to be far away and a long stretch of time with many possible opportunities. But the gap of time closes with the passing of time, and many of the perceived opportunities vanish if one has not taken preparations and action earlier on in life to allow them to come to pass. A conscious use of time means to live in the present moment but, still, to keep the future in mind and to take action to set one's path in the direction one wants his or her life to develop. As previously mentioned, it is never too late to take up responsibility for one's life, but also never too early. Now is always the best time to start, or continue, consciously on one's life journey.

Another difficulty, according to Schmid (2000b), is to fear the loss of time and to attempt to realise too many opportunities at once. This action will lead to stress, disappointment and a general negative life experience (p. 74). Trying to constantly "make the most of it" is not a prudent use of time as understood in the context of the art of living. A conscious use of time also entails the conscious decision to experience leisure time and to seemingly "waste time" by doing nothing, or just by following one's desires and having fun. However, Schmid states that making time for these aspects of life is as much a part of an art of living as is a productive use of time. As in most aspects of life, the art is to keep a balance between leisure and productivity.

From an educational perspective, helping students to understand certain complexities can have a significant impact: (i) to learn how to manage one's time properly, (ii) to limit one's expectations of what one can achieve and what one expects of oneself in a certain amount of time and (iii) to understand the concept that there is a right time for anything but that now is not always the right time for everything. Further, making especially young people aware of how the perceived gap of time can close opportunities if some actions are not taken early on in life can help them to make prudent decisions in time and reduce anxiety and distress later on. Some often commonly ignored topics by young people are, for example, the aspect of health and the delayed impact of one's behaviour (drinking, smoking, etc.) on one's body and health, or the issue of taking preparations for retirement, which have to start early in life to allow for more freedom and flexibility later on.

To live experimentally

The second technique Schmid (2000b) proposes is to live in an essayistic manner, to experiment in life (pp. 79–86). He refers back to Montaigne, who was not only the father of essay writing, but who lived an essayistic life as well by approaching all sorts of questions in life from different angles. He experimentally approached different ways to deal with situations and obstacles in life and shaped his life and his personality through these experiments. (Sarah Bakewell's book *How to Live* offers a good insight in Montaigne's life and his answers and suggestions for living a good life.)

Schmid (2000b) names two traits that go together with living experimentally: *imagination* and *curiosity* (pp. 82–3). Similarly, he describes two ways of being experimental in life. The first way is to actively imagine new ways of living, new ways of acting and reacting, and to make attempts in various directions in similar situations. The other way is to allow oneself to be tempted by new situations in life – not solely to keep to the known, but to be curious about, and open for, what one might find down a different road of action.

To have the courage to make experiments in life and attempt new ways of living can shape one's self through imagination and curiosity; it can help to stay open minded and flexible in the face of new challenges and changes in life. Educationists can support these traits of imagination and curiosity, as well as make an attempt to show their students the qualities of open-mindedness. They can challenge their students to *invent themselves*, which is nothing else than shaping one's own self and living an artful life.

The art of rage

Schmid (2000b) discusses the affect of rage as representative for dealing with affects in general. His reason to focus on rage lies in its role as the single most destructive human emotion. Mainly based on hurt feelings and mental or physical pain, rage is an affect with an immense power of destruction for relationships and the self-concepts of other people. If held on to and nurtured, rage can turn into hatred, which not only can close certain doors in life forever but also impact on one's self and personal core in negative and destructive ways. (pp. 87–96)

The nature of rage and ways of dealing with it and anger have been discussed by various philosophers of the art of living. Schmid refers to Aristotle, Seneca, Montaigne and Kant as examples to present different ways of dealing with it. Aristotle, for example, valued rage generally as a positive affect, as only a passionate heart can experience rage. However, he pointed out that one needs to be selective in when to become angry, towards whom, why, how long and in which way. For him, only on the basis of rational considerations is a righteous rage more positive then destructive (p. 87).

To introduce a contrary opinion, Schmid (2000b) draws on Seneca, whose position was to suppress any surge of rage and anger, as he did not see any positive value in them (pp. 87–8). Even the smallest arising of this emotion has to be controlled and not allowed to grow into uncontrollable rage. The way to deal with rage leads through reason only; one should monitor one's emotions and act immediately to contain anger.

Schmid (2000b) turns to Plutarch, who advocated a balance for all affects and proposed to practice habits and coping strategies for dealing with anger and rage on a daily basis and to keep them on a prudent level when they arise (p. 88). He also advised avoiding situations that might provoke rage in the first place.

Finally, Schmid (2000b) calls on Montaigne and Kant to propose a moderate dealing with rage (pp. 88–90). Montaigne, according to Schmid, was no stranger to rage, but he tried to express it in a short and private manner. To give rage its space and not suppress it was a matter of health for him, as unventilated rage can, as indicated earlier, lead to hate and negative mental and physical consequences

Schmid's concept of the art of living

for the individual. Schmid states in this context that giving one's anger space is not only healthy, but might even support a generally serene lifestyle. As mentioned previously, a prudent balance and coping with one's emotions, especially rage, is important for an art of living.

However, a theoretical awareness of the matter can only help so much. To artfully cope with one's rage, Schmid (2000b) discusses a number of strategies that can help in various situations (pp. 90–4). He calls the first method "*Prämeditation*" [pre-meditation] (p. 90), which is to picture and think through future situations that bear the potential for rage or anger. This thinking through can prepare oneself for an upcoming confrontation or hurt and help to better compose oneself when the expected situation comes to pass. It also allows the individual to hermeneutically reason through the meaning and development of a situation and might help to change one's attitude about the situation or the topic at hand. At least, one can prepare oneself for the expected emotions and will not be surprised and overrun by them, which makes it easier to keep calm and control one's emotions.

Further, Schmid recommends the strategy of *division*, which is a rational choosing of when to get angry and when not to in an Aristotelian manner. Also, *postponing* one's reaction can be helpful for a situation to deescalate and for rage to cool down and resolve itself. However, one needs to make sure to give it space later on and not start harvesting it to let it turn into hatred.

To *deal with the physical aspect* of anger and rage, one can go for a walk, a run or pace back and forth rapidly to reduce the level of adrenaline in one's circulation. Also, *turning one's rage towards something else* can be relieving and helpful, for example, a sparring session with a punchbag or similar. Additionally, Schmid offers to consider *diversions*, such as focusing on an object of interest, listening to music or watching a show, to give one's anger time to dissolve on its own (p. 92). Finally, forms of *compensation* – for instance, finding relief in loud laughing – is a method that can provide relief for all sorts of anxieties.

For all these methods, a rational outside perspective (i.e. consciously "stepping out" of the situation; retreating from an emotional to a rational level of self-reflection) is necessary to break the chain of reactions and seize control of one's affects and the situation at hand, as Schmid points out (p. 93). From an educational point of view, giving students opportunity to test and train these strategies – for example, in form of role-playing, might be a proper way of teaching this technique for an art of living.

The art of irony

For Schmid (2000b, 97–103), irony is the art of living with contradictions. He states that through irony one can gain a *distance* from an affair which allows the individual to be unaffected by the consequences of contradictions, which could lead to severe distress or despair if taken too seriously. Irony requires a form of *humour*, which can act as a shield for affairs that are of an intrinsically conflicting nature. These conflicts or contradictions can be between desires and actual reality; expectations of different roles, such as family and work life; or contradicting opinions between individuals, which cannot be proven one way or the other.

The art of irony, according to Schmid, can balance contradictions, and it allows an individual to live with them without the need to change what cannot be changed. Irony can be applied to all sorts of affairs, including self-reflection and the course of one's own life. An ironic view of one's own limitations and shortcomings can help the individual to accept oneself and the circumstances of one's life without feeling pain or humiliation for these shortcomings. It allows a level of (self-)acceptance that can be far more healthy and positive for one's well-being than self-doubt and an undue lack of self-confidence.

Irony can also hint at a *different reality* (pp. 98–9); it can raise awareness that the way things are at the moment is not the only way life could have played out and that things might easily change and be different next time. Schmid (2000b) summarises that irony has the potential to allow conflicting affairs to co-exist, to accept unchangeable situations and deal with them from a position of a humorous distance, as well as to open one's mind for other possibilities (pp. 102–3). However, irony holds the danger of accepting unbearable circumstances in a stoic manner, although they could be changed. Therefore, irony in the context of the art of living has to be used in a critically and prudent way. The development of practical wisdom can help to decide when irony is properly used and when one should take a situation seriously.

The skill to use irony can only be developed through practical experience. Irony can be encountered in multiple ways: in dialogue, in literature, in situations of daily life, as well as in theatre plays or in a classroom setting. Teaching irony cannot happen in a single session, but needs development and continuous forming and cultivation. Educationists can introduce their students to various forms of irony and slowly shape their understanding for the deeper levels of this art. However, as is the case with every form of art, it needs practice and can be more and more refined over the span of a lifetime.

Negative thinking

As final technique, Schmid (2000b, 104–10) argues for an attitude of *negative thinking*, which he places against the often-proclaimed panacea of modernity: positive thinking. He critiques positive thinking as bound to fail. It not only implies that every form of even miniature failure is negative and needs to be countered by thinking positively, it also expects constant and invariable success in all aspects of life. This expectation is bound to fail, and, therefore, positive thinking not only invites negative experiences and disappointments, but creates them.

Negative thinking, on the other hand, always expects the worst possible outcome and the worst behaviour of people, and, therefore, according to Schmid, it creates positive experiences and surprises. This form of thinking prevents disappointments and prepares the individual for a worst-case scenario. Schmid (2000b) describes this form of thinking not as simple pessimism, but as being open for the possibility of failure while keeping a preserving and cheery attitude, which keeps a distance from too high expectations (pp. 109–10).

Although some of Schmid's explanations of his understanding of negative thinking go in line with other concepts and worldviews of harbouring low or no expectations to prevent disappointments and being open for positive surprises (see Section 9.1), the extreme angle taken here, with always expecting the worst, seems to overshoot the mark. Keeping one's expectations on a reasonable level, or even to try to let go of one's expectations altogether – as much as possible (see Section 9.1) – is solid advice against disappointments and conflicts. However, according to the concept of the self-fulfilling prophecy (Merton 1957) and positive psychology research in terms of optimism (Seligman 2010, 83–95), having a generally positive attitude towards life and the outcome of affairs one is involved in will increase one's actual success rate. Part of it is due to subconscious influences and one's desire to act in line with one's expectations, which affects one's behaviour and handling of a situation and influences the outcome in the direction of one's expectations.

Not negative thinking, but an attitude of fewer expectations, less "taking things for granted" and a tendency of optimism in life might be a proper alteration of Schmid's considerations. It acknowledges the rightful critique of excessive positive thinking, but also heeds human psychology. (See Section 9.1 for more details about mind-sets, expectations and attachments.)

Education for the art of living

The primary objective of an education for the art of living is to support individuals to gain their own freedom. Moreover, it is to help them shape this freedom to make it liveable and to enable them to shape their own lives into works of art. The focus, therefore, lies on *Bildung* – in the meaning of having the knowledge, education and skill to be able to care for one's self, shape one's own self and make sensible choices. Where possible, this should be acquired through *self-bildung*. The knowledge and skills that need to be learned by the subject of the art of living to achieve the necessary *Bildung* includes *scientific* knowledge, which could possibly be of relevance for one's own life; the *hermeneutic* knowledge and skills that enable an interpretation of life and life surroundings; and the *know-how* and practical knowledge of how to live one's life. These three facets of *Bildung* and education can empower the individual to make reflected choices, which is fundamental for the art of living as shown earlier. Attention is needed not to influence the pupil in the process of education in a way that would make choices for him or her, but to enable the pupil to make his or her own choices (Schmid 2000a, 310–12).

Schmid considers further areas of an education for the art of living. First, *education for prudence* has its origin in "the self-interest of the individual to learn how to live, and how to acquire the necessary prerequisites for it"[42] (p. 312). The aim is, beginning with the individual's experiences and questions, to broaden the pupil's horizon step by step and to train all the aspects and elements that are necessary to care for one's self and to live in a sensible way. Second, Schmid names the training or formation of *sensibility*. This happens through the practice of paying attention to everyday events, which sharpens one's senses and perception. This entails a *physical knowledge*, which Schmid also calls "corporeal knowledge"[43] (p. 312). On this basis follows a *structural knowledge*, which is mainly provided by the traditional school subjects. However, a direct connection between them and one's own life is not always obvious due to an end-in-itself attitude, which is often assumed in schools. Still, these subjects typically unfold knowledge about the fundamental structures of life and the world, including their historical context and present social relevance.

The condition to be able to acquire this scientific knowledge is the *knowledge of signs* in the form of language, writing and an understanding of numbers. This allows, on the one hand, the participation in the informational world and, on the other hand, provides the foundation for hermeneutic skills, which, for example, can be trained through the interpretation of texts and stories. Finally, the development of the pupil's *imagination* is of importance to open the mind for other, less obvious opportunities and to broaden the view for multiple possible future developments. An education and training in all these areas can lead to a creative understanding of the self, the world and others. It provides the basis for the ethical dimension of the art of living through a reflected and prudent self-interest.

As mentioned earlier (Section 5.5), experiences are essential for learning processes regarding the art of living in general and acquiring life-knowledge in particular. Norms, values and beliefs, which are always part of teaching processes, need to be reflected in educational settings to train one's critical perspective. The *self-bildung* and critical self-reflection of the teacher, as well as his or her character, are of the highest importance. He or she needs to be able to balance the use of power and the relationships of power in educational situations properly. According to Schmid, only an authentic practitioner of the art of living can effectively lead others through the learning process to develop their own, individual art of living. (See Section 9.2 for more details.)

Summary

Schmid's approach to the art of living has been presented in this chapter as a holistic concept that takes into account the whole of a human's life cycle. Schmid draws on earlier philosophical approaches and discusses them in a current (post-) modern context that takes into account challenges for today's people and societies, such as globalisation, cyberspace, cultural diversity and sustainability.

Beyond the translation and summary of Schmid's philosophy in English language, various aspects have been discussed from an educational point of view. It has been shown that *Bildung* and education are a fundamental part of Schmid's art of living concept, and it has also been indicated how various aspects of this concept affect educational theory and practice. It is important for the argument in this book to have a good understanding of Schmid's theory, including the

Schmid's concept of the art of living 91

depth and broadness of his philosophical thinking. A holistic education for life theory can only be built on a broad philosophical basis. Although only a limited summary of Schmid's philosophy could be presented here, it shows his eclectic thinking and the significance of his theory for people today.

Before the importance of this concept for educational theory and practice will be explored further, it is important to discuss the philosophy of the art of living in relation to the earlier presented aspects of positive psychology to show how certain aspects of both areas support each other but also to reveal their shortcomings.

Notes

1 The articles from Burke and Aylesworth are both online media without section and page numbers. For clear identification of the cited paragraph, section headings (e.g. Modernism) and paragraph numbers will be supplied.
2 All translations of material from Schmid are my own unless otherwise noted.
3 " [. . .] einer anderen Moderne, deren Anliegen die Ausarbeitung einer Praxis der Freiheit ist"
4 Schmid uses the German term *Subjekt* in reference to an individual striving towards his or her own art of living. In German, the term has an active and a passive connotation. It might have been more intuitive to use 'individual of the art of living' as translation, but I have opted for a more literal translation here as in Schmid's argument, the subject (person/individual) pursuing an art of living is shaping his or her own self and, therefore, becomes the subject (passive) of this shaping process. Hence, the phrase 'subject of the art of living' will be used in this book to show this reciprocal active-passive relationship of one's self to oneself.
5 "*Wie kann ich mein Leben führen?*"
6 Original: "Arbeit der Sorge". In this part of Schmid's theory a clear influence of Foucault's work can be seen. Compare Section 2.2 and the concept of the "care of the self" by Foucault (1984).
7 Choice is understood literally in this context and for the purpose of the argument: people have choices in life, and they have to make choices and decisions. Choice, therefore, has aspects of both *freedom* and *demand*. See Section 5.2 for a more detailed discussion of *choice* and *freedom* in the context of the art of living and education.
8 It needs to be pointed out that terms such as "choice", "freedom" and "opportunity" have different meanings in various contexts. The understanding of these terms in this context is as literal as possible without any political or ideological connotations intended.
9 See, for example, the preamble of *The Universal Declaration of Human Rights* (United Nations 1948).
10 See, for example, Codd (1993) and Larner (2000).
11 Schmid (2000a, 198) uses the German word "*Gespühr*" and describes it as the ability to raise awareness for inter-relations of situations and circumstances.
12 "Die Kenntnis übergreifender Zusammenhänge, ihrer Herkunft, ihrer 'Gründe' und ihrer möglichen künftigen Entwicklung, um die Lebensführung dazu in Bezug zu setzen."
13 Schmid uses mostly the term 'reflected art of living' when he refers to a philosophical understanding of this term. It is mostly a synonym for 'philosophical art of living', but with a connotation of his own exploration of this topic.

14 "Was das Selbst aus sich und seinem Leben macht, ist eine Frage seiner Selbstaneignung, mit der es sich der Inbesitznahme durch Andere, aber auch durch schicksalhafte Verhältnisse selbst dann entzieht, wenn es ihnen nicht entkommt."
15 "*moderne Elemente*" (italics in original).
16 Original terms: Moral, Moralistik, Ethik.
17 "*Was soll ich tun? Was sollen wir tun?*"
18 "Die als *Lebenskunst* verstandene Individualethik besteht schliesslich im kunstvollen Vollzug der Existenz auf der Basis der Reflexion jener Bedingungen und Möglichkeiten, die für den Vollzug Bedeutung haben; anstatt das Selbst und sein Lebenkönnen vorauszusetzen, zielt die reflektierte Lebenskunst auf die Heranbildung des Selbst und das Erlernen der Lebensgestaltung."
19 I am avoiding the term *definition* in this section to prevent misunderstandings. Where this term is used later on in reference to the art of living, it is always aimed at the philosophical concept itself and not meant as a definition of a good life. This is conforming to Schmid's use of the terms *definition* and *description*.
20 "*Hermeneutik der Existenz*".
21 "*Ästhetik der Existenz*".
22 "Lebenskunst ist die Ernsthaftigkeit des Versuchs, aus diesem Grund [der Verantwortung für unser eigenes Leben] sich das Leben beizeiten selbst anzueignen und vielleicht sogar ein 'schönes Leben' daraus zu machen."
23 Schmid uses the German term "*bejahenswert*" (2000b, 178), which means 'worth of being wishable for', 'worth of saying *yes* to something'.
24 "das finale Argument".
25 "*Wie kann ich mein Leben führen?*" The German word *führen* in this context includes a connotation of actively giving direction, to lead in a certain direction.
26 "Praxis der Freiheit".
27 "*In welchen Zusammenhängen lebe ich? Wie lassen sich Zusammenhänge herstellen, in denen es sich leben lässt?*"
28 Compare the philosophy of Foucault (1984) in terms of power structures.
29 "*Welche Wahl habe ich?*"
30 "*Wer bin ich?*"
31 "*Welches Verständnis vom Leben habe ich?*"
32 "Durch die Arbeit der Interpretation wird geklärt, was für das Selbst Bedeutung hat, was nicht, was als wichtig und unwichtig erscheint und auf welche Weise der Vollzug des Lebens daran jeweils zu orientieren ist."
33 "*Was kann ich konkret tun?*"
34 Schmid uses the German terms "*Selbstsorge*" and "*Sorge um sich*". The translation used here leans on Foucault's (1984) notion of the care of the self.
35 "Andere [sind] nicht bloß als Mittel für eigene Zwecke zu gebrauchen, sondern sie [sind] selbst zur Sorge um sich zu befähigen."
36 Reality is another difficult concept that would need further discussion beyond the scope of this text. For the purpose of this argument, what is meant here is, for example, to be able to discern the intentions behind an action of another person properly and not to assume intentions that have not been there, or, as a second example, to properly identify causality between situations or events to be able to intervene in an intended way.
37 "Interpretationswelten".
38 "*autonome Hermeneutik*".
39 Schmid uses the terms "*Grundlegungshermeneutik*" and "*Anwendungshermeneutik*".
40 At this point I want to explain that the characteristics of the German language allow an easy creation and definition of words with new or altered meaning. Here, Schmid creates the term "*Lebenwissen*" (and other terms at various points in his concept). This creative aspect of the German language and Schmid's use of the

same is challenging for the translation of his theory. I have tried to find expressions that are as close to the meaning intended by Schmid as possible, followed by a more detailed explanation where necessary.
41 Schmid's original German terms ar: *Die Zeit gebrauchen, auf den Versuch hin leben, Kunst des Zorns, Kunst der Ironie* and *Negativ denken*.
42 "das Eigeninteresse des Individuums, selbst leben zu lernen und sich die nötigen Voraussetzungen dafür anzueignen".
43 "leibliche[s] Wissen".

6 *Lebenskunst* and positive psychology in dialogue

This chapter[1] is a critical comparative analysis of the philosophical concept of the art of living (with a focus on Schmid's concept *Lebenskunst*) and positive psychological research about the good life from an educational point of view. The angle taken in this chapter will be based on the assumption that there are commonalities and overlaps between philosophy, psychology and education. In the end, all three disciplines explore the thinking, feeling, behaviours, teaching and learning – among other topics – of human beings; therefore, all three have one essential overlap: the human being itself. This chapter will explore the extent of common ground between positive psychology and some philosophical concepts (especially Schmid's approach) of the art of living, where they differ and where they might be complementary. It will become apparent that both disciplines provide beneficial insights for the topic at hand and that the findings in this chapter will strengthen an educational conceptual approach to the art of living.

6.1 The relevance of the art of living and positive psychology today

Some reasons have been provided in previous chapters for the increased interest in questions of living a good life, the art of living and positive psychology today. Schmid (2000a, 9), for example, states a pattern throughout history, where uncertain times – especially uncertainty with regard to appropriate behaviour, values and norms – lead to uncertainty in life. This uncertainty triggers questions about how one should live, what purpose life has, what values one should have in life and why one should act in accordance with certain values. Schmid identifies a degeneration of values and especially a loss of validation of these values and norms in (post-)modern societies. As stated earlier, the loss of the validation of traditional norms and values came to pass through the deconstruction of religion and governmental authority, as well as the rapid globalisation and change of our modern world, which increases the need for guidance and stability (see Section 5.3). Schmid's final argument (one's own death and the finality of life) for taking up the responsibility for one's own life and the desire to make it a beautiful one is more pressing today than ever. Through the loss of a belief in God and any form of afterlife, the notion of death can become much more powerful and fearsome for modern people.

Csikszentmihalyi's (2008, 10–14) consideration about the actuality of these questions, as outlined in Chapter 4, is based on a social assessment of life in postmodern America. In accordance with motivational theories, for instance, Maslow's hierarchy of needs, he claims that some basic requirements need to be fulfilled for humans to become interested in questions about the good life at all. These basic needs are mostly of physiological and social origin: examples are food, sleep, shelter, company and belonging, as well as respect for and from others. Csikszentmihalyi points out that when these problems are solved, people tend to start developing new desires, which they believe need to be fulfilled to enjoy a good life. He observes that most of these upcoming needs are influenced by cultural beliefs, which today consist of money, cars, big TVs, expensive food, luxury holidays and such. The problem he identifies with this behaviour is that human nature is able to accustom easily to new situations (a new car, good food) and subsequently new desires arise, which again are believed to be necessary for happiness and well-being in life to come to pass. A spiral for the need to improve one's life, instead of taking pleasure and contentment in what one has, becomes apparent. This vicious circle is often supported by the media, advertisements and other systems of the cultural setting one lives in.

Although Csikszentmihalyi is mainly referring to the United States, most of his considerations can be applied to the modern (Western) world in general: the consequences of globalisation, unchecked capitalism and inequality affect many countries and societies today. However, Csikszentmihalyi states that finally people will start to realise that this form of life does not provide the happiness and contentment they hoped to achieve in the first place. This, then, is the point when people start to ask the question: "Is this all there is?" (p. 13). One field people can turn to, to answer this question, is religion – either in the form of standard confessions or of alternative beliefs of an Eastern origin or esoteric nature. Still, Csikszentmihalyi claims that today the existing religious systems can only provide a temporary solution:

> The form in which religions have presented their truth – myths, revelations, holy texts – no longer compels belief in an era of scientific rationality, even though the substance of the truths may have remained unchanged. A vital new religion may one day arise again.
>
> (p. 14)

In this quote, Csikszentmihalyi indicates what he believes to be one of the main reasons why humanity in total was not able to improve their level of happiness and contentment despite all technical and social developments in the last centuries. He states that the truth about living a good life, which is *"that the control of consciousness determines the quality of life"* (p. 20, italics added), can be traced back all the way through the existence of human records. He provides an alleged quote from the ancient oracle of Delphi, "Know thyself", and Aristotle's notion of the "virtuous activity of the soul" (p. 20) as examples of early ideas that seem to go in line with his own work on flow and enduring happiness in life. The reasons for the limited progress made, despite the existence of this knowledge over time, are that

> the kind of knowledge – or wisdom – one needs for emancipating consciousness is not cumulative. It cannot be condensed into a formula; it cannot be memorised and then routinely applied. [. . . It] must be earned through trial-and-error experience by each individual, generation after generation.
>
> (p. 21)

The second reason appears to be that the knowledge about how to control one's consciousness is dependent on the cultural context and needs to be adjusted and reformulated each time a cultural change occurs. The existing knowledge, although still relevant, does not reach and correspond to today's people anymore.

Another factor for the current popularity of happiness might be the multitude of possibilities. The technical development in the last 200 years led with increasing speed to a *Lebenswelt* [life world or experienced reality] with sheer uncountable opportunities and an unmatched freedom of choice for today's people. The downside of this development is the number of choices each individual has to make every single day. A whole set of skills is necessary to interact with new technology, cope with the challenges that arise and make informed decisions and prudent choices. Media-literacy[2] and the ability to judge the value of advertisements for one's own life are only two that spring to mind. The amount of choices and the pace of postmodernity, which is, according to Schmid (2000a, 101), an intensification and an over-acceleration of the modern age, can lead to the same uncertainty as does the loss of traditional values and norms. In fact, these two phenomena might be connected, as some values and especially some norms are not applicable to today's changed *Lebenswelten* [life worlds] and everyday experiences anymore.

Both Csikszentmihalyi and Schmid, although coming from different angles, reach the same conclusion: the contemporary cultural context plays a major role in the popularity of questions about the good life. This is not surprising as an increased general interest indicates a communal background for this development instead of factors on an individual basis. Still, the art of living has been a continuous topic of interest throughout time for individuals as well as cultural instances such as philosophy, religion and other spiritual belief systems. Another corresponding point between Schmid and Csikszentmihalyi is the notion of a possibly necessary change of culture. Csikszentmihalyi (2008, 14) indicates in the citation earlier that a "vital new religion may one day arise again"; Schmid (2000a, 103), on the other hand, proposes the development of a *new* or *different modernity*, which should preserve the freedom of postmodern societies, but shift the focus from a fixation on pleasures in life to a more reflective way of living.

However, it is also important to point out the differences of the philosophical approach versus the psychological perspective. Overall, the psychological point of view seems to focus on the development of the individual and to emphasise enduring happiness as the utmost goal for a good and meaningful life. The philosophical concern seems to be more holistic in two regards: first, it focuses more on a culture, or even humankind as a whole – although Schmid's concept also includes many references on an individual level; and second, most art of living concepts do not state happiness and well-being as the only goals for a good life. On the contrary, even a life without happiness at all can still be regarded as a good life. The discrepancies of the interpretations of the good life will be discussed in more detail in the next section.

6.2 Concepts and definitions of a "good life"

The term *good life* has a multitude of possible readings and interpretations in philosophy, as well as in psychology and in everyday language, as discussed in Section 3.6. To avoid misinterpretations, Schmid (2000b, 19) distinguishes between the *good life* and the *beautiful life*. The good life, for him, is the expression of the current popular interpretation of living a life of pleasures and amenities. Similar to Csikszentmihalyi and Seligman, he sees such a life as the wrong path and as a life which is empty and dead. The beautiful life, however, is marked by an active and conscious influence of the individual on his or her own life (Schmid 2000b, 10). It is the attempt to take responsibility for one's own life and shape it accordingly to one's values, beliefs and imagination.

In contrast, Csikszentmihalyi and Seligman assume that enduring happiness is the utmost goal for human beings and, therefore, the purpose and definition of a good life. They emphasise enduring happiness to differentiate their concept from a pleasurable life, which would seek a maximisation of short-term pleasures instead of long-lasting happiness. Enduring happiness is achieved through enjoyments and flow and related to Aristotle's idea of *eudaimonia*, as discussed previously.

Another term employed by Seligman (2010, 250–60) in this context is the "meaningful life", which is, in his definition, a good life lived with the purpose of serving the greater good – this can be, for example, a group of people or humanity in total. Still, the question remains if what is measured as happiness in positive psychology today does reflect the extent of the idea of happiness and *eudaimonia* that is discussed in psychological and philosophical literature. In line with Biesta's (2006, 12) enquiry about the direction of the relationship between measuring and values,[3] the question here is if we measure what happiness is or define happiness as what we can measure. Biesta rightly points out that we are currently living in an age of measurement and that the current emphasis on assessment suggests that everything worthwhile should be able to be measured and, therefore, can be measured. The consequence of this belief is that if something cannot be measured, it is not worth being pursued or taught. This view is highly questionable and leads to a neglect of important aspects of teaching and certain needs of students, such as personal development, pursuit of wisdom and the value of spirituality for human beings (see, for example, Section 9.1).

As has been shown in Chapter 2, there are various philosophical, spiritual and religious approaches to living a good life. However compelling the idea of enduring happiness and well-being as an overall goal for each individual might be, it cannot be assumed that a happy life is the same as the good life. Even when we assume that each individual is strongly motivated by a desire for lasting positive emotions in one's life, it seems to be a far stretch to employ gratifications in form of flow experiences as the silver bullet or the only way to achieve this goal. Further, going back to the different interpretations of a good or beautiful life, in the end it is the value system and the beliefs a person has which decide the outcome of one's normative judgement about one's own life. Somebody might believe, for example, that happiness and positive emotions are evil or sinful and cannot be considered good at all; consequently, this person would not consider a life as a good one if it had many of these qualities. Someone else might have experienced many hardships in his or her life, which were never pleasant, nor would they reflect any kind of enjoyment through a state of flow. However, these hardships might have shaped and developed the self and the character of this person in a way that he or she in the end could say: "I am content with who I am and how I evolved through this life – it was a good one." There are many different ideas and opinions about the nature of a good or beautiful life, which seems plausible, as every individual is unique,[4] despite social and cultural influences and multiple connections with one's environment. Therefore, Schmid's more holistic approach to the topic and his individualistic definition of a beautiful life seems to be favourable. Nevertheless, due to the proximity of education and motivation, and for the sake of keeping a holistic perspective, it is important to keep in mind that striving for enduring happiness is a significant motivational factor for human beings.

6.3 Concepts of the self

This section will show that the overlap between the philosophical and psychological notion of the self is rather limited, but that psychological research not only supports the idea of the existence of an entity inside each person, which can be identified as one's *own self*, but also contributes structural knowledge to this discourse. For an educational approach to the art of living, which is based on philosophical concepts that not only require the existence of a person's self but also depend strongly on its qualities, it seems important to analyse the meaning and scope of this term and how it is understood in the respective disciplines.

The self is an important term in Schmid's theory of the art of living, especially in the concept of the care of the self, which places the shaping of one's own self as the key element for a beautiful life. The philosophical discussion about the nature of the self, however, is highly conflicted and anything but unitary.[5] Schmid does not give a final definition himself, but he makes some anthropological assumptions, which he claims to be essential for his art of living concept, and he names some qualities of the self as it is understood in his work. Schmid's (2000a, 83–7) anthropological assumptions are that human nature is *contradictory* (e.g. one can love and hate with the same intensity); it has a *social* component (one acts in relation to others, and power[6] is an underlying principle); and it has an *ecological* dimension, which means that the human being influences the environment, but one is also influenced *by* the environment. Further, human nature entails the dimension of *choice*, which implies that an individual can decide – more or less reflected – about oneself; the dimension of *self-awareness* (human beings are rational and able to identify connections); the dimension of *care* (in the meaning of prudent and forward-thinking behaviour, which compensates for shortcomings in other areas humans might have compared with animals); and the dimension of *experiences*, which implies that human beings are open to experiences, flexible in terms of change and able to draw conclusions because of their experiences. It is also necessary to mention that for Schmid the "human nature" is always a *cultural* one: humans (generally speaking) do not live alone, but in groups and societies; therefore, the social and cultural aspect is essential for each human being.

On the background of these anthropological assumptions, Schmid's notion of the self is a *self-reflective* one. The subject or individual (*hypokeímenon; subjectum* – p. 239) is able to look beyond the immediate situation and circumstances and contemplates his or her own situation from an outside perspective. For Schmid, the self has a subject character and an object character; it contains an *I*, which is the actual, current instance talking or thinking about oneself, and a *oneself*, which is the reflective object part one is talking or thinking about. Two relations connect these two instances of the self: (a) an epistemic self-consciousness one, which is a cognitive self-reflective relation, and (b) an ethical-aesthetic self-shaping one, which is a forming and transforming relation towards one's own self. Hereby, relation (b) is conditional on relation (a). Thus, he states that one's self is the subject and its own object at the same time with a self-reflective and a self-forming relation.[7] What follows is that the I is shaping one's own self; therefore, one's I changes, which leads to a state of *self-alienation*. This alienation is followed by an orientation towards the other (new) self to come back to oneself. Schmid describes this process as a spiral one, as the individual is not turning to the former self, but to the changed one. This spiral of self-shaping and self-annexation is the essential process of the art of living. It is favourable, as one has to be open to change instead of fearing the loss of identity, which often can have a limiting impact on people's self-development. For Schmid, the self preserves itself through continuous change (pp. 239–42). Therefore, change is an integral part of Schmid's self-concept to form a beautiful self and a beautiful life.

Schmid implicitly solves the question of identity by pointing out that the state of self-alienation is not to be avoided. On the contrary, in the context of the art of living it is even to be pursued "to multiply the self and to base one's self-consciousness on the multiple experiences of otherness, [which leads to] a self-consciousness that has no need anymore to protect one's own identity too fearful"[8] (p. 242). Schmid trades the concept of identity for the concept of a coherent self, where the connecting parts of the self combine to an organic whole, which stays coherent even if the individual parts are dialectic and continuously changing (pp. 242–4, 252–7). Constant integration of change into one's own self is necessary to construct coherence. A lack of care for the self would lead to dissolution of the self and the subject, but through coherence the self forms and shapes itself, and so one shapes one's own life into a work of art. As mentioned previously, this shaping process frames the core of Schmid's art of living concept *Lebenskunst*.

The self-concept in positive psychology, compared with Schmid's philosophical approach, is rather limited. One reason for this shortage might be that the focus on happiness as the ultimate goal does not necessarily need to take into account the shaping and transformation of one's self; although, flow, as the single most potent technique to increase enduring happiness, entails personal growth. Another reason might be that the question of the self is traditionally a topic of personal psychology, social psychology and, more recently, neuropsychology and therefore might not be considered necessary to be discussed in positive psychology in more depth. To provide a broader background for a dialogue between the disciplines about this topic, a brief outline of the more common aspects of self-concepts in the psychological discourse will be given before summarising Csikszentmihalyi's adaptation for positive psychology.

The phenomenon of the self is a rather complicated matter and can be approached from various directions. One of the most recent developments in psychology is *A Social Brain Sciences Approach to Understanding the Self* (Heatherton, Krendl, Macrae, and Kelley 2007). The objective is to identify the parts of the brain involved when aspects of the self are active. According to Heatherton et al., there is no one single location in our brain for the self and its functions, such as thinking about one's own identity, personal traits and attributes, or recalling memories that are linked with one's self-concept (p. 4). These functions and memories are spread out through our brain, and the combination of all these functions and memories form what we perceive as our self. However, Heatherton, Krendl, Macrae, and Kelley (2007) also state that memories relevant for, or connected with, one's own self are stored differently from other memories: people are more capable of recalling memories connected with their own self than other memories; self-related memories are easier and quicker to recall than other memories[9] (p. 5).

Although these results underpin the phenomenon of the self itself, they do not explain the content and structure of one's self-concept. The latter area is closer to the field of personal and social psychology. One of the first sophisticated theories about the self in psychology was proposed by Carl Rogers[10] in the 1950s. In short, Rogers distinguished three components of the self-concept: the *self-image*, which is one's own perception of oneself; the *self-esteem* or *self-worth*, which reflects how one accepts and values oneself; and the *ideal self*, which is the vision of how one would like to be. The overlap of self-image and the ideal self determine the amount of self-esteem: if both fit together nicely, one's self-esteem is higher than when both images are incongruent. It needs to be noted that Rogers conducted this theory on a phenomenological basis and, therefore, he builds a bridge between psychological and philosophical approaches.

Lebenskunst *and positive psychology* 101

A more recent concept is the self-complexity model discussed, for example, by McConnell and Strain (2007). Interestingly, they state that there is a relation between one's self-concept content and one's level of well-being; they claim that the "understanding of [this relation...] is critical but far from complete" (p. 52). The self-complexity model is an attempt to merge self-concept content (thoughts and opinions about oneself; compare Rogers' self-image) and self-concept structure (aspects such as roles and relationships). An example would be the hypothetical person John (see Figure 6.1), who might be a successful young student; he is on good terms with his family and quite extroverted when going out with his friends. Therefore, the self-concept he would draw for himself could contain different roles (aspects) such as "family member", "student", "peer group" and different content (attributes) such as "helpful", "social", "outgoing", "intelligent" and "successful". John might attribute some of these contents with one role and some with more. In Figure 6.1, one can see that he associates "social" with the family and the peer role; this attribute connects these two aspects of his self-concept, whereas the student aspect stands alone.

McConnell and Strain (2007) describe some phenomena regarding the self in connection with well-being, which can only be summed up at this point[11] (pp. 57–64). First, there seems to be a negative correlation between the number of aspects (e.g. roles) and well-being: more aspects in one's self-concept have a dampening effect on one's well-being. An explanation for this might be an increasing level of stress and a diminished experience of control over the development of one's own self through increasing numbers of self-aspects (p. 63). Second, McConnell and Strain explain a concept they call "spill over" (p. 59), which describes the effect that a positive or negative impact has on one of the attributes, which are connected to more than one aspect, and influences the well-being of both aspects. If, for example, John receives negative feedback about him being social in a peer setting, this will also affect his self-image of the family aspect; therefore, both aspects will have a combined reducing impact on his self-esteem. If he receives positive feedback, accordingly, it will have a combined positive effect. Feedback on not connecting attributes will only have a singular impact on one's self-esteem. Third, an individual with a more complex self-structure is

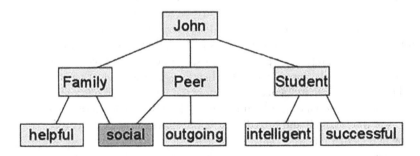

Figure 6.1 Example: John's self-concept.

less affected by the spillover effect, as feedback on special attributes affect only a smaller part of the self, whereas individuals with only one or two aspects are highly affected.

The following quote from McConnell and Strain sums up the nature and purpose of self-concepts from a psychological point of view:

> In sum, it seems that self-concepts are highly organized memory structures featuring critical attributes that, because of their exceptional accessibility, serve to guide the interpretations of behaviors and characteristics of one's self and of others. [. . . Many] self-regulation theories posit that comparisons among self-aspects serve to regulate social behavior and also account for the experience of affect from one's successes and failures.
>
> (pp. 55–6)

Csikszentmihalyi's (2008, 33–6) notions about the self are, at least in his book *Flow*, quite superficial. He states that "the self is in many ways the most important element of consciousness, for it represents symbolically all of consciousness's other contents, as well as the pattern of their interrelations" (p. 34). Therefore, the self is part of the consciousness and contains all content (memories, impressions, perception) that is part of the consciousness and the interrelations between these memories, impressions and perceptions. Further, he claims that the self foremost represents the "hierarchy of goals" (p. 34) one builds up on the basis of one's own memories and experiences. According to Csikszentmihalyi, one is only aware of a small part of one's self at any given time: one's body, an idea or a goal one tries to achieve, for example.

Comparing Schmid's philosophical contemplation of the self with the psychological approach shows that psychological research seems to focus on physiological and neurological aspects as much as on the structure of one's self-concept, including interactions of structural aspects and contents. The philosophical approach is mainly concerned with the contents – if one wants to use the psychological distinction in this context – or the quality of the self. Both are important research areas for understanding the self and its formation, but not all aspects are relevant for the contemplation at hand. Schmid's thoughts about the qualities of the self are more important for an educational approach to the art of living than structural or neurological considerations. However, we can learn from psychology that what one experiences as one's own self does have a representation in one's brain – not a single area, but various functions and relevant stored memories. Further, memories are an important part of one's self-concept – especially memories that are encoded as relevant to the self. Therefore, educational processes (learning and experiences) can influence and support the formation of one's self, especially when the educational object (content, idea, skill) is considered relevant for one's own self by the pupil and linked with one's self-concept. A conclusion one can draw here is that an educational art of living approach needs to pay attention to the relevance of lessons for the student's self-concept. After all, the shaping and growth of the self are core concepts of the art of living.

From a philosophical point of view, as from a psychological one, there is so much more to say about the self, its formation and its implications. Perry (2002), for example, discusses questions about personal identity, memory, continuity of one's self over time and the formation and aspects of the self itself in depth. His contemplations expand into the structural domain of the self-concept, and he partly reaches conclusions that are in line with psychological results. However, it is not possible to reflect on the whole discussion here; therefore, the interested reader might refer to Perry (2002), Sorabji (2006), Taylor (1989) and other literature mentioned earlier for more details.

6.4 Social influences on individual human beings

A consideration of postmodern understandings of the human being as either an individual or a social being is quite significant for an art of living concept. Schmid's (2000a, 73–5) approach defines the individual not only as the subject *and* the object of the art of living, but also as *the single point of reference for a normative evaluation of one's own life*. If one's own life is perceived as a good or beautiful one should depend on the individual's norms and values alone and not on the opinions of other people or on social conventions. The premise is, as discussed in the previous section, the existence of an entity in every individual, which is identified as his or her own self. However, as pointed out in Chapter 1, one's surroundings and the social environment undoubtedly influence the development of one's self, but in the end one is capable of agreeing or disagreeing with social norms and conventions and, hence, is able to form one's own opinion – that is, if one has acquired a certain level of *Bildung* and hermeneutical skill, which points out the importance of the art of living as has been discussed earlier. As one's own self and, therefore, one's own life is the object that is shaped in the art of living, and one's own self is also the shaping entity – the artist – consequently one's own values and beliefs provide the basis for one's evaluation and judgement of the outcome of this shaping process: one's own life. One reason for Schmid to use the term "beautiful life" instead of "good life" is to emphasise the relevance of an individual's own beliefs, values and taste and to avoid misunderstandings through varying interpretations of "good" (2000b, 9–10). However, *the Other* and the relationship between the subject of the art of living and the Other are important factors in Schmid's (2000a, 258–71) concept. The aspects of prudence and practical wisdom require the individual to take the Other and his or her desires into account. This consideration is the foundation of Schmid's ethical concept for the art of living (see Section 5.3). Schmid does not claim the human being to be an individual distinct from society and social surroundings, but, on the contrary, to be an *individual with an inherent social component*. A human being is a social animal but unique in its existence, with an identifiable notion of one's own self and, therefore, an individual.

The interrelations between an individual, a group and the cultural context seem somewhat different from a positive psychological point of view. According to Csikszentmihalyi (2008), it is necessary for individuals "to overcome the anxieties and depressions of contemporary life, [. . . to] become independent of the social environment to the degree that they no longer respond exclusively in terms of its rewards and punishments" (p. 16). In this notion, Csikszentmihalyi indicates a similar direction as Schmid does: one needs to be one's own reference for what is desirable and how to live a good life. The underlying assumption for this claim, however, appears more drastic than Schmid's notion of the individual as a social being. Csikszentmihalyi requires the individual to provide his or her own rewards to reach the previously indicated level of autonomy, which appears necessary for a happy life. But he also claims that it is more difficult to reach this level of autonomy than it might seem. The goal is to achieve control over one's own experiences, which "requires a drastic change in attitude about what is important and what is not" (p. 16). One reason is that individuals in social contexts most often learn to postpone gratifications to an unspecified point in the future, which emphasises the importance of future outcome to be of higher value than the actual present. Individuals in cultural settings often learn early that everything they are supposed to do – according to the cultural norms and demands – will be important for their own future and rewarded at a later point in time. Taking into account motivational comments such as "You will need this when you want to get a job" or "This will help you become rich when you are grown up", which most will have heard in school or childhood at some point, make this claim empirically comprehensible. In addition, Csikszentmihalyi points out that cultures and social settings are *dependent* on this kind of reward and punishment system to keep the cultural subjects in line and the society alive (p. 17).

The problems for an individual's good life and happiness, as Csikszentmihalyi points out, are the suppression of individual desires (which are important to increase flow experiences and enjoyments) and the fixation on future rewards (which sometimes is the promise of an upcoming "good life" itself) that prevent people in social settings from increasing their level of enduring happiness. Although it has been shown previously that the "good life" is not necessarily a "happy life", the drive for happiness, especially enduring happiness, is a strong motivational factor for human beings in general. Therefore, social control and reward systems limit the freedom of individuals and their options for living a good and beautiful life. This said, the answer cannot be to reject social affiliation and to retreat in hermitage – at least not on a general level. The difficulty is, as previously indicated, to live as an autonomous member of a social group, mostly independent of the group's expectations and reward system.

Although cultural influences can have a huge limiting impact on the experience of flow – for example, through suppression, alienation or anomie (pp. 85–6) – one's immediate social setting, one's own family, can be quite beneficial for an individual's capacity to increase flow experiences: for example, through an "autotelic family context" (p. 89). This term describes a family setting which is supportive for developing an autotelic personality. People with an autotelic personality "seem to enjoy situations that ordinary persons would find unbearable" (p. 90) and, therefore, are more capable of experiencing flow and enjoyments, despite their situation and the circumstances they are living in, than other people.

The family context which supports the development of such an individual is marked by five traits: *clarity* with regard to rules, consequences and expectations; *centring* on the here and now instead of focusing on future outcomes of learning and behaviour; the possibility to *choose* from a variety of opportunities; *commitment* of the parents, which helps the child to develop trust; and *challenges* provided by new and more complex opportunities through the parents (pp. 88–9).

Another controlling factor evident in cultural settings (especially in modern Western cultures) is the myth of pleasures being the path to enduring happiness and a good life. As shown throughout all philosophical and psychological theories presented earlier, including hedonism, purely sensational pleasures are not regarded as capable of providing enduring happiness and the experience of a good and beautiful life. Although one could argue with Schmid's individual-based theory that pleasures could suffice for living a good life if the individual regards a life of pleasures as a beautiful one. However, despite such an individual choice being possible, it is unlikely to be a way of living a good life for most people. This stands in contrast to what people are often made to believe in most current (Western-oriented) cultures. As shown previously, there is no significant increase in enduring happiness and contentment through accumulation of sensational pleasures (see Section 4.3). Among others, this leads to the question in which cultural setting one wants to live and how one should form a society to make it fit to support the natural human desire to live a good and beautiful life. Schmid (2000a, 95–106), for example, calls for the development of a "new modernity", which takes into account the value of human happiness and the ability to live a good life.

Some implications following from these considerations for an educational approach are that (a) educationists have to be aware of the effect a future-based educational approach can have on one's pupils. More desirable would be a setting and method of teaching that suggest the immediate relevance of the matter at hand for the pupils' life and their own self and a way of educating (to avoid the term "teaching" here) that might even lead to repeated experiences of flow and enjoyments. (b) Socialisation is always a part of education and, as stated earlier, necessary for human beings to live in a social context. The challenge is to allow for a social education that enables the pupil to question his or her own cultural beliefs and values and to become an autonomous individual who is able to choose his or her place in and contribution to society based on prudence and practical wisdom. Terms such as *Bildung* and *critical thinking* spring to mind in this context. (c) Educational settings that support the development of an autotelic personality can help pupils cope better with challenging situations in life and might enable them to experience more enjoyments despite their individual situations. Chapter 9 will engage with these thoughts in more detail.

6.5 Control over consciousness and the care of the self

The core of Schmid's concept of *Lebenskunst* is the care of the self (see Sections 2.2 and 5.4) and, consequently, the labour of care: an individual's self needs to form itself through self-*bildung* and self-development up to a point that leads to self-mastery. This process of the labour of care, which Schmid calls *askesis*, shapes one's own life (possibly) into something beautiful. One of the key aspects is an individual's active engagement in this process: one's life does not shape itself; without effort of the individual, it can only pass by unshaped and unrefined. Further, the aspect of labour indicates substantial effort, and shaping one's own self is a lifelong process.

A good life with a focus on enduring happiness, on the other hand, according to Csikszentmihalyi (2008, 20–2), can be achieved through control over one's consciousness, which leads to control over the quality of one's inner experiences and, therefore, to flow and enjoyments (see Section 4.5). For Csikszentmihalyi, this is also the way to self-mastery and to a relative autonomy from social punishment and reward systems (see the earlier section). As examples, he lists spiritual traditions – for instance, the oracle of Delphi, Stoic philosophy and some Christian aspects, as well as Eastern traditions such as the Indian yogi, Taoism and Zen Buddhism – to show that the control over consciousness has a long history throughout time and cultures. Csikszentmihalyi provides two reasons for the necessity of reinvention – or better to say *reformulation* – of ways to achieve this control and to demonstrate the benefit this practice can provide. First, this kind of knowledge cannot be condensed into a formula and simply be learned or memorised, but it has to be experienced and understood on a more fundamental level. Second, through permanent changes in the cultural context, former teachings and ways to gain control over consciousness do not apply or are not understood anymore.

Comparing these two concepts, one can find similarities of what is deemed necessary for a good life. Recalling the theories about the concept of the self (Section 6.3), one's self is not only part of one's consciousness, but it includes everything that passes through consciousness. Therefore, control over consciousness is control over one's self, which again leads to self-mastery. Gaining control over consciousness, according to Csikszentmihalyi, has to be learned through practice and experience, which is very similar to Schmid's notion of the labour of care. Although Csikszentmihalyi and Schmid employ different terms and approach this from different directions, it seems possible that they both describe aspects of the same phenomenon. This is remarkable but not surprising, taking into account that they both aim their research at a concept for a good life. One of the biggest challenges of these considerations – not only for an educational approach, but for modern cultures in general[12] – is to create social settings that allow individuals to find their own way of controlling their consciousness and of developing their own art of living, despite continuing changes in the cultural context and without prescribing a singular, supposedly valid formula. A meta-theory of how to live a good life is necessary, for which Schmid's work provides a good starting point. Also, an educational theory that proposes content, methods and settings to provide the required knowledge and skills but is also flexible enough to respond to different and changing cultural settings and individual requirements needs to be developed. The first steps in this direction will be taken in Chapters 7 and 9.

Summary

Considering the very different approaches positive psychology and the philosophy of the art of living take towards the nature of the human being and a definition of a good life, it is not surprising that the findings differ somewhat. However, by reading between the lines and comparing terms and concepts, a great deal of concordance can be found between these disciplines. It might even be possible that both approaches show various aspects of the same phenomenon – *eudaimonia*. If this is the case, qualitative research results in the psychological area would support Aristotle's claim of this phenomenon being inter-cultural and consistent over time. This would confront some postmodern critiques of universal philosophical and anthropological approaches and provide a foundation for a general educational approach as argued for in this book.

Although the definition of what a good or beautiful life is differs in the concepts discussed earlier, it can be agreed that Schmid's concept subsumes the idea of a good life in the notion of being the maximisation of enduring happiness as defined in positive psychology. Further, the drive for enduring happiness is a strong motivational factor for most human beings, although practical attempts to reach this goal are often ill considered and misleading. However, it is not unlikely that an individual engaged in the art of living experiences increasing amounts of flow due to the shaping of one's own life according to one's interests, to being strongly involved with every aspect of one's own life and to one's subsequent personal growth.

Both Schmid and Csikszentmihalyi point out that in the end the individual has to strive towards self-mastery (through the labour of care with respect to control over consciousness). Although the human being is always a social being, an individual needs to become independent of society's punishment and reward systems to be able to develop his or her own art of living and a good life.

In sum, both approaches seem to contribute to a more complex picture of the human being and the endeavour to live a good and beautiful life. Therefore, the dialogue in this chapter provides significant input for educational considerations such as teaching methods, relevant content and the influence of family and educational settings on the development of autotelic personality traits and experiences of flow. Despite some limitations of the psychological view of enduring happiness as the gauge for living a good life, both philosophy and psychology have been shown to be relevant for the development of a holistic education for life concept, as was set out as one aim for this study. Based on the discussion so far, an argument can now be made for the importance of the art of living for an education that aims for "the best possible realization of humanity as humanity" (Dewey 2001, 100).

Notes

1 Parts of this chapter have been published earlier: Teschers, C. (2015). The Art of Living and Positive Psychology in Dialogue. *Educational Philosophy and Theory*, 47(9), 970–981. The journal is available online at www.tandfonline.com.

2 Media-literacy, as it is understood here, does not only refer to knowledge and skills about how to use computers, the Internet, TVs, radios and other interactive media such as touch screens, ticket machines and similar, but also the ability to use them in a prudent and safe manner.
3 Biesta discusses in the section "Valuing what we measure or measuring what we value?" the influence measurements can have on values in a society, especially when the discourse about which values to employ is diminishing.
4 Compare the philosophy of Hannah Arendt, for example, in Biesta (2006, 82–9).
5 Perry (2002) wrote a strong philosophical argument about various aspects of this topic in his book *Identity, Personal Identity, and the Self*. See also Charles Taylor's (1989) *Sources of the Self* for an extensive discussion of the self and identity. Further, the book *The Self?* by Galen Strawson (2005) offers articles from various authors about a phenomenological approach to the self.
6 Compare Foucault.
7 Compare Kierkegaard's (2000, 351) notion of the self as "the relation's relating itself to itself".
8 "Die Selbstentfremdung ist nicht etwa ein Zustand, der aufzugeben wäre, sondern einer, der in der Lebenskunst geradezu zu suchen ist, um das Selbst zu vervielfältigen und sein Selbstbewusstsein auf die vielfältige Erfahrung des Andersseins zu gründen, ein Selbstbewusstsein, das nicht mehr nötig hat, allzu ängstlich die eigene Identität zu hüten."
9 Heatherton et al. refer, for example, to studies from Timothy Rogers and colleagues (1977) and to Symons and Johnson (1997).
10 An overview of Rogers' self-concept theory can be found at www.simplypsychology.org/self-concept.html; a more in-depth discussion has been conducted by Hall and Lindzey (1957).
11 For more detailed information and references to studies proving these statements, see McConnell and Strain (2007).
12 See, for example, Schmid's chapter about "the search for a different modernity" [Auf der Suche nach einer anderen Moderne] (2000a, 95–106).

7 An educational approach to the art of living

Having discussed and critiqued the philosophical and psychological background of the art of living, this chapter[1] signifies a turning point in this book and will now discuss practical implications of the art of living for education and schooling. The following chapters will argue for an interpretation of education that is more holistic and features a stronger humanistic image of students and human beings than is common in current public and political discussions. This chapter will further include a discussion of ends and aims in education, the role and importance of the art of living for these ends and a further critique of Schmid's concept from an educational viewpoint.

7.1 Reasons for an educational approach

Throughout the course of this book, various philosophical and psychological approaches to the art of living and to interpretations of a good life have been presented. At this point, one might ask why it is important or necessary at all to add an educational approach as well. A trivial answer would be that knowing about the art of living and teaching the art of living are two different things. Additionally, on a more fundamental level, it might be asked if teaching how to live a good life is possible at all. Therefore, a more thorough answer is needed. The first question that has to be addressed from an educational perspective is the question if it is possible at all not only to teach *about* the art of living, but to teach *anything that can help to develop* one's own good life and one's own art of living. When, further on in this chapter, it will have been established that this is the case, subsequent questions need to be contemplated as well: what are the skills and knowledge that can be taught, how can they be taught, which settings suit best, which methods are most beneficial and so forth.

When considering most of these questions, one has to have an underlying idea or concept of the art of living, a theoretical framework, to base one's answers on. Various concepts have been presented earlier, and it will be argued again that Schmid's approach is a good foundation to build on; however, I will also comment on some of its possible shortcomings for educational purposes in light of other philosophical concepts. Further, the dialogue between philosophical and psychological approaches (see Chapter 6) can provide significant input for an educational perspective as well. Education and schooling are often used synonymously, although they are not equivalents; they are understood here as different concepts. Therefore, when considering the possible settings for teaching the art of living, one also has to address the purpose of schooling and its place in the wider educational field (see Chapter 8 for a discussion of this topic).

However, coming back to the initial question of why an educational approach is necessary in the first place, a second answer can be given, which is also related to the notion about schooling presented earlier. This answer is mainly a combination of the question of the overall importance of the art of living for human beings and society and of the intention and purpose one attributes to education in general. To approach the first part of this question, one treads on highly philosophical ground: what is the purpose of human life, what are we here for and is leading a good and beautiful life part of our inherent human plan and purpose? It will become apparent that Schmid's concept of the art of living provides a solid foundation for the outlined questions, as his concept suggest a simple, but not easy, answer: there is no such thing as one answer to living a good life, but every human being has to find his or her own answers and shape his or her own life accordingly. This will, hopefully, result in a life that this individual can appreciate as a good and beautiful one (see Schmid 2000b, 7 and Section 5.1). Therefore, developing one's own art of living, understood in Schmid's terms, *bears the answers* to these questions of life; hence, engaging in the art of living – conscious or ignorant of its theoretical background – is highly significant for human beings.

Also, from a more pragmatic perspective, Aristotle (1095a15–20) argues that the utmost goal that human beings can achieve is *eudaimonia*, which can be described as an overall attitude of serene happiness, and that most, if not all, human beings strive to reach *eudaimonia*. Therefore, happiness is a strong motivational factor for human action and decision-making. On the other hand, which actions and decisions lead to serene happiness for an individual is, again, the field of the art of living. This leaves the question if education should be concerned with the quality and purpose of pupils' lives at all. This will be discussed in the following section.

7.2 An end of education

In the public as well as in the academic discussion, many ideas about the purpose of education have been voiced, but there is hardly any consensus. The ideas vary from transferring knowledge (sometimes called instruction); over-socialisation and reproduction (tradition) of society and culture; to critical thinking and life-long learning. Education, in fact, includes all those purposes and many more. The historical circumstances, the reality of the current society and the living environment of the individual determine which objectives are regarded with higher priority and come to the fore (Dewey 2001, 116). The question is if an overall aim for education can be identified at all. In *Democracy and Education*, Dewey (2001) certainly denies the existence of "some one final aim which subordinates all others to itself" (p. 116). However, he identifies three main streams of thought that subsume most of the aims people attributed to education in his time: the *natural, individual development* (Rousseau n.d./2004), *socialisation* (or *social efficiency*), and *personal mental enrichment* (or *culture*). Although the terms he uses might be slightly misleading if they are read in current social contexts, the underlying concepts are nevertheless still relevant for the present time: the clear, single-sided emphasis on socialisation and economic benefit in contemporary educational systems, which are often strongly influenced by neo-liberal social and political tendencies, produces similar difficulties for democratic societies and the development of human beings today as in Dewey's historical circumstances.

Dewey discusses the three general aims of education earlier and points out their strong sides and their weaknesses. He supports some key aspects of the natural development of the individual, as described in Rousseau's (n.d./2004) *Emile*:

> The three factors of educative development are (a) the native structure of our bodily organs and their functional activities; (b) the uses to which the activities of these organs are put under the influence of other persons; (c) their direct interaction with the environment. This statement certainly covers the ground. His [Rousseau's] other two propositions are equally sound; namely, (a) that only when the three factors of education are consonant and cooperative does adequate development of the individual occur, and (b) that the native activities of the organs, being original, are basic in conceiving consonance.
> (Dewey 2001, 118)

On the one hand, Dewey criticises Rousseau's belief that the three "factors of educative development" are independent from each other, and especially his view that one's organs and natural faculties can develop "irrespective of the use to which they are put" (pp. 118–19). He summarises that Rousseau's critique of the educational practice of his time was righteous by pointing out the importance of the individual nature of each pupil as a fundamental educational condition. But Dewey also claims that Rousseau was wrong in stressing this point to become the final end of human development and the sole aim of educational intervention.

On the other hand, Dewey argues that the opposite view of "social efficiency as aim" (p. 123) is equally flawed, as its supporters often neglect the importance of individual and inter-individual diversity. They also, at least in Dewey's time, often did not take into account the quickly changing environment in industry and the need for flexibility, but instead proclaimed a training "for too specific a mode of efficiency[, which] defeats its own purpose" (p. 125). However, no educational system can afford to neglect the need to train its students in a way that enables them to participate in economy and industry and to earn their own living. As a second aspect of social efficiency, Dewey names "civic efficiency, or good citizenship" (p. 125), which includes all traits that "run from whatever make[s] an individual a more agreeable companion to citizenship in the political sense" (p. 125). Some of them are, for example, to be able to create and enjoy art, to participate in recreation and leisure and to formulate and abide by laws. Finally,

112 *An educational approach*

Dewey summarises social efficiency as something that is more or less close to the contemporary understanding of socialisation:

> It must be borne in mind that ultimately social efficiency means neither more nor less than capacity to share in a give and take of experience. [. . .] In the broadest sense, social efficiency is nothing less than that socialization of mind which is actively concerned in making experiences more communicable; in breaking down the barriers of social stratification which make individuals impervious to the interests of others.
>
> (p. 126)

Moving on to Dewey's considerations about culture, he describes it as "something personal; it is cultivation with respect to appreciation of ideas and art and broad human interests" (p. 127). It is a personal refinement in opposition to the "raw and crude" (p. 126). However, he points out that this personal refinement must not be conceived as something solely "inner":

> What is called inner is simply that which does not connect with others – which is not capable of free and full communication. [. . .] What one is as a person is what one is as associated with others, in a free give and take of intercourse. This transcends both the efficiency which consists in supplying products to others and the culture which is an exclusive refinement and polish. [. . .] And there is perhaps no better definition of culture than that it is the capacity for constantly expanding the range and accuracy of one's perception of meaning.
>
> (pp. 128–9)

Dewey argues against the opposition of "self-sacrifice" and "spiritual self-perfection" and instead advocates that "it is the particular task of education at the present time to struggle in behalf of *an aim in which social efficiency and personal culture are synonyms instead of antagonists*" (pp. 128–9, italics added). Dewey (2001) summarises that partially stated aims, focusing either on the individual's nature, culture or on socialisation, fall short of providing an overall end of education, as these aims come into conflict with each other and on their own do not take into account all aspects of educational circumstances in reality. However, combining these aims by recognising

> that natural activities mean native activities which develop only through the uses in which they are nurtured, the conflict disappears. Similarly [. . .] social efficiency as an educational purpose should mean cultivation of power to join freely and fully in shared or common activities. This is impossible without culture, [. . .] because one cannot share in intercourse with others without learning – without getting a broader point of view and perceiving things on which one would otherwise be ignorant.
>
> (p. 129)

An educational approach 113

What evolves here is an argument for a holistic approach and an overall aim of education that takes into account the human being with both its nature and its ability to culture one's mind and form one's character.[2] Dewey proclaims a proper end of education to be "the promotion of the best possible realization of humanity as humanity" (p. 100); this end is, however, hardly pursued in real-world situations, as the focus lies often on the short-term or immediate benefit and advantage for the students in the present cultural setting.

A different argument about ends and aims in education is presented by R. S. Peters (1973). He proclaims that most "arguments about the aims of education reflect [. . . merely] basic differences in *principles of procedure*" (p. 131, italics added). In his observation, disputes about aims are often nothing more than disputes about values and "manners of proceeding" (*teaching methods*, p. 125) instead of targeting the "matter" (*contents*, p. 126) of educational intervention. Although this might have been true in the 1970s, considerations of economic outcome and usefulness for companies and industry are strong influencing factors in the social and political discussion today. However, it is helpful to distinguish between schooling in particular and education in general to evaluate Peters' argument in current social contexts. Even though public and political discussions refer to "education" more often than not, the actual arguments mostly concern policies of teaching in school settings, that is, schooling. The wider areas of education, such as upbringing and socialisation in the parental home or social environment, learned skills and knowledge in everyday life outside of schools and self-acquired content and *Bildung* on the basis of pursued personal interests, for example, are mostly not taken into account in a public discussion about teaching, learning, curriculum and school politics. Today's societies most often assume that life skills are learned "somehow" automatically and all that remains in the domain of public interest is the contents of an agreed-upon school curriculum.

In this regard, Peters' notion of "disputes between educationists, which take the form of disputes about aims" (p. 125) as actually being mostly disputes about values and manners of proceeding can still be accepted today when interpreted as aims of schooling in this context. Nevertheless, Peters (1973) also acknowledges that a change of values and proceedings often affects the contents as well (p. 131). Therefore, aims-talk, as Noddings (2005) calls it, is not futile but has a very real impact not only on teaching methods, school policy and the hidden curriculum, but also on the "matter" of teaching – the official curriculum – as well. Further, as politics and policy-making by definition are concerned with aims and outcomes, aims-talk cannot be ignored by educational theory and practice. Instead, it should guide the public and political discussion to ensure the best possible outcome for students. In the end, teachers and educators regularly have to bear the responsibility for students and their achievements.

Peters, however, argues against educational aims altogether, which must be read here as aims for education in general. He proposes that education has an intrinsic value and should be pursued for itself, as "there is a quality of life embedded in the activities which constitute education" (Peters 1973, 131). According to Peters, the talk about even "omnibus 'ends' does more than obscure [. . . the

114 *An educational approach*

justification of education]; it also encourages an *instrumental* way of looking at the problem [. . ., but] 'life' must be for the sake of education, not education for life" (p. 131). Peters proposes education as an end in itself, rather than a means to an end.

For Peters, the declaration of general aims of education as, for example, "self-realization, the greatest happiness of the greatest number" or the idea of the social citizen, is not only a harmless stretch "of a limited model of means to ends," but a dangerous undertaking, as terrible things have been done by passionate (and fanatic) upholders of generalised aims and beliefs (pp. 130–1). Peters' notion is a valid one, as long as the proposed general aim is based on the teacher's (society's) values and position and is intended to preserve these values and pass them on to the students regardless of their individual circumstances and personality. However, if the aim is formulated with the student's position in mind and allows the student to question the underlying value system, this is a different matter entirely. Such an aim would need to be flexible in its outcome and would hardly lead to means and procedures that are ethically questionable, as the best interest of the student, not of the teacher or the society, lies at the heart. The demand of flexibility is not only built on the variety of individual ways of living at any given point in time, but is also due to the diversity of cultural backgrounds over distance and time. This aim could be reciprocal and not only uses education as a means, but also as an aim in itself for the sake of one's own good life, which closes the circle with Peters' argument.

Hence, an overall end of education from an art of living perspective can be formulated as follows:

> *Education should enable students to develop their own art of living: to live a good and beautiful life, according to their own judgement and under the circumstances they are living in.*

Based on this aim, education needs to begin with and centre on the pupil; it needs to focus on the subject (individual), not the object (content) of the teaching–learning interaction. Dewey argues for two main stakeholders of education: on the one hand the society, and on the other the individual human being. In light of Schmid's theory of the art of living, the interests of the first are included in the development of the second through the qualities of prudence and practical wisdom and through the notion of the individual's own best interest. As argued earlier (Section 5.3), an individual with a developed sense of prudence and practical wisdom has to take into account the desires and needs of the people around him or her and has to act accordingly. Additionally, one's own self-interest requires the pupil to master the knowledge and skills that allow him or her to live as effortlessly as possible in the current society, which includes serving its purpose and demands as long as they are in line with one's own norms, beliefs and values. On the other hand, as *Bildung* is a requirement for developing one's own art of living in a lifelong process and education is an integral part of the concept of

Bildung, this aim supports life for the sake of education as much as possible without obstructing individual choice and self-guided development.

Seeing education – and schooling – from this angle is quite different from the current political agenda of many modern countries and societies. As stated earlier, the good life of the individual lies at the heart here, not the growth of the national economy. The qualities of prudence and practical wisdom, as discussed in Section 5.3, ensure that the Other and the greater good of society are taken into account as much as one's own good. According to Schmid, this should lead to a more considerate interaction between people and more care for each other than the everybody-fight-for-yourself attitude that often seems to dominate current politics and policy-making.

As a consequence, the outcome of transferred knowledge and learned skills might not vary much from what is taught in schools today; although some changes in content will be necessary to cater for a stronger individual development of the self and self-care. In manners of proceeding, however, changes are most likely, and there will certainly be a difference in pupils' experiences of schooling and education, and hopefully, an improvement in their ability to shape their own lives.

7.3 The importance of the art of living for education

As shown earlier, the end of education is not (or should not be) in the first place to teach young people a profession and the necessities to become a useful and functioning part of the current society with the main intent of growing and contributing to a country's economy and industry. The aims resulting from the end of education, as discussed earlier, are rather to allow human beings (a) to grow and develop their capabilities; (b) to make sense of the world and the culture they are living in; (c) to reflect on their own self, their own beliefs and values; and (d) to flourish in a way that enables them to actively shape their own lives into potentially good and beautiful ones. The philosophy of the art of living is important to identify which skills and knowledge, as well as teaching methods and settings, are necessary or beneficial to achieve these aims.

However, a question that needs to be addressed first is if teachers and educationists have the right at all to intervene in a student's life in relation to the art of living. That educational practice in any way is an intervention in a student's life can be acknowledged without question: to teach or educate someone means to cause a change in this person's thinking, knowledge or level of skills, which is to intervene in this person's life and being. Unfortunately, it would go beyond the scope of this book to discuss all aspects of rights and responsibilities in relation to teaching and education adequately. However, it can be argued with Schmid that educationists not only have the right, but also the duty, to help their students develop their own art of living. As has been argued in Sections 5.4 and 6.4, the care of the self demands, through prudence and practical wisdom, that one also cares for others and to help the people around oneself to develop their own art of living.

Further, based on the discussion in Section 7.2, it can be argued that an education for the art of living is in line with an education for the best possible realisation of humanity as humanity, which can be achieved through the development of each individual. Therefore, educationists, especially if engaged in the art of living themselves, have to support the development of a student's own art of living – for their own good and the good of society. However, great care has to be taken not to manipulate a student to follow a particular course but to enable him or her to make reflective decisions and to find his or her own direction in life. This can be quite challenging for educationists, as one is always influenced by one's own beliefs, values and norms. But a reflective teacher, who engages in the art of living, will realise that what might be good for himself or herself might be quite the contrary for the living reality of a student. This is especially true if the social and cultural background of the teacher and the student differ significantly. However, these considerations will be revisited again later on.

Coming back to the more tangible aims of education as stated earlier, the contribution Schmid's theory of *Lebenskunst* can make to the first aim (a) of growth and the development of capabilities becomes apparent in the notion of the prudent care of the self. To be able to grow and form one's own self, it is necessary to have some knowledge about oneself in the first place. Knowing oneself includes knowledge about one's own history, one's faculties and the desires and ideas one has, as these reveal the contents and inter-connections of one's self (see Section 6.3). The first aspect of Schmid's (2000a, 246) care of the self is to be *self-receptive*. It is the experience of one's own self as oneself, which belongs not to others but to oneself alone; it is also the awakening of one's own self-interest. The ability to consciously perceive oneself and to be receptive of one's own self is, therefore, the first step educational intervention has to focus on. What has to follow, then, according to Schmid, is *self-reflection*, which will cause a transition from self-perception to self-awareness and is also a fundamental skill for aim (c). The ability to reflect upon oneself can be supported significantly by a guiding educational approach; the newfound self-awareness will help the pupil to see one's own life from a distance, which enables him or her to realise one's own circumstances, conditions and opportunities. In a final *self-productive* step, the pupil will learn how to shape one's own self and one's own life, which concludes, on its highest level, in the realisation of the care of the self and subsequently one's own art of living.

However, the realisation of the art of living is not as simple and straightforward as outlined in the paragraph earlier, even if the core concept seems indeed not to be overly complicated. The question is: What else is needed to actively shape one's own life in a way that one can experience it as a good and beautiful one? One condition is formulated in aim (b): to make sense of the world and the culture one is living in. The second step of the care of the self (self-reflection), as outlined earlier, can only lead to a realisation of one's own circumstances, conditions and opportunities if one can make sense of what one perceives and reflects upon. Schmid's (2000b, 286–92) answer to this challenge is *hermeneutics*: hermeneutical skills and knowledge are part of the care of the self, and hermeneutics is in itself the art of finding one's way through life and make sense of what one is experiencing in the world. Hermeneutical skills are also required to make informed *choices*, which will be discussed later on in more detail.

As mentioned earlier, a key skill for aim (c), the reflection on one's own self, one's beliefs and one's values, is obviously the ability for *self-reflection*. The pupil needs to learn how to make himself or herself the object of one's own reflection. But although this skill is necessary, it is not sufficient at all to realise the aim discussed here. To reflect critically on the values and beliefs one is confronted with in the culture and society one is growing up in requires a certain kind of knowledge to be able to put these values and beliefs into perspective. It requires a way of reflection that engages with these external ideas critically. Schmid (2000b), in this context, employs the concept of *Bildung* [(self-)cultivation] as the foundation for comprehension and understanding (pp. 310–17). *Bildung*, in the German understanding, is more than factual knowledge alone; it also includes the formation of one's character and a notion of practical wisdom (see Section 8). The way of reflection, mentioned here, can be found, according to Schmid (pp. 310–17), in the notion of cultivating *critical thinking*.

The term *critical thinking* has a number of different interpretations ranging from a technicist, skill-based understanding, to critical theory as understood by Habermas and the Frankfurt School, along with postmodern, postcritical and poststructural interpretations. For the argument made here, critical thinking will be understood as a rational skill that allows one to think critically and analytically about an affair or a situation one is confronted with, as, for example, a claim for a certain "fact" to be true or a logical argument to be right. Aspects of other interpretations of this term might be more closely related to the concept of hermeneutics (Gadamer 1975; Ramberg and Gjesdal 2011; Weinsheimer 1985), as it is understood here. However, one's ability to think critically and the use of one's rational faculties cannot be separated from a person's being and self. Therefore, critical thinking is always connected with the hermeneutical process of interpretation, the creation of meaning and the shaping of one's own self. The distinction made in this study is for critical thinking to have a rational and logical emphasis, whereas hermeneutics includes the wider field of interpretation and the creation of meaning that happens continuously – sometimes more, sometimes less consciously – in people's everyday lives.

The final part (d) of the end of education, as described earlier, is harder to grasp and more difficult to break down into practical educational goals. To flourish and to shape one's own life in a way that may result in a good and beautiful one might be as diverse as the number of living human beings. However, *to be able* to flourish and to shape one's own life accordingly might prove to be much less demanding than to cater for the diversity these skills and knowledge can lead to. As argued earlier (see Section 5.4), according to Schmid, the care of the self is the core of the art of living. Therefore, the aims (a) to (c) are essential for the individual to approach a flourishing way of living. But Schmid (2000a) refines his terms further in this context: he refers to the care of the self as "*kluge* Selbstsorge" [*prudent* self-care] (p. 256, italics added). The German term "klug",

118 *An educational approach*

which is significant for Schmid's philosophy, does have two connotations: *prudence* and *practical wisdom*; Schmid continuously refers to both meanings in his philosophy. Hence, prudence and practical wisdom are important qualities whose development needs to be supported in educational settings. Both terms are also closely related to the concept of *Bildung*. Further, Schmid emphasises the importance of "Lebenswissen" [life-knowledge], which is an empirical, practical form of life's know-how and not a scientific meta-knowledge about life (2000b, 303–10). This kind of life-knowledge needs to be accumulated over time, but the development and growth of this knowledge can be supported by educationists through structured or designed experiences.[3] A condition for flourishing that might stress the limits of education is the freedom every individual needs to be able to make choices and to shape one's own self and one's own life. However, the concept of freedom has different dimensions, some are internal, others external. One's internal boundaries can certainly be stretched through education, which is an inherent function of learning, and it might be possible for a pupil to influence his or her external constrictions once one's mind has found internal freedom (see also Section 9.1).

7.4 An educational critique of Schmid's concept *Lebenskunst*

Although it has been discussed earlier (see Chapter 5 and Section 7.1) that Schmid's approach to the art of living is a suitable starting point for an educational perspective, there are some limitations from an educational point of view that need to be addressed. Some issues that will be discussed in this section are as follows: the discrepancy of a holistic art of living approach versus educational practicability; the scope of *Bildung* necessary to live a beautiful life; the question if it is not already possible to live a good or beautiful life with the educational systems and curricula in place; which areas of knowledge are significant for an educational approach at all; and the question of the impact a change of focus would have on individuals and societies.

Schmid seems to propose a holistic philosophical concept by emphasising the responsibility of the individual to decide upon his or her own values and beliefs and to shape his or her own life. Educational processes, however, are always based on a certain selection by a teacher, who is influenced by his or her own, as well as culturally transmitted, values and beliefs. Also, an educational approach needs to take into account the different cultural teaching settings and social circumstances in which pupils need to be able to develop their own art of living. Schmid does not address these issues in sufficient depth, as his take on the art of living focuses on the individual human being. He acknowledges the social component, but argues that in the end it is up to the individual to decide if he or she wants to embrace the cultural values and settings one is born into and raised with or not. This requires one, however, to be aware of these norms and values and to reflect critically upon them, which is part of practising a reflected art of living. Although this basic assumption is true for all human beings in every culture, as

An educational approach 119

an educationist one is always restricted by the social norms and cultural circumstances one happens to work in. Although the end of education, as stated earlier, should be the same, the settings, methods and even contents of educational intervention will most likely differ. The first challenge here would be to outline *methods, settings and contents* that indicate the boundaries of significant educational intervention for an individual art of living. This will be addressed in more detail in Chapter 9.

The second issue, pointed out earlier, is the question of the scope of *Bildung* that needs to be achieved to enable pupils to actively shape their own lives and potentially live a beautiful one. To explore this issue, a deeper understanding of the concept of *Bildung* will be helpful. As explained earlier, the term *Bildung* has three dimensions in the German understanding: knowledge, character formation and practical wisdom. A person with *Bildung* is a self-cultivated person who transfers learned knowledge through reflection and contemplation into shaping one's own character and acquiring practical wisdom. This self-cultivating process can be supported and guided by a mentor or teacher: for example, through asking critical questions and encouraging the pupil's thinking process. But how much knowledge needs to be acquired? How much cultivation is necessary for an art of living? An answer to these questions cannot be absolute, as they are tightly linked with the cultural and social setting; the individual's innate and developed skills and faculties; and, subsequently, the content of knowledge, as discussed earlier. However, as will be shown later on (Section 9.1), the content of significant knowledge can at least be categorised to make sure that all necessary areas of knowledge are provided. Equally, skills can be identified, which are necessary to enable the pupil to transfer knowledge and cultivate himself or herself in form of character shaping and acquiring practical wisdom. And, finally, when these fundamental skills are learned, the pupil has the active potential to gain enough *Bildung* through *Selbstbildung* [self-*bildung*; self-cultivation] to shape one's own life and one's own self. In fact, at this point one is already on the way to developing one's own art of living. It must also be said that there is no end to *Bildung*, the same as to the art of living; it is a *potentially lifelong process of personal growth*.

A valid question to ask in this context is if it is necessary at all to change anything in current educational systems and settings to enable pupils to live a good and beautiful life. The answer is a solid "yes and no". Human beings are in general very adaptable and able to achieve all sorts of things under impossible circumstances, and the shape of most educational systems and societies is hardly impossible for living a good life. However, tweaks and improvements are always possible, and the rapid developments in the last 50 to 60 years, which have involved huge changes in the living environment and the social setting for most people, call for a reassessment of current educational systems as well as current social beliefs and norms. Depending on one's ideology and the underlying values one has in mind while reviewing current educational systems, methods and contents of curricula, the conclusion of such an attempt will provide very different results.

The majority of today's reviewing processes seem to rely on the underlying assumption that the educational system should contribute to and strengthen the

120 An educational approach

national economy and cater for the needs of businesses and industry. As argued earlier, this perspective is important for every society to take into account, but it is certainly not the only aspect of importance for educational systems. Therefore, a review of these underlying beliefs and values is in order: the question one should ask is "In which society do we want to live?" Philosophical concepts, such as the art of living, can be of major importance for answering this question and, thus, are a good guideline for reassessing educational structures.

As has been pointed out previously, this review process from an art of living perspective might not result in a radical change of nations' curricula and schooling systems, but it will more likely propose a fine-tuning and in some cases a long overdue clear out. The fine-tuning will, for example, take into account life skills – other than reading, writing and maths – that are important for a good life and the well-being of human beings (cf. Noddings 2005). It might also suggest a closer interconnection between school subjects and contents to improve the relevance for a student's own life and his or her immediate circumstances. However, an art of living approach cannot prescribe how and what should be taught, as one always needs to take into account the social and cultural environment and cater for the diversity of human beings in general, as argued earlier. Hence, a certain openness and flexibility would be beneficial for every kind of educational theory, curriculum and practice. To close the loop with Liebau's (1999) question raised in Chapter 1: when one reviews educational systems and curricula, one should not just ask what education can do for society, but rather what society can do for education and the good life of its members.

In terms of content that is deemed relevant for the development of an art of living, Schmid (2000a, 319–22) proposes six areas of learning that should be included in school curricula: *the human being as individual; the social human being; difficulties and burdens of human life; striving for fulfilment and meaning in life; religions, beliefs and cultures of humanity;* and *the personal shape of life and global* perspectives. It is certainly disputable if Schmid's list includes all important aspects of a human life cycle, as he claims, but this list is, at the very least, a good starting point to explore this field.

Undoubtedly, every human being has an individual component, an idea of his or her own self and identity (see Section 6.3). This identity stays always in relationship to the external world, including objects; other individuals; and social and cultural norms, beliefs and hierarchies. A human life is marked by a multitude of challenges, everyday choices and burdens, such as the necessity for food, water and sleep, as well as common needs, for instance, social acceptance and support. Additionally, external influences, including unemployment, financial problems, death of friends or family members and so on, have to be dealt with.

As argued earlier (see Chapter 6) striving for happiness and well-being is a strong motivational factor for human beings, and this striving is often accompanied by a search for fulfilment and meaning in life. Traditionally, this search for meaning in life is connected with spirituality, religion and other cultural beliefs, which vary greatly on a global scale. Finally, the life of every human being takes shape over time: if one is shaping one's own life in an active way or if one is passively driven by society and external influences is again up to the individual.

However, in most modern societies one's life and everyday experiences are not only influenced by one's immediate surroundings, but through global events as well. At the same time, we experience a rise of opportunities in an increasingly globalised world, which is significant for an active shaping process of one's own life. The more difficult parts for educational practice are to fill these abstract areas of learning with contents, give meaning to them and to which topics are part of which category or categories. Some of the more sizeable topics have been identified by Noddings (2005), such as good relationships, parenting, prudent economic behaviour (for example, saving money or being careful with credit cards) and being prepared for work as part of one's life.

The final question raised in this section concerns the impact such a change of focus in educational systems would have for individuals in particular and societies in general. An answer here is, again, very dependent on the social and cultural setting one is working in and on the practical implementations of an art of living–driven educational practice. However, a few assumptions can be made on the premise that educational intervention is able to improve the ability of pupils to live a good and beautiful life. First of all, it is most likely that people who are better equipped to live a good and beautiful life have an increased average of individual happiness and contentment. Enduring happiness and positive emotions, on the other hand, contribute to higher resilience and better coping abilities (Seligman 2010, 3–6). Subsequent increasing levels of tolerance and communal support are quite possible, especially if the development of prudence and practical wisdom is taken into account. As an art of living educational approach needs to be flexible to cater for individual differences, pupils need to learn how to help themselves and how to learn what they need to know for the life they want to live. Therefore, they are well equipped for lifelong learning processes and significant changes in their future living environment.

On a society level, a wider diversity of lifestyles and ways of living, or at least a broader acceptance for them, can be assumed. The development of prudence and practical wisdom might, through more tolerance and the care for others, lead to less crime, more communal support and maybe even more equality in and beyond society. It would be interesting to see if this development would also spread on a global scale. In any case, a more prudent use of ecological resources can be considered beneficial for one's own long-term best interest and, therefore, might lead to an overall more sustainable behaviour. Considering the speed of development in the last century, a widespread implementation of an art of living education could have a significant influence on societies in one generation's time and would make an immediate contribution to people's individual well-being and good life. Current political and social processes, however, make this time frame seem quite ambitious.

Summary

In this chapter, an argument has been made for a shift of focus in educational theory and practice towards an education that is aimed at the development of an individual art of living for one's students. This larger aim or vision has been divided into four more tangible aims for educational intervention: to grow and develop a student's capabilities, to help him or her make sense of the world and culture he or she is living in, to learn how to be self-reflective and, finally, to support a student's flourishing and development of a good and beautiful life. Some aspects have been shown of how Schmid's philosophy can support these aims in education through, for example, hermeneutics, *Bildung* and practical wisdom. Also, various areas of learning have been pointed out that should guide teachers as curriculum decision-makers, not only for teaching art of living classes but also any aspect of the curriculum. These aspects will be taken up again in particular in Chapter 9, where practical implications will be discussed in more detail.

Notes

1 Parts of this chapter have been published earlier: Teschers, C. 2013. "An Educational Approach to the Art of Living." *Knowledge Cultures* 1(2): 131–44. The journal is available online at https://addletonacademicpublishers.com.
2 Dewey's notion of culture and personal mental enrichment (as discussed on pages 126–129) calls to mind the German concept of *Bildung*, which will prove to be important for the educational concept proposed later on.
3 Rousseau's *Emile* is only one example of designed experience education. More practical examples can be found in outdoor and adventure education, as well as other experience-based educational approaches.

8 Beyond schooling

The discussion in the last chapter revealed difficulties of an interchangeable use of *education* and *schooling*, as it is often done in current public and political discussions. As has been mentioned before, a case will be made in this study for a broader understanding of education. Consequently, this chapter will explore the relationship between education and schooling in general, discuss some of the concerns that have been raised about schooling and explore some practical implications of the art of living for schooling and education. The aim of this chapter is to establish an understanding of education that goes beyond schooling but also informs schooling through the wider philosophical and theoretical background presented in other chapters.

8.1 Education and schooling – a German perspective

Schooling, as mentioned earlier, is an aspect of education, but it is not all there is. Education includes a broad range of situations, topics, tasks and interactions of which schooling covers only a small, although significant, part in the lifespan of an individual. In the German tradition, according to Liebau (1999), the understanding of the term *Pädagogik* [pedagogy/education] is based on three fundamental terms: *Erziehung* [upbringing], *Bildung* [(self-)cultivation] and *Entfaltung* [flourishing].

Liebau (1999, 25–8) states that the current understanding of *Erziehung* has its origin in the Enlightenment, where Kant (n.d./1900) claimed: "man can only become man by education [*Erziehung*]. He is merely what education [*Erziehung*] makes of him" (p. 6). Central points of the Enlightenment movement in the German and French context have been, similarly to the English tradition, economic aspects of labour, property and achievement, with an emphasis on an education and socialisation towards developing sensible habits as a citizen. But in addition to these, "political questions in terms of living together as a civil (world-) society and the problems of an education [*Erziehung*] to freedom and tolerance" (Liebau 1999, 25, my translation)[1] have been discussed. Therefore, it is not only achievement and socio-cultural rules that are at the centre of socialisation and upbringing, but also ideas of freedom, tolerance and a concern for the development of society on a global scale that influence the understanding of education in the German tradition. Liebau concludes that "only a prudent education [*Erziehung*], which at the same time respects the freedom of the pupil and the freedom of other people, can lead to prudent human beings and to a prudent society" (p. 26). The aim of *Erziehung* [upbringing] in this context is the "maturity [of the pupils, understood] as economic, moral and political autonomy" (p. 28).

The consequences of this aspect of education for schooling are, on the one hand, to offer a place and an opportunity for all citizens to gain qualifications and, on the other hand, to make achievements comparable, which leads straight to assessments and selection processes in schools. The challenge to mediate between these two functions of modern schooling is quite controversial but probably hard to resolve without a change in society as a whole. However, this is only the first of three aspects of education, but, unfortunately, often the most salient and dominant in current politics and school policies in modern societies.

Bildung, as the second aspect of education, has its origin in German Idealism: in contrast to the notion of achievement, it is "the life-long labour on the perfection of one's own person [that] lies at the heart of the classical concept of Bildung" (p. 28). It is the development and cultivation of one's own self that takes precedence, as it is believed that through the perfection of individuals the development and perfection of humankind in total will come to pass. This relation, according to Liebau, has two consequences: *the healthy self-interest of the individual* to further one's own *Bildung* is to be encouraged as it is in the best interest of society, and each individual has *a responsibility to pursue Bildung* for the same reason (pp. 28–33).

The concept of *Bildung* as it is understood today has been strongly influenced by Wilhelm von Humbold at the end of the 18th century, who connected scientific and humanistic approaches to conceiving the world with the notion of aesthetics. Therefore, *Bildung* is closely linked with art, music and theatre, but it also refers to the beauty from within: "this one has Bildung, who orients oneself to the standard of aesthetic and moral perfection, and who strives to shape one's own self accordingly" (Liebau 1999, 29). In the end, it is the development and perfection of humankind that is of concern to the German Idealists, and, therefore, they take the economy and governments to be of lesser importance and merely as supportive institutions that are necessary to allow citizens to pursue *Bildung* and their own perfection. *Bildung* is also one of the key aspects of Schmid's concept of the art of living.

The role of schooling in this context is quite different from the previous assessment: as *Bildung* is a lifelong process, schools have to provide the foundation for each individual to be able to engage in a continuous process of self-*bildung*. Instead of focusing on facts or scientific knowledge, learning how to learn needs to be emphasised, not to acquire advanced technical skills and qualifications, but to enable lifelong humanistic learning. It also needs to be pointed out that this level of learning needs to be accessible and achievable for all individuals as, despite "all the inequality in society, it is the equality of humans as human beings that forms the basis for the concept of public Bildung" (p. 31).

Finally, the third term forming the understanding of education and pedagogy in the German tradition is *Entfaltung* [flourishing]. To flourish, to develop what is given at the moment of birth, is the notion of the early Romantics. The "perfect child", lost through the shaping and norming processes of *Erziehung* [upbringing/socialisation] and *Bildung* [self-cultivation], is the starting point of "a quest for a second childhood, fortune and paradise – that is in the present and actuality [Gegenwärtigkeit]" (p. 33). It is this image of the child in early romanticism, which is quite different from empirical children, that stands for "the complete, non-alienated, socially not distorted human being" (p. 33). In this context, Liebau states that "Erziehung has no other meaning than to release and to express this ideal design of one's self, which is inbuilt in every human being" (p. 34). Further, *Erziehung* is not limited to teachers and educationists anymore, but everyone takes part in the upbringing and socialisation of young people – and all other people one interacts with. In this sense, education happens everywhere and mostly anytime.

The focus of this notion of flourishing points to the subjectivity of each individual (which, again, is a strong parallel to Schmid's ideas about the development of an individual art of living): everyone has his or her own strengths, weaknesses and set of abilities. These are largely innate, but it is the part and responsibility of society to support, not hinder, the harmonious development – flourishing – of these faculties. Part of this support is not only educational interaction, but, above this, the circumstances of one's everyday experiences (pp. 35–6).

Therefore, schools need to pay attention not only to what happens in classrooms, but also in hallways and the schoolyard during the breaks as well as before and after school. In addition, it is not only the contents but also the circumstances of learning that form the everyday school experiences. Hence, it is important how the school building is designed, as well as the layout and decoration of classrooms and all other accessible areas. With an eye on Schmid's (2000a, 322–4) remarks on holistic schooling and the idea of education happening everywhere and through everyone, one should even include support staff, such as administrators, cleaners, caretakers and gardeners, and take their tasks into consideration for a comprehensive school design.

The term education or pedagogy in the German tradition, and as it is used in this book and for Schmid's considerations about the art of living, is based on the concepts of *Erziehung*, *Bildung* and *Entfaltung*. The historical development of these notions not only influenced the understanding of education, but also Schmid's understanding and discussion of the art of living. Some ideas and major points of the art of living as discussed by Schmid are, or have been, significant parts of the basic understanding of the concept of education. However, current trends in schooling neglect many of the humanistic elements of this concept and seem to focus, in a very limited way, on the aspect of *Erziehung* in the tradition of the Enlightenment. I would argue that it is time to rethink the aims and end of education for human beings and society and to reintroduce more strongly again the wisdom and cultural achievements of two centuries of human history into current (Western) school design and policies.

8.2 De-schooling and the art of living

The de-schooling critique

The call for reshaping or rejecting schooling, however, is not new. Ivan Illich (1972) and Peter Buckman (1973), for example, argued in the 1970s against what they saw as a wrong development in schools and their negative impact on society. Illich, who takes a strong position in his book *Deschooling Society*, argues for de-schooling, and even de-institutionalising of society on a grand scale. Although not a follower of neo-liberal beliefs, he also argues for less compulsory control and structure in people's everyday life in general, and in education in particular, and for more freedom of choice. However, as he writes in a different historical context, his position is not to encourage market freedom and to limit governmental authority, but to help citizens to get over their self-adopted helplessness and take up responsibility for their own lives and their own education. Even if the strong approach outlined in his book can, and should, be questioned and critiqued – especially with regard to the current neo-liberal context that could easily lead to misinterpretations of his original ideas – Illich offers various points that are important to consider and relevant in the context of schooling and the art of living today.

The first point he makes is the dominance of schooling in education and educational processes in modern societies (Illich 1972, 7–10). The institution of school is widely recognised as the one and predominant place where education (supposedly) can be acquired. This belief, together with the assumption that education is mainly the same as skills and scientific knowledge, as well as schools' single authority over providing qualification certificates has far-ranging consequences for societies and especially for less advantaged citizens. According to Illich, poor families are robbed of alternative ways of learning and achieving relevant job qualifications, as alternative ways and areas of learning are not recognised as relevant for professional development. However, he also points out that most relevant skills for a successful working life are not learned in school, but in everyday life (p. 28). Even skills such as reading, writing or speaking a second language properly are hardly learned well in school, but more so through out-of-school opportunities and support.

Illich argues that school curricula are not well suited to teach skills, and, therefore, are both inefficient and very expensive (p. 17). Alternative models, such as apprenticeships or flexible courses that can be chosen whenever interest and life circumstances demand further learning, seem to be preferable to him. Another of his points is that certificates are mostly bound to time spent in school rather than one's achievement and effort (pp. 19–23). One further critique point is Illich's (1972, 38) observation that schools, generally speaking, reproduce society. Additionally, the widely shared belief that making money is the end goal of all education and schooling and that certificates are just the currency of, or "price tags" (p. 34) on, one's education seem still to be dominant today. At this point one might want to consider the historical and local circumstances: some of his arguments seem to be very specific to the American school model in the 1960s and 1970s and less applicable to other, more contemporary systems. Also, some of Illich's critique could be misunderstood as in line with a neo-liberal agenda, which was not his intent at all, and Lister (1973) addresses some other dangers as well, which will be discussed in the next section. However, many of Illich's points, and the critique made by his colleges, are still relevant today, and some of it might already have had an impact in changing education systems since the 1970s.

Buckman's (1973) critique of schools is offered in more moderate but nevertheless significant terms. He understands education as a "process of understanding the world, of acquiring the confidence to explore its workings" and as "an essential part of maturity" (pp. 1–2). Schooling, however, does not fit this description, and, therefore, is very different from education in this broader understanding. Buckman voices an argument for more flexibility in people's professional development as well as in schooling and learning. He argues for the need of lifelong learning and sees schools as not being able to cater for this necessity. However, although this claim was probably right at the time when this argument was made, and might even be true in many schools and systems around the globe today, it does not mean that schools are per se unable to prepare for a life of ongoing learning and development. It is at least possible to imagine settings and learning processes that support the development of lifelong learning in school environments if they are not already (at least partly) implemented in progressive schools like Summerhill (Neill 1992; Cassebaum 2003), Helene Lange school (Helene Lange Schule Wiesbaden 2012) or schools in the tradition of Montessori pedagogy (Raapke 2006), for example.

Further, Buckman (1973, 5–7) points out the practice to incapacitate children and to subjugate them under a teacher's ruling. This critique, again, targets some systems more than others, but overall schools are still some of the least democratic and most repressive places young people have to experience. Buckman argues that no adult, after leaving school, would suffer this kind of treatment and the limitations that come with attending school. As a possible alternative to this kind of practice, he refers to adult and community learning centres: these learning environments are, similar to early childhood education centres, mostly interest based, pupil centred and need no grades or exams at all.[2] As Illich points out, the only reason for grades and exams in schools is a distinction for later employment, although one's grades are often unrelated to one's actual ability and performance in a particular job. He suggests that one's qualification for a job should be determined completely distinct from one's educational and schooling history, for example, through specific tests or assessment centres at the time of employment.

Finally, Buckman (1973, 7) directs the reader's attention to the relationship between learner and teacher, which is hugely important for learning processes. This is a point taken up in more recent years by Ellsworth (1997), for example, who argues in this context, even though in different historical circumstances, that teaching, as it is commonly understood, is not possible at all, but the relationship

128 *Beyond schooling*

between teacher and student, and the way a student is addressed by the teacher, makes a difference for learning.

Possible ways out

In her later book *Places of Learning*, Ellsworth (2005) also argues for a different understanding of pedagogy and education. She uses examples of media and architecture to advocate for a pedagogy through "the force of the experience of the learning self" (p. 12). Ellsworth proposes that the learner should be seen as a *learning self*, who shapes his or her own self through the process of learning. This learning self – which is closely related to Schmid's view of the individual's self-concept – is in constant transition through the experiences that "set us in motion toward an open future" (pp. 17–18). The question for pedagogy and teaching should be *how to create learning spaces and situations that cater for these kinds of experiences*. Some of the aspects to take into account to answer this question would be the actual teaching space, the (physical) teaching material that can be bodily experienced by the learner and sensational and emotional experiences in relation to the learning object. Ellsworth (2005) does not critique schooling in particular, but she tries to change people's thinking about teaching, learning and pedagogy/education towards a more holistic and experience-based interpretation, which focuses on the development of the learning self, instead of a fixed knowledge-based curriculum. Her emphasis on the learning self and her experience-based approach is quite close, in some aspects, to Schmid's idea of self-shaping individuals and Foucault's care of the self. Ellsworth does not simply critique the existing ways of thinking, but offers possible practical approaches to teaching through movies, poems, memorials and other materials and spaces, designed with the intent to be educational.

Other initiatives to move beyond the problems outlined earlier have been proposed by Lister (1973), who offers three measures to move forward, away from the present system[3] to a more flexible one that provides alternatives for education – not only for the rich, but for all people:

1 An end to compulsion and the promoting of voluntarism. This would also involve the provision of real choice for learners which, in turn, would mean putting the funds, or the credit, for education in their hands, and an expansion of advisory services which would help people to satisfy their need in the more flexible and varied system of the future.
2 Deformalizing instruction and putting more stress on informal and incidental learning – that is learning related to experience. This would mean an end to the schooling system of sequential curricula and graded exercises – a system which fragments reality for the majority of people. [. . .]
3 Creating opportunities for life-long learning (permanent education). This would expose the most insidious message of the hidden curriculum of schooling – that education ends when formal schooling ends. (p. 23)

Although the third point is becoming more widely realised – the extent depending on the country – and lifelong learning is a term not only used by just academics anymore but in the public discussion as well, not much has happened to implement the first two measures. Schooling is still compulsory in most modern countries; alternative educational streams, such as apprenticeships or home schooling, often lack significant support; and formalised instruction, including the related process of certification, has more significance in today's developed societies than ever before. Ironically, the last goes hand in hand with the so-called *credential inflation*, which is the devaluation of achievements and certificates gained in the education system (Werfhorst and Andersen 2005).

However, these proposed changes carry some dangers as well if not accompanied by social and structural changes. Lister (1973, 24, 27) mentions, for example, that moving towards a voluntary education system could intensify the gulf between schooling and education if common beliefs and values are misguided. As this partly resembles a common market situation, which is close to the line of neo-liberal beliefs, deregulation and increased competition could lead to the contrary of the desired effect; it could lead to decreasing variety and streamlined teaching, which focuses on the best outcome of job-relevant subjects. This is especially the case as long as relevant job qualifications are still based on school certificates and one's personal schooling history, instead of one's actual qualification for the particular job in question. Therefore, de-formalisation and the abolition of school certificates, as requested by Illich (see earlier), need to go hand in hand with developing alternative education systems.

More recently, the German philosopher Frieder Lauxmann (2004) explored the idea of wisdom and came to similar conclusions about how economic and modern beliefs have devalued the idea of wisdom and corrupted modern education systems. His critique, similar to Buckman's, is moderate but significant: his main position is that a thriving modern society needs both *a flourishing economy and people who are able to think beyond* (p. 17). He argues that this conflicting situation is needed for a society not only to develop, but also to survive at all. A single-minded focus on economy, as is increasingly the case nowadays, will lead to the desolation of society.

Lauxmann interprets wisdom as "knowledge without knowledge" (p. 24, my translation).[4] According to Lauxmann, "wisdom manifests in the not provable, not pre-formed and often not comprehensible truth", which cannot be found in a textbook or the Internet, but which is of a "very different nature" (p. 24). Wisdom cannot be taught, but a teacher can be wise and teach in this manner. Lauxmann proclaims that one cannot possess wisdom, but wisdom "happens, it shows itself, it takes place" (p. 24). His main critique of modern schooling and education systems are the increased focus on scientific and facts knowledge (to use Schmid's terms here) and a lack of space and time for leisure, contemplation and *falling in love with the world*, which is, according to Lauxmann, the only way to find wisdom (Lauxmann 2004, 25–9). This is also the reason for wisdom being rarely popular in current school settings: it is not measurable or testable, and it is not easy to come by. However, wisdom has a connection to truth, which is of a very different quality than anything knowledge can provide, and wisdom brings forth the good for the one who is wise and for his or her surroundings. Therefore, striving for wisdom, in school as well as outside of formalised learning, is important and rewarding not only for individuals, but also for society as a whole (see Section 9.1 for more details about the relevance of wisdom).

8.3 The art of living and schooling

Having established the relationship between education and schooling, and having discussed some of the (de-)schooling critiques, the question now is: How does the art of living fit into schooling? It has been argued in Sections 7.2 and 7.3 that the ideal of the art of living lies at the heart of education, and this chapter, so far, outlined some of the critiques of current school systems, mainly targeting the inflexibility, inequality and disruptiveness of schooling for people's lives. It has also been shown that there are possible ways out of the current inadequacy of schools to prepare for people's life challenges and experiences. These ideas mainly focus on a different understanding of, and thinking about, education and schooling in terms of content and practice as much as in structure and its place in society.

The art of living can play a role in this context in two ways: it can serve as an underlying, guiding ideal or context in which to orientate school practice, curricula and teaching, and it can become a changing force, not only for schooling and education systems, but also for society in general. In terms of the latter, as indicated earlier, schools are mainly reproducing society, not changing it. However, with the distinction between schooling and education in mind, education can make a difference and should be pursued on all levels and for (and by) all age, social and gender groups. The idea of lifelong learning has reached the public sphere – even if still focused on professional development – and herein lies the opportunity for an increasing personal development and level of *Bildung* for people today, which again might lead to further changes in the structure of, and thinking about, education and schooling in society: this could lead to an understanding of education that could be called *education for life* or *life-pedagogy*, which focuses on the well-being, the good life and the development of an individual art of living of future students.

Coming back to the first role the art of living can play for schools, various aspects of education have been identified in Sections 7.2 and 7.3 that are strongly connected with the concept of the art of living and that can be incorporated in schools in much stronger ways than it is done today. Schmid (2000a, 318–22) also identified six areas of learning, which should not only be part of a curriculum, but could be a unifying theme throughout the curriculum: *the human being as individual; the social human being; difficulties and burdens of human life; striving for fulfilment and meaning in life; religions, beliefs and cultures of humanity;* and *the personal shape of life and global perspectives* (see Section 7.4 for more details). Certainly, such a theme should not limit the content of the curriculum, but create an interconnected experience of learning for students.

It can certainly be disputed whether Schmid's list includes all the important aspects of a human life-circle, as he claims, but this list is at the very least a good starting point to explore this field. Also, as has been argued earlier (Section 7.4), the areas noted are certainly significant aspects of a human's life.

Schmid discusses these areas of learning in the context of a suggested new school subject: "*Lebensgestaltung*" [shaping-of-life; lifestyle] (p. 318). This subject is based on the idea of the unifying theme mentioned earlier; it is about connecting the fragments and splinters of perception and knowledge young people experience inside and outside of school into an integrated, sense-making and life-shaping whole. The mentioned areas of learning are supposed to loosely encircle a human's path from birth to death and help the students to situate themselves, think about their lives and futures, widen their perception in everyday life as well as on a global scale, and help them to artfully shape their lives in ways that they deem fit and judge as good and beautiful (see Section 9.1 for more details).

Beyond these areas of learning, Schmid also draws attention to the teaching methods and didactics used, which are as significant as the content itself (p. 322). He underlines the personal experience for the learner in contrast to abstract theoretical knowledge transfer. Similar to Illich and others, he follows the notion that (at least when questions of life and living well are addressed but even beyond that) teaching and learning should not be primarily achievement oriented but focus on the experience and development of the human being. Grades and assessments about one's progress in terms of self-reflection or wisdom or one's quality and amount of experiences are counter-productive at least, if not impossible at all (Section 9.2 will discuss these and the following points more thoroughly).

Moreover, a structure that does not focus on achievement but on the personal experiences of students creates a freedom where they can ask questions that are relevant to their own self-concept and where they can discuss these questions openly. According to Schmid, a fundamental factor for teaching is, for example, to further reflective thinking through a "self-reflective approach" to teaching that puts the teaching process itself in the focus of reflection (p. 323). A possible discussion that leads beyond the classroom to include the whole school, the ways of dealing with school and the social structures around it into the reflection process can open the view for conditions of and opportunities for one's own *Lebensgestaltung* [shaping-of-life] and art of living (p. 323).

Schmid also draws attention to the personality of the teacher: "that the personality of the pedagogue and his/her ability for self-reflection is of even higher importance here than in education in general goes without saying" (p. 323). Further, Schmid emphasises the areas of *Bildung*, general knowledge, life-knowledge and philosophy, as well as knowledge about good teaching methods and didactics as some of the necessary traits for teaching in the area of the art of living. Only someone who engages in the art of living and takes responsibility for one's own life can be a helpful teacher on the way to an individual art of living. He also lists a number of areas of expertise a teacher needs to be familiar with, which will be discussed in more detail in Section 9.2.

Summary

In this chapter, I introduced Schmid's (and the German) understanding of education (pedagogy) on the basis of *Erziehung*, *Bildung* and *Entfaltung*. Consequences for schooling and the relation between education and schooling have been discussed, and it has been pointed out that schooling is, although significant, only a part of a person's educational journey. One's education, in the broader understanding described earlier, only concludes with a person's death and, therefore, the ability for lifelong learning and self-*bildung* is one of the most important skills to be learned during a young person's upbringing and school life. The development of one's own self through *Bildung* goes hand in hand with the development of one's own art of living. As discussed before, it has been shown here again that Schmid's art of living concept provides a useful theoretical background as well as helpful suggestions for a practical implementation of an education for life concept.

Notes

1 All translations of material from Liebau are my own unless otherwise noted.
2 Compare progressive school concepts, such as Summerhill or Rudolf Steiner schools.
3 Although written in 1973, Lister's points are still relevant and instructive for today's schooling systems.
4 All translations of material from Lauxmann are my own unless otherwise noted.

9 Life pedagogy – an education for life concept

The discussion in the previous chapters has shown that Schmid's approach to an art of living concept has much to offer education today, especially when one takes seriously the end of education previously argued for to enable (young) people to live the best life they possibly can under the circumstances they are living in. This aim in education is not new; it has been promoted – explicitly or implicitly – by educationists such as J. H. Pestalozzi, Maria Montessori, A. S. Neill, Helene Lange and Nel Noddings (Pestalozzi 1997; Raapke 2006; Neill 1992; Helene Lange Schule Wiesbaden 2012; Noddings 2005). It has also been shown previously (Chapters 2 and 5) that concepts of the good life and striving for "happiness", or *eudaimonia*, are substantial aspects of human life. Education in any form, in schools and beyond, needs to support students to thrive and flourish as much as possible – not only for their own good, but also for the good of society and humanity as a whole (see Chapter 7).

But how are educationists and teachers supposed to give this support? Which theoretical concept gives guidance and underpins practical approaches, like those done at Geelong Grammar School in Australia or at the Wellington College in Berkshire, UK? As indicated earlier, some answers can be found in progressive educational concepts and theory. However, despite other student-centred approaches, a fundamental educational theory that centres on the development of a student's own art of living and good life is still lacking.

So far, various philosophical and psychological approaches in light of educational theory have been analysed. The following chapter will provide a first step towards a subsequent *education for life* concept. Some of the fundamental theoretical areas will be explored, such as hermeneutical skills, the concept of *Bildung*, religion and spirituality, as well as practical implications, including a teacher's personality, teaching methods and school and classroom settings.

As previously argued, a shift of focus is needed in educational theory and practice away from mainly economic considerations to a more student- and human-centred approach (Section 7.2). Current demands of the (post-)modern age, with its increased pace of life and the challenge of having multitudes of choices every day raise the importance of this shift of focus even further and, likewise, open the space to consider alternative conceptualisations of education.

9.1 Pedagogical content and practice

In the course of this book, various aspects of the art of living and how to live a good life have been explored. This section will now be dedicated to a discussion of some of these aspects in relation to an education for life concept. As mentioned before, an education for life is understood as a student-centred approach and focuses on the well-being and flourishing of the individual by supporting the development of an own art of living. On the basis of Schmid's considerations about the art of living, as well as positive psychology research and some educational concepts, key skills, knowledge and other factors, which are necessary or helpful for developing an own art of living and that support personal flourishing, will be identified. Ways of educational interaction to support the development process of students in this regard will be discussed as well.

Skills and knowledge

When considering which skills and what knowledge are important for (young) people in current societies to learn, one is faced with a difficult task. (Scientific) knowledge today exceeds the learning capacity of human beings by far. Even to know "everything of relevance" in a single area of expertise, such as construction, law, medicine or information technology – to name only a few examples – is close to impossible. Moreover, to anticipate how professional areas will develop in the near future is hard to predict, and much of the knowledge that is considered "cutting edge" today will be obsolete in the near future as developments and inventions move on. Therefore, focusing mainly on scientific and facts knowledge in school curricula and other areas of educational practice is short-sighted and destined to be insufficient.

However, this does not mean that scientific knowledge, general knowledge about the world and other important areas of expertise should be ignored. A solid knowledge base on a broad variety of topics not only helps to orient oneself in everyday life and to find one's area of interest in the job market and life itself, but it also supports informed decision-making and contributes positively to the political and social discourse of one's society. As Dewey (2001) pointed out, education – in the broadest meaning of the word – is a necessary condition for a democratic society.

Still, without increasing the number of compulsory schooling years to an infeasible amount, it will not be possible to acquire a solid knowledge base in all areas of significance for people today. Consequently, strong emphasis needs to be placed on self-learning and self-development skills. It goes without saying that students who are able to fill the gaps in their knowledge when they encounter them and who are also able to distinguish between knowledge that is relevant or irrelevant to them are much better equipped for a quickly developing and changing world than students who are not. The role of formal education today, in terms of scientific knowledge, can only be to reveal the scope of possible knowledge (Schmid 2000a, 312); it is the role of each student to decide, based on one's interests, which areas of knowledge to pursue.

Beyond the skills for lifelong learning and (scientific and general) knowledge, a holistic educational concept needs to take into account a wider range of aspects of human life. Noddings (2005), for example, refers to areas such as companionship, making a home, bringing up children, religion and awareness of the impact of the different roles one has to play in life as areas of importance for well-being and happiness. Schmid (2000a, 298) introduces the term *life-knowledge* (see Section 5.5) in this context: a life know-how that is gained through the experience of life and prepares for living a good life. Life-knowledge, in Schmid's reading, is a conglomeration of knowledge that is gained, for example, through synthesis of hermeneutical, scientific and experience-based knowledge and allows the individual to live in a managed, orienting, shaping and serene way (p. 298). It combines detailed knowledge about all significant aspects of daily life with general knowledge and offers an overview of broader aspects and interrelations between personal, social and political life. This kind of knowledge allows dealing with daily life effortlessly and lends orientation to direct one's life and development. Ways for educationists to support the development of relevant life-knowledge is to allow for and specifically create learning situations that give students a hands-on perspective and personal experience in all sorts of scientific knowledge areas and aspects of life.

A good implementation for a highly integrated personal experience with a vast variety of learning areas is, for example, John Hunter's *World Peace Game*.[1] This game allows students to experience all sorts of personal, social, political, strategical and environmental situations; it allows for conflict, debate, discussion, negotiations and solutions. Students can explore strategies and learn about consequences. This is a highly complex game, and not every subject and experience can be facilitated in this way. However, playful learning environments in general offer opportunities for experience learning, as games, per definition, are hands-on, engaging and offer exploration of skills and strategies in a safe environment.

Other skills and areas of learning, which are part of the *World Peace Game* and that are also important in an education for life context, are social skills that allow the student to live successfully and peacefully in a social society. This includes sympathy for people around oneself – their state of mind, emotions and needs – which is also often called empathy. It includes skills and readiness for negotiations and compromise; knowledge of social rules and conventions; personal flexibility to interact with different people and to deal with different expectations; and it requires the ability to take responsibility for one's own actions and for one's role in the wider social context.

These skills are hardly learned from textbooks, and, therefore, more creative and interactive learning environments and settings are called for. Many, but not all, of these skills will be learned in the course of normal interaction in everyday life. However, educationists in school and other settings should consider these aspects and provide learning environments that cater explicitly or implicitly for the development of these skills mentioned earlier.

Further, to be able to move effortlessly in a socio-cultural context and still be able to develop one's own art of living based on one's own values, beliefs and

136 *Life pedagogy*

norms, one needs to be able to practise self-reflection and critical thinking.[2] These skills are not necessarily acquired in a "normal" family context and in everyday life; therefore, an education for life calls on schools and other educational institutions to create learning spaces and opportunities for developing these faculties. Recent developments in the area of *philosophy for children*, for example, can offer helpful insights of how to create these learning spaces (Daniel and Auriac 2011).

Finally, the area of *self-knowledge* needs to be emphasised in this context. Much can be learned through self-reflection about oneself, one's beliefs, one's assumptions and one's view of the world. However, some aspects of life and the human condition are not easily accessible and are sometimes even counterintuitive. Helpful insights can be gained through the study of psychology and positive psychology research findings, as discussed in Chapters 4 and 6. To be aware of significant functions and aspects of how our brain works can help in two ways: first, to improve one's own experience of life and, second, to avoid pitfalls for unnecessary grief, as well as manipulation through others (e.g. people, media and advertisements).

Concluding this section, it needs to be pointed out that these areas of learning presented in this section are not to be seen as exhaustive, but as a starting point for an exploration of what is necessary for people to develop their own art of living and live a good and beautiful life. Many areas, such as scientific and general knowledge, will have to be adapted constantly as the development of human knowledge and science moves on. Other areas, including social and critical thinking skills, need to be adapted to the cultural and social circumstances of educational interaction. Further, some areas have not been touched on so far, which are of high importance for the current modern and postmodern age: media-literacy and inter-cultural competencies are only two examples. Finally, the key areas of learning for an art of living today, as identified by Schmid (2000a, 319–24) and described in Section 7.4 and Chapter 8, are highly significant as well: the human being as individual; the social human being; difficulties and burdens of human life; striving for fulfilment and meaning in life; religions, beliefs and cultures of humanity; and the personal shape of life and global perspectives.

Hermeneutics

The role of hermeneutics for the art of living has been discussed before in Section 5.5. This section will be focused mainly on implications of the previous discourse for education, as well as on some recommendations for teaching practice.

Hermeneutics is understood here in light of Heidegger, Gadamer and Habermas: it is both an epistemological and ontological concept. Hermeneutics is a technique that allows a human being to interpret what is perceived and to make sense of one's perceptions. This process of "making sense" of the world and giving meaning to the world as one perceives it influences and shapes one's own self through the beliefs one creates and holds. One's perception, on the other hand, is influenced by one's beliefs. This forms a so-called *hermeneutical circle*: perception; interpretation through hermeneutics; shaping one's own beliefs and

Life pedagogy 137

one's self through constructing meaning; and, finally, influencing one's perception through the lenses of one's beliefs and one's worldview.

It becomes apparent that hermeneutics is essential not only to make sense of the world and culture one is living in, but also to actively shape one's self and to influence the world one is living in. Schmid (2000a, 288) introduces the term "interpretation-worlds" in this context to emphasise the influence of one's own perception and interpretation of one's experience of life and the world. However, understanding gained through hermeneutics is also important to influence one's surroundings in a directed way, which might lead to the intended outcome. Both aspects of hermeneutics are an integral part of the concept of *Bildung* and, therefore, important for developing one's own art of living.

To live somewhat successfully in any social circumstances, a certain level of interpretation skill is needed and can be attested to by virtually every human being. However, the level of skill and the significance of insights one can gain varies and can often be extended. Higher levels of hermeneutical skills[3] can lead to more autonomy and control over one's life circumstances and one's experience of the world.

According to Schmid, interpretation is mostly dependent on symbols in any form (pp. 286–92). Most common is language, but other symbols are relevant as well, be they numbers, pictograms or musical notes. To find a public bathroom, for example, it might be very helpful to identify and draw meaning from the pictogram of a little man or a woman in many cases. Finding one's way in foreign cultures with unfamiliar symbols might prove more difficult. More challenging, however, is to identify and make sense of human behaviour and expressions in social situations such as body language, facial expressions, voice modulation and eye expressions.

The challenge for educationists in terms of hermeneutical skills is not only to teach language, reading, writing and maths, but also to allow for inter-subjective experiences in various social settings and situations. Visiting a political discussion, spending a day in court or actively scrutinising emotional social situations are only some ways to create room for experiences in this area. Another easier-to-facilitate way is to discuss educational narratives, high-class literature (such as Herman Hesse, Thomas Mann, Dostoevsky, Goethe or Shakespeare) or popular TV soap operas. Although often manipulative and constructed, the last can provide modern examples which might be closer to students' everyday experiences and reality of a wide range of human emotions, behaviours and interactions. Further, through critical interaction with certain media, students can also learn media-literacy skills and how to identify and critically reflect on (hidden) messages, norms and values in certain programmes.

Other methods for hermeneutical experiences in educational settings could be role-playing, dialogue or observations during student discussions (i.e., assign students the role of observers during a discussion about any topic and let them give feedback afterwards about their experiences and observations).

The significance of hermeneutics for an education for life concept is to sharpen one's perception, increase one's skill to make sensible interpretations and to accumulate life-knowledge and practical wisdom. This allows the individual not only to interact more purposefully and effectively with his or her environment, but also supports the development of wisdom, as will be discussed later on.

Bildung

The concept of *Bildung* has also been discussed previously in Chapter 8. However, according to Liebau (1999), *Bildung* is one of the three central concepts of education and, according to Schmid (2000a), a key aspect of the art of living. Therefore, it is essential for educationists to consider how to support the formation of *Bildung* for students in any educational setting.

As described previously, there are three aspects to *Bildung*: knowledge, self-formation and practical wisdom. To impart *knowledge*, especially scientific and factual knowledge, is a genuine task of schooling. However, general knowledge about life and the world seems to be considered of less importance of late, as this is seldom assessed in national standard exams or is part of international OECD comparative tests, such as PISA.[4] Nevertheless, general knowledge is important not only to live a good life, but also to be successful in life.

Rarely taken into account, partly due to its difficult and non-assessable nature, is what Schmid (2000a, 297–303) calls *life-knowledge*: it is not knowledge about life, but applied knowledge through hermeneutics *from life for life*, as described before. It is practical knowledge gained through experience, perceptions, sensations and hermeneutically processed scientific knowledge, among others, and is applicable to real-life situations. This aspect distinguishes life-knowledge from more theoretical scientific or facts knowledge, which is predominant in most curricula. Life-knowledge is mostly dependent on experiences, either through educational games and settings, as can be found in outdoor, adventure and experience education,[5] or through real-life experiences by visiting as many different environments as possible. This might include, but is not limited to, visiting theatres, zoos, planetaria, sea life aquariums and various sorts of workplaces, including universities, during one's time of compulsory formal education.

Life-knowledge, though related to practical wisdom, is not the same. *Practical wisdom*, as the second aspect of *Bildung*, has a normative quality of right and wrong. It is not only important to know *how* to do something, but rather to know *what* to do in a certain situation from a *practical, moral and social* perspective. Practical wisdom is not pure reasoning; it includes an emotional aspect, a "gut-feeling" of what is right and wrong. In this, it is more practical than pure reasoning, as it is much harder to think through all possible consequences of one's proposed actions and filter them through Kant's categorical imperative than to develop a *feeling* for what might be right or wrong in a certain situation and be guided, more or less instantly, by this feeling. Schwartz and Sharpe (2010) characterise practical wisdom as follows:

1 A wise person knows the proper aims of the activity she is engaged in. She wants to do the right thing to achieve these aims and wants to meet the needs of the people she is serving.

2   A wise person knows how to improvise, balancing conflicting aims and interpreting rules and principles in light of the particularities of each context.
3   A wise person is perceptive, knows how to read a social context and knows how to move beyond the black-and-white of rules and see the gray in a situation.
4   A wise person knows how to take on the perspective of another – to see the situation as the other person does and thus to understand how the other person feels. This perspective taking is what enables a wise person to feel empathy for others and to make decisions that serve the client's (student's, patient's, friend's) needs.
5   A wise person knows how to make emotion an ally of reason, to rely on emotion to signal what a situation calls for and to inform judgement without distorting it. He can feel, intuit or "just know" what the right thing to do is, enabling him to act quickly when timing matters. His emotions and intuitions are well educated.
6   A wise person is an experienced person. Practical wisdom is a craft, and craftsmen are trained by having the right experiences. People learn how to be brave, said Aristotle, by doing brave things. So, too, with honesty, justice, loyalty, caring, listening and counseling. (pp. 25–6)

Therefore, practical wisdom combines certain kinds of knowledge (facts knowledge, practical life-knowledge, knowledge about expectations) with improvisation, perception, empathy, emotions and experience. The key for developing practical wisdom, according to Schwartz and Sharpe (2010), is experience. They claim, by referring back to Aristotle, that practical wisdom is a craft that can be learned by experiencing and repeatedly exercising it. This requires teachers, who themselves can exercise practical wisdom or can provide encounters with people who are good at exercising it. In this context, knowing one's own limits is an important quality for educationists (see Section 9.2 for more details about teacher requirements).

The third aspect of *Bildung*, *self-formation* or *self-cultivation*, is, in the end, up to the student. Teachers and educationists need to be very cautious not to direct students in a way that will lead to manipulation and external formation of their characters. However, this does not mean to abandon any influence, as this would be quite impossible in any case: educational practice is always an intervention in a student's life. The key is to help students develop critical thinking, reflection and self-reflection skills. This will allow students to filter external values and norms, put them into context and build their own set of norms based on their beliefs and values.

Finally, students need to be able to increase their level of *Bildung* on their own; the German word for this is *Selbstbildung* [self-*bildung*]. This includes the ability for lifelong learning (accumulating knowledge in proposed areas), being able to increase one's hermeneutical skills and deepening one's level of practical wisdom. These faculties will enable a student to shape and care for his or her own self and his or her own life.

Wisdom

Wisdom and practical wisdom are, as the terms indicate, quite closely related. However, some differences can be discerned. Generally speaking, practical wisdom seems to be an aspect of wisdom applied to everyday life. As described earlier, it allows for a broader understanding of a situation, takes into account the people (and other agencies, such as animals or the environment) connected with this situation and helps to identify the morally and socially right course of action. *Wisdom*, on the other hand, is often described as a broader concept that implies the ability for practical wisdom, but reaches beyond: it entails high levels of self-knowledge and humbleness; a good feel for one's role in the world; the ability and practice of "deep" thoughts (i.e. thinking a topic through on many levels); a deeper understanding of the world; and further insights, such as an acceptance of one's own insignificance in the broader picture of the world and the universe.

However, there are many different descriptions and interpretations of wisdom: ancient philosophy (Aristotle, Socrates, Diogenes), current philosophy (Lauxmann 2004; Schwartz and Sharpe 2010), educational and psychological interpretations, religious perspectives (Christianity, Buddhism, Hinduism, Islam, Judaism) and cultural definitions (Confucius, Daoism). The borders between practical wisdom and wisdom and between wisdom and spirituality are somewhat blurry; however, wisdom seems to fill the room between practical wisdom and spirituality (not religion) to some extent.

One interpretation of wisdom can be found in descriptions of wise men in Eastern texts from Confucianism, the *Dao De Jing* and Buddhism (Laozi n.d./1993; Lau 2009; Mello 1992; Nakagawa 2009; Tucker 2003). There, men of wisdom are often characterised as calm, non-violent, free from hatred and fear, righteous, just, knowing themselves and mastering themselves and carefully discerning between right and wrong.

Interestingly, being knowledgeable is not a necessary part of being wise. Peter Roberts (2012, 9–10) points out, referring to the *Dao De Jing*, that certain kinds of knowledge can even hinder wisdom and living a good life. He also refers to Dostoevsky, who emphasises the qualities of intuitive knowledge (wisdom) over science (pp. 9–10). Other philosophers who argue along these lines are Frieder Lauxmann (2004) and Nicholas Maxwell (2012). Lauxmann (2004), for example, states in the context of, as he claims, the changed relationship of philosophy (love of wisdom) to wisdom that

> enjoyment, which exceeds the joy through the experience of wine and music, [which has been described by Jesus Sirach (190BC) as the experience one has when reading philosophy], is hard to come by when reading some of today's more important philosophical texts. Have philosophers, therefore, done anything wrong? They probably have forgotten to heed their hearts while working with their minds. Wisdom, understood rightly, is not the domain of knowledgeable people; it is open to all, who have an open heart

for the intellectual and material beauties of the world. If considered in this way, however, philosophy and wisdom have drifted apart and became mostly independent [from each other].

(p. 12)

In this quote, Lauxmann critiques not only the relationship between current philosophy and wisdom, but also indicates that wisdom is more dependent on appreciation than on knowledge. Similar to Maxwell (2007), he critiques further the increasing dominance of science in education and academia due to the demands of industry and economy, which might lead to a decline in creativity and social innovation, as these are areas of the arts and humanities, not science. Much more could be said about the critique of current developments in education and society; however, the scope of this section does not allow for a full discussion of this topic.

Turning back to the relationship between wisdom and education, Maxwell (2012) argues for a shift in educational and academic practice from *knowledge-inquiry* to *wisdom-inquiry*. As reasons for this reformatory shift, he claims that most of today's human-made problems – such as "modern warfare and terrorism, vast inequalities in wealth and standards of living between first and third worlds, rapid population growth, environmental damage" (p. 665), among others – are a direct consequence of applied scientific knowledge without wisdom. He states that "wisdom *can* be taught in schools and universities. It *must* be so learned and taught. Wisdom is indeed the proper fundamental objective for the whole of the academic enterprise: to help humanity learn how to nurture and create a wiser world" (p. 666).

At this point it needs to be said that Maxwell's interpretation of wisdom is different from Lauxmann's understanding. Maxwell (2007) defines wisdom as

> the desire, the active endeavour, and the capacity to discover and achieve what is desirable and of value in life, both for oneself and for others. Wisdom includes knowledge and understanding but goes beyond them in also including: the desire and active striving for what is of value, the ability to see what is of value, actually and potentially, in the circumstances of life, the ability to experience value, the capacity to use and develop knowledge, technology and understanding as needed for the realization of value. Wisdom, like knowledge, can be conceived of, not only in personal terms, but also in institutional or social terms. We can thus interpret [wisdom-inquiry] as asserting: the basic task of rational inquiry is to help us develop wiser ways of living, wiser institutions, customs and social relations, a wiser world.
>
> (Maxwell 2007, 79)

Maxwell seems to have a more practical understanding of wisdom, which is closer to the side of practical wisdom, whereas Lauxmann's (2004) definition goes more in the direction of the spiritual end of wisdom: "Wisdom is a way of thinking that evolves through falling in love with the world" (p. 26). He describes four factors that loosely encompass the way of thinking that can help wisdom to flourish:

1. Wisdom cannot be stored, it happens;
2. it is unsystematic, therefore not programmable [i.e. cannot be taught by instruction];
3. it flourishes only through love for the world;
4. it brings forth the good. (p. 26)

When comparing this quote with the notion of wisdom proposed earlier in the context of Eastern philosophy, some overlap can be seen here, and the distinction from Maxwell's understanding becomes apparent. However, both interpretations have value and can provide guidance for education. Maxwell's call for a reform of academic enquiry is as important as Lauxmann's idea of wisdom for living a better life. In fact, both seem to aim at the same goal: helping humanity to become more fully human, helping people to live better lives and bringing forth the good in and for the world we are living in.

Another definition from a Confucian viewpoint has been proposed by Lin (1976), who describes wisdom as a balancing act between realism, idealism and humour:

> So then, wisdom, or the highest type of thinking, consists in toning down our dreams or idealism with a good sense of humor, supported by reality itself.
> (p. 5)

To sum up this section, wisdom can and should be part of formal education. Educationists should strive not only for bare knowledge, but also for wisdom, which goes hand in hand with developing an art of living and living a beautiful life. Similar aims and directions can be found in various religions and value systems in many parts of the world. As argued earlier, wisdom seems to border on spirituality, and to develop wisdom at the level Lauxmann envisions, aspects and techniques of spirituality can be of much help. The next section will therefore engage with these aspects of human life and their implications for an education for life.

Spirituality and education

Besides philosophical contemplations about the art of living, religions and spiritual traditions have laid claim to ways of how to live a good life. Where religions tend to be prescriptive, spirituality and mysticism seem to be more open for different individual ways of accomplishing this goal. As mentioned earlier, one of the challenges in our current age is the validity of norms, values and (religious) belief. Globalisation has led to an increased exchange and interaction not only between people, economies and governments, but also of norms, values, religious beliefs and confessions. Travelling to foreign countries, the Internet and widespread migration brought various cultural and religious traditions in closer contact with each other, and they provide multiple opportunities for people on a global scale to get to know religious and cultural belief systems that are different from the one they were born into. This confrontation with other belief systems and the readiness of information about them can easily lead to confusion and uncertainty about which worldview, norms and values might be the right ones to choose for oneself.

This uncertainty of what to believe, if to follow a religion at all, and, subsequently, the question of how to live one's own life, as pointed out by Schmid (2000a), increase the importance of an art of living for people today. However, as the art of living concept by Schmid is centred on the individual (see Chapter 5), the decision whether someone believes in one god, multiple gods, follows a religion at all, becomes an atheist or devises his or her own mixture of beliefs and convictions has no preference in the context of the art of living, as long as each decision is a conscious one and is based on reflection, prudence and practical wisdom.

As religion is a difficult topic and often emotionally charged, many objections and concerns could be raised at this point. However, the art of living does not actively favour any one religion or belief over another, so most concerns that could be brought to the fore in this context would be of an ethical nature and not a critique of the art of living itself. The qualities of prudence and practical wisdom, which lie at the heart of the ethics of the art of living, as discussed in Section 5.3, can provide answers to these points. In addition, it has to be acknowledged that the way religion is practised sometimes – all religions and cultures have to be included here – can be in conflict with prudent and wise decision-making, which is another argument for the importance of strengthening the skills related to the art of living. More important for the argument in this book, however, is the fact that practised faith, religious beliefs and spirituality in general can contribute positively to one's level of well-being, happiness and health (Lau 2009, 719; Seligman 2010, 59–61).

Spirituality is understood here as an engagement in questions beyond the sensational perceivable reality. One does not have to follow an established faith or religion; one only has to engage with the idea of going beyond what one can perceive with one's common five senses. To strive to engage with what is "beyond" in any way is to engage in spirituality. As mentioned earlier, spiritual practice has various positive effects for the individual, such as increased levels of well-being, happiness and health, as well as reducing the ageing process of one's brain, for example, through meditation (Lau 2009).

Spirituality is also the combining notion behind most, if not all, religions past and present. Religious beliefs vary in overall direction and detail, but most of them concern themselves with the divine (god, transcendence), or at least with a realm beyond perceived reality (nirvana). One could argue that the notion of spirituality is the encompassing quality human beings strive for when engaging in religion and religious practice. One could say, further, that this striving for spirituality, which is often paired with the search for meaning in life, is indeed one expression of the holistic striving of human beings for *eudaimonia* and the good life.

144 *Life pedagogy*

Drawing on this notion of spirituality and its relation to religion – religious beliefs are a form of spirituality, but spirituality is not necessarily a form of religion – we can now continue to discuss the relationship between education and spirituality. Marian Souza (2009) claims that the

> question for Australia [and other Western cultures] in the 21st century is not how we can become richer: it is how we can use our high standard of living to build a flourishing society – one devoted to improving our wellbeing rather than just expanding the economy.
>
> (p. 677)

This claim emphasises, again, the importance of the art of living, not only for each individual, but also on a broader scale: "a flourishing society". De Souza offers spirituality as one possible answer to this question:

> if spirituality is nurtured it gives the individual a sense of belonging and a sense of place which, in turn, provides the individual's life with some meaning and purpose. . . . This belonging [and the sense of having 'a place'] can bring with it a kind of ownership as well as a sense of being one of many; of being part of a whole. Further, it could inspire a feeling of responsibility to self and community and, therefore, provides a sense of purpose which, then, can give life meaning and value. *The essence lies in the feelings of being connected, of being part of something more than self.* Consequently, if contemporary educational programs and environments are designed to foster young people's spirituality and allow its expression, they should promote wellbeing.
>
> (p. 679, italics added)

De Souza links spirituality not only with the well-being of individuals, but also with local communities and a healthy, flourishing society. This approach provides a strong argument for giving spirituality a place in schools – provided that the well-being of citizens and a flourishing society is the goal of a country, other than solely trying to increase its wealth, which has been proven to be non-beneficial for people in terms of happiness and well-being (Csikszentmihalyi 2008; Seligman 2010; Wilkinson and Pickett 2010).

Beyond the possible increase of well-being for the individual and the positive outcome for a society, spirituality, as understood here, is also an important way of gaining self-knowledge; finding out about one's own beliefs, values, hopes and desires; and, subsequently, of developing one's own art of living. Although spirituality might not be necessary to live an artful and beautiful life, developing one's own spirituality can be most helpful in finding one's own way in life and, therefore, should be part of any (holistic) educational model.

Building on this notion, Lau (2009) promotes spirituality as part of an "holistic education", and he points out that spiritual exercises and meditation about concepts, such as mindfulness and compassion, have also very immediate (even measurable) benefits: the cultivation of attention and increased concentration;

reduction of stress and more positive feelings in and towards school and learning; better connection of mind, body and spirit; increasing intuitive knowledge, insight and creativity; and, drawing on Gardner's (2006) book *Five Minds for the Future*, increased capabilities for good leadership.

Mind-sets and attachments

One attempt to bridge the gap between Eastern and Western philosophy has been made by Anthony Mello (1992), who was an internationally well-known Jesuit priest and spiritual teacher; he published various books, held spiritual conferences and founded the Sadhana Institute of Pastoral Counselling in Poona, India. Although he studied psychology, theology and philosophy, his public writings are not of an academic nature but rather have a spiritually guiding quality and could be considered works of wisdom. Some of the key points of his teachings are *the role of awareness, the impact of attachments on happiness and well-being, the power of one's own beliefs and convictions,* and *the role of external and internal experiences.*

The following citation is an example of his teaching style and is also meant as an example of possible teaching methods in terms of wisdom and the art of living. According to de Mello's friend J. Francis Stroud, this is what de Mello said about his work (and his friend) at an occasion when he was asked to describe what he was doing:

> A man found an eagle's egg and put it in a nest of a barnyard hen. The eaglet hatched with the brood of chicks and g[r]ew up with them.
> All his life the eagle did what the barnyard chicks did, thinking he was a barnyard chicken. He scratched the earth for worms and insects. He clucked and cackled. And he would thrash his wings and fly a few feet into the air.
> Years passed and the eagle grew very old. One day he saw a [. . . magnificent] bird above him in the cloudless sky. It glided in graceful majesty among the powerful wind currents, with scarcely a beat of its strong golden wings.
> The old eagle looked up in awe. "Who's that?" he asked.
> "That's the eagle, the king of the birds," said his neighbor. "He belongs to the sky. We belong to the earth – we're chickens." So the eagle lived and died a chicken, for that's what he thought he was.
> (Mello 1992, 3)

With this story, de Mello wanted to tell his friend that he believed him to be "a 'golden eagle,' unaware of the heights to which [. . . he] could soar" (p. 3); he also tried to show his friend what he (the friend) was thinking about himself. De Mello tried to make people *aware*, to wake them up and connect them with their spirituality. He describes people who are not in touch with their spirituality and wisdom – which are most people – as asleep and driven; he urged people to wake up and become aware of their own beliefs and expectations that make them suffer. In this notion of the power of the mind and one's own beliefs, one can find strong Buddhist influences. One of the techniques he was using, and that can be seen in the example earlier, is the short story. This technique of telling educational stories, stories which try to convey an insight about life or aspects of life, has been commonly used by spiritual guides, wise gurus and Western novelists alike.[6]

Coming back to de Mello's philosophy, he places awareness, similar to Buddhism, at the centre of the spiritual journey to enlightenment, spirituality or "waking up" (p. 6). He also emphasises that it is not the teacher (or anyone else) who will be able to help someone to follow the path to awakening or to living a good life; only the individual can move in this direction through the practice of awareness and self-reflection, the same as each individual is responsible for his or her own experiences, feelings and thinking (pp. 7–8).

As indicated earlier, attachments and expectations are two major reasons for people's suffering. Berlant (2011, 23–4), in her book *Cruel Optimism*, argues in a similar direction when she states that attachments to something (an object of desire) can have a potential negative impact on one's flourishing and well-being. De Mello (1992, 17) states in this context that there are only two ways out of this misery of attachments: suffering so much in life that one decides at some point that it is enough and lets go of all attachments and expectations that led to disappointments and hurt in the past (which he describes as "waking up"), or listening to the truth – in the deeper meaning of the truth of wisdom, not scientific knowledge – which comes to pass through awareness and leads to awakening as well.

The underlying assumption of de Mello's philosophy, which has its origin in Buddhist thinking, can be quite difficult to accept, but it is also liberating at the same time: everybody is responsible for their own experiences – for their own feelings of pleasure, happiness and hurt – and this also means that everyone is able to change the influence external circumstances have on their internal experiences and the way they perceive reality. *Spirituality is finally the ability to alter the quality of one's experiences in the world.* The external circumstances might not have changed, but the internal perception can change and lead to a different experience of the world and reality. As mentioned earlier, this idea is closely related to what Roger (1998) describes in the context of stress and strategies of stress avoidance. It also has parallels with the concept of the hermeneutic circle, as described previously. Likewise, Csikszentmihalyi (2008, 43) points out that the one strategy that is most likely successful in improving one's quality of life is to change one's own expectations and inner experiences by exercising control over one's consciousness.

However, as mentioned earlier, spirituality is not a necessity to develop an own art of living and to live a beautiful life. Still, according to Mello (1992, 16–19), spirituality is nothing else than to chance upon wisdom through the practice of awareness. Moreover, control over one's own mind, beliefs and consciousness[7] can alter one's perception of life and the feelings attached with experiences made. Therefore, and for the reasons mentioned in the previous section, a holistic educational approach should offer opportunities for students to engage with their own spirituality and to practise awareness and mindfulness.

9.2 Requirements for teaching the art of living

As discussed in Chapter 5, the shape of a beautiful life and how to live a good life need to be defined and discovered by each individual for himself or herself. Likewise, teaching "the art of living" is equally impossible, as not only aims, norms and values in life differ from person to person, but also living circumstances and cultural aspects are multifold. However, teaching *about* the art of living and teaching skills and knowledge that are important (either necessary or helpful) *to develop one's own art of living* is quite possible. Some of the skills and knowledge that fall under this category of being important and that can be supported through educational interaction have been discussed in previous chapters. Also, some suggestions and recommendations have been made for suitable and non-suitable teaching methods and settings. This section will now summarise some of these insights with a specific, but not exclusive eye, on schooling.

The teacher, his or her personality and developing an art of living

According to the German understanding of education (Chapter 8), everyone can be a teacher to someone at any given time. In this sense, anyone can potentially contribute to one's understanding of the world or understanding of oneself and thus contribute to the development of one's own art of living. Additionally, taking into account the current emphasis on scientific knowledge and assessment in school curricula and policy, it is more likely than not that actual significant knowledge about life and how to live well is learned outside of schools and rather accidentally from people who are not formally teachers. These can be parents or family members, sometimes peers, or chance meetings with strangers. Informal teachers can also be novelists, songwriters or other non–face-to-face role-models, such as the Dalai Lama, the Pope or Nelson Mandela.

This learning by example, as it mostly is, requires that the person who can help someone on the way has already mastered a certain level of skill or knowledge in an area beyond one's own current stage. In terms of the art of living, this means that these "teachers" are on their way themselves, intentionally or not, to develop their own art of living. It is also hardly surprising to encounter these people, as, according to Aristotle (n.d./1996), the striving for *eudaimonia* (serene happiness) is the utmost goal of human beings, and, therefore, exploring ways that let one live a good life (however one defines "good" for oneself) is a strong factor for human decision-making and personal development.

The crux is that so far little formal guidance is given, and it is also difficult for young people to determine if someone's course is leading in the right direction – for this person or for oneself. As Socrates pointed out about learning virtue (Chapter 2), one needs to have virtue to determine if someone else has virtue; therefore, if one has not reached virtue yet, one cannot determine if a teacher is a true and worthy teacher of virtue. It seems to be similar for teaching the art of living. As positive psychology research shows (Chapter 4), people often make false decisions which they think to be beneficial for their level of happiness and well-being as their social circumstances make them believe this would be the case. They lack the skills and knowledge to see through these misconceptions and find the right path.

Which conclusion can be drawn now for the requirements of a teacher's personality, knowledge and skill? In the first instance, one needs to distinguish between teachers who are charged with teaching about the art of living and deliberately support the development of an own art of living in their students and teachers who are focusing on other subjects but are still part of the educational school setting. Different requirements have to be met by an "art of living" teacher[8] than by, say, a maths teacher. Where a maths teacher needs to have a deeper understanding of mathematics and teaching methods that are best suited for learning maths, an art of living teacher needs to be knowledgeable in other areas.

Some of the requirements for an art of living teacher are, according to Schmid (2000a, 323–4), to at least be on the way of developing his or her own art of living; to be self-reflective; to care for his or her own self; to be knowledgeable (in the meaning of having *Bildung*); and to have a philosophical background. Schmid emphasises the importance of a foundational study in philosophy to enable art of living teachers to properly engage with questions about ethics and morality; to learn critical-hermeneutical thinking, as well as other methods to reflect upon terms, concepts and problems; and to develop their own conclusions. The technique of the Socratic dialogue is only one example of philosophic enquiry which could be well suited for a teacher to self-reflect and also help students to reflect upon their beliefs and opinions.

To acquire knowledge and *Bildung*, according to Schmid, an art of living teacher should have more than just a basic understanding of a number of areas (p. 324): (i) *anthropology*, for insights about human nature, conditions and possibilities; (ii) *cultural studies*, to be aware of different ways of living and the background of different cultures; and (iii) *religious studies* will provide differentiated knowledge in the area of belief and spirituality. He or she also should have insights in (iv) *psychology*, and here especially in *positive* and in *developmental* psychology. The former will allow for a better understanding of areas such as happiness, pleasures, well-being, flow, enjoyments and the role of meaning for enduring happiness, as discussed earlier; the latter will further one's understanding of feelings, emotions and ways of thinking of one's students. Further, (v) *sociology* provides insights and understanding of the special situation of individuals in current modern societies. Knowledge in the area of (vi) *media science* allows the teacher to explore the role of media today, including their know-how and the opportunities they can provide for the development of one's own art of living. One should also have an understanding of (vii) *law* to advise students about their possibilities and constrictions of shaping their own lives in the current society. Finally, (viii) *ecology* will provide knowledge about environmental complexities that can affect one's own life and about how one's choices in life can affect the environment one is living in.

In terms of personality, art of living teachers, more than most other teachers, need to be caring and interested in the positive personal development of their students. However, they also have to be able to step back and give their students the freedom and space to explore different concepts and ideas and to follow pathways other than the ones they prefer. Art of living teachers need to keep a balance between guidance and freedom; they need to be open to different and new ways, views and ideas. The mentioned skills of self-reflection and self-awareness will be most helpful to keep this balance.

Beyond art of living teachers themselves and in the larger setting of a school, as will be discussed later, every teacher – and every other member of staff for that matter – should have the opportunity and support to develop their own art of living. This will not only benefit them on a personal level, but also create a positive and stimulating environment for students to thrive in. Additionally, it will support a holistic and inter-connected learning experience for students, as proposed by Schmid and discussed later.

Pedagogical approaches for teaching the art of living

In terms of methods and didactics, only a few thoughts shall be given here, as more research is needed to support more specific recommendations.

Two requirements are important to support personal development in the way as intended by an education for life: *trust* and *open space*. To allow students to be open about their questions and uncertainties in areas that matter to them on a personal level, they need to be free of fears (as much as possible) and have trust that their questions will be taken seriously and not lead to negative responses from a teacher or their classmates. Therefore, a trusting relationship needs to be built between teachers and students and between students themselves. Being open, approachable, relaxed and friendly can be beneficial personality traits for art of living teachers to have. Empathy and sensibility can prove to be helpful for a teacher to gauge the atmosphere in a class and to support a friendly and trusting relationship between the students themselves.

Open space is understood here as the ability of students to have the freedom and a place to express their questions and inquire about topics of their interest in relation to their present point in life, rather than tightly following a predefined curriculum. Schmid (2000a, 322–3) proposes that for this freedom to evolve, the aim of this subject cannot mainly be about grades and assessments. On the contrary, progress in personal development should not be in any kind comparable or expressed in grades or comments in grade books or reports. Only personal, encouraging messages from the teacher might be possible. However, taking into account motivational theory, it might also be counter-productive should a student start to act in certain ways to provoke positive feedback from the teacher. Other feedback methods – anonymous group feedback,[9] for instance – might be more suitable.

Schmid proposes further to bring " 'authentic' representatives of various religions and worldviews, social groups and institutions" (p. 323) into the classroom to connect school and society in a more direct way. These authentic representatives can be far more illustrative than other methods of presentation. He also suggests making the subject of the art of living, the class situation and the school in total the subject of discussion and critical reflection. This can be a helpful exercise to provide feedback for teachers and schools, but also for the students to learn to critically interact with social norms and institutions instead of obediently accepting the status quo. With Dewey in mind, this can also be helpful for citizenship education in democratic societies.

General guidelines for methods to use in an art of living classroom setting would be to prefer interactive methods, such as discussions, rather than traditional teacher monologues; experience-based teaching, for instance, excursions or presenting examples, more than using textbooks or similar; and to utilise methods from experience and adventure/outdoor education, for example, in the tradition of Kurt Hahn (Röhrs and Tunstall-Behrens 1970). These experiences can be eye opening for students and teachers alike, as mentioned previously.

Various educational theories emphasise the importance of connecting areas of learning with existing student experiences, as well as creating learning experiences based on the student's current interests and state of personal development. One example can be found in Montessori pedagogy: according to Raapke (2006), Maria Montessori pointed out that pupils learn best *when they want to learn*. Schools can support the natural curiosity and interest of students by providing learning environments that allow for a range of learning areas through prepared self-learning units and by giving the students the freedom to follow their interests and to choose the task that is most appealing for them at this current moment. Certainly there are limits to this freedom, and Montessori pedagogy also provides certain structures around free learning sessions, but in general to orient teaching and learning environments on the students' interests and to provide real experiences (beyond textbook learning) seems to be a common theme in progressive education concepts. Other examples can be found in Pestalozzi's (1997) theory of *head, heart* and *hand*; Froebel's Gifts in his kindergarten pedagogy; and Dewey's (1963) book *Experience and Education*.

To provide a recent example based on inter-disciplinary research, I would like to point to an interview with Gerald Hüther (2013), a German neurobiology professor, about his new book *Jedes Kind ist hoch begabt: Die angeborenen Talente unserer Kinder und was wir aus ihnen machen* [Every child is high achieving: The inborn talents of our children and what we make of them]. Hüther argues for a different view on children and high achievement. He states that what is defined as high achieving is dependent on the present social setting and cultural norms. In Germany, and most Western societies, high achievement is defined in intellectual, cognitive and analytical areas. Abilities such as exceptional control over one's body, good climbing skills or the ability to make people's hearts sing are not valued in our current society, but they possibly might be in other cultural settings. Based on this view and the latest insights of neurobiology in terms of brain development and capability, Hüther developed a new school model that focuses on the development of the students' talents, or "potentials", as he calls them. He uses progressive teaching methods instead of traditional classroom settings, which he calls "learning-offices," where children can choose according to their interests what they want to learn and when. Similar to Montessori pedagogy,

Life pedagogy 151

learning is treated as a fun activity and based on intrinsic motivation instead of external rewards through grades and prizes.

In terms of happiness and well-being, Ian Morris' (2009) book *Teaching Happiness and Well-Being in Schools* offers a wide range of proposed methods of various aspects related to this topic. Morris focuses in this book on the outcome of positive psychology research and only provides a limited spectrum of topics for the art of living and an education for life. However, the methods he mentions can partly be applied to other topics and learning areas as well.

In the end, methods employed in art of living classes need to build on the experiences of students instead of being mainly outcome focused. They should support self-reflection and critical thinking, which can be expanded towards the school, teaching in general, the role of schooling in society and the way one interacts with other people in school and society, as mentioned earlier. The aim of art of living classes is to support the creation and shaping of the student's own lifestyle (in the meaning of the way of living) and to help him or her grow into that, which is life (Schmid 2000a, 323).

Teaching settings and school context

Areas of learning and ways of developing an art of living can be multifold. As the art of living is about shaping one's life in a way that might lead to a good life, experiences and life itself are the major teachers in this field. However, as argued earlier, some guidance can be helpful, and to give guidance, one needs a place and a setting. As education can happen everywhere and anytime (see Chapter 8), a whole range of settings can be envisioned for supporting the development of a student's art of living. A modern word for an old concept would be "coaching". Being a life coach has become a profession, and life coaching can happen in one's living room, a cafe, on the phone, in an office or in seminars and group sessions. However, the basic concept behind life coaching is mostly guided reflection on a face-to-face basis with one person (the coach, guru, master, teacher) providing the space and time for a student (young and old) to engage in questions of personal relevance while asking questions that support (self-)reflection and personal development. To be a suitable life coach for developing an own art of living, one needs to fulfil the same requirements as outlined previously in this chapter.

If not in a one-on-one setting, group settings appear suitable as well to develop the skills and gain the knowledge one needs to engage in an art of living. These sessions can be situated in distant retreats in beautiful spots somewhere in the wilderness, in special seminar rooms somewhere in a city or simply at schools or colleges. The nature of the setting is not too different from classroom settings, with the exception that out-of-school groups come together with explicit interest and intention, whereas a school setting is often compulsory. To make a school setting as supportive as possible, the following aspects could help.

As mentioned earlier, art of living classes need to take place in an environment of trust and open space. A friendly environment without pressure from assessments or similar is paramount. It also would be helpful to make these classes at

152 Life pedagogy

least partly voluntary with the possibility to opt out of single sessions if a student's mind is in a state that would prevent him or her from benefiting from the class or even to experience distress. As art of living classes often touch on private matters and topics of personal interest, the emotional and mental condition of students and the teacher is of importance and needs to be taken into account. As personal development cannot be forced but has to be actively pursued, any kind of compulsory attendance to these classes can only be counter-productive for the individual and most likely for the group as well.

Beyond the classroom, the whole school setting is important. As discussed in Section 7.3, for an education for life it is important that students see the connections between different subject matters taught at school. Not unconnected and distinct topics provide a broader understanding of the world, but to see the connections and inter-relations of different subjects with each other can help students connect the knowledge provided with their own life reality. This lends importance to these matters and increases the significance for students to engage with these topics. It not only helps them in their personal development and understanding of the world, but might provide additional motivation for topics that would otherwise be perceived as boring or insignificant.

Personal relevance is also one of the main factors for intrinsic motivation. As research in motivational theory has shown, intrinsic motivation (motivation of the individual to do something for its own sake) has much better long-term outcomes than extrinsic motivation (doing something to gain a reward or to avoid punishment) (Bénabou and Tirole 2003; Deci, Koestner, and Ryan 1999; Deci and Ryan 1985). Therefore, helping students through the interconnection of subject matters to make better sense of the relevance of individual subjects in the larger picture of life, and to help them see the relevance and meaning of these subjects for their own lives, will increase their intrinsic motivation and lead to better performance and learning outcomes. Further, as has been discussed in Section 6.3, content that is considered relevant for one's own self-concept is more readily accessible and more permanently remembered than other content. Combining these insights with Schmid's theory of *fundamental choices* (Section 5.2), which become part of one's self-concept, would imply that learned knowledge that is relevant for any of one's fundamental choices should be memorised in this more accessible and permanent way.

If the organisation of schooling and teaching in this way is done correctly, the highly contested (for a number of reasons) practice of grading students should be abandoned as well. Not only in the context of art of living classes, but also in the wider school context in general. As research has shown, grades are not only a non-suitable instrument of self-assessment, but also degrade interest in a topic, reduce intrinsic motivation, decrease creativity, induce fear of failure and potentially lead to lower performance (Bénabou and Tirole 2003; Butler and Mordecai 1986; Lipnevich and Smith 2008). As Lipnevich and Smith (2008) found out, relevant feedback for students to maintain intrinsic motivation and show their best performance is descriptive and "specific to individual work" (p. 31). Test groups who received grades or praise had significant lower outcomes in the final test which was designed to indicate long-term interest and motivation. However, their research findings also indicate that when grades are unavoidable, individual praise from the teacher can counter most, but not all, of the negative impact of grades on students' intrinsic motivation.

Consequently, if school is understood to prepare for life in a world where lifelong learning is unavoidable, specific descriptive feedback should be used instead of praise or grades. For the second function of grades – to provide a measure of comparability between individuals for employment reasons – a different way should be found: for example, through individual job assessments, or assessment centres, as already proposed by Illich (1972).

In terms of developing an art of living, as mentioned earlier, a school environment that is interfused with questions of life and the development of people's art of living will provide much more support for an education for life than just addressing these questions for an hour or two per week. Schools could offer personal development seminars and sessions for teachers and staff, add relevant books to their libraries and encourage an atmosphere of open exchange and support. The design of school buildings, the courtyard and school grounds could include aesthetic elements, decorations and pieces of art, such as sculptures or paintings. These could be done by local artists or by students themselves, for example, in art and sculpture classes. A recent project in Germany, "Kultur macht Schule" [culture meets schools], showed that cultural teaching methods, that is, active participation in art, music, theatre, circus activity and similar, not only lead to higher levels of identification with one's school, but also to better participation and grades in classic subjects such as maths, sciences and languages.[10] Everything that helps to grow a student's identification with his or her school can be helpful to increase an open and fearless environment. One example of a successful implementation of a mostly fearless school environment is Summerhill, founded by A. S. Neill (Cassebaum 2003; Neill 1992; Vaughan 2006).

In terms of the curriculum, making space for questions of life and lifelong learning is as important as keeping in mind providing connections between subjects. Topics for subjects in particular years should be matched to allow for overreaching themes and easier inter-relations. One example of a curriculum that allows for certain levels of inter-connectedness between subjects is *The New Zealand Curriculum* (Ministry of Education 2007), as it caters for encompassing term themes that can be incorporated into most or all subjects.

Implications for teacher education

This chapter, so far, has been intended to be a first step for an education for life concept, which will have to be developed in subsequent work. However, the aspects considered in this and the two previous chapters might provide a starting point for teachers, principals and schools to review their aims, values and teaching concepts. An education for life concept, as proposed here, is not limited to the aspects of the art of living and how to live a good life, but aims to be a holistic educational concept that takes into account all aspects of human life and development. Not only art of living teachers, but every teacher, can and should reflect critically on one's own methods, aims and values in terms of supporting young people to learn what is necessary to live a good and successful life by developing their own art of living.

Beyond schools, this also applies to universities and especially teacher education programmes. Korthagen (2010) summarises the research about teacher education effectiveness as disturbingly lacking in terms of actual teacher behaviour in classrooms. His main point is that teaching is a profession that has aspects of a craft, and current cognitive- and theory-based content in teacher education seems to be rather ineffective at having an actual impact on teacher behaviour and practice.

Korthagen proposes a three-level model of teacher education, which starts with the "gestalt" level, then the "schemata" level and finally the "theory" level. His main claim is that teachers first of all develop "gestalts", which are learned acting patterns based on certain situations and the experience and history of the teacher in question. These gestalts seem to be related to what Pierre Bourdieu calls "habitus" or "habita" (plural). These gestalts or habita are mostly responsible for a teacher's action and reaction in a classroom setting. To influence a habitus, the teacher needs to reflect upon one's action and build a cognitive schema of this action: why he or she acts in this why, what is the purpose, how does it fit into the wider aim of the subject and proposed learning outcome. According to Korthagen, only after building this cognitive schema is it possible to challenge it with theory and concepts and alter one's initial set of responses accordingly. In a final step of level reduction "schematized or even theoretical knowledge can become self-evident, and the schema or theory can then be used in a less conscious way" (2010, 103), which would make it an altered gestalt or habitus.

Therefore, Korthagen calls for a change in teacher education towards a more experience-based way of teaching to allow gestalts to be identified, schematised and finally challenged with theory. This call for a more experience-based teacher education practice is interestingly quite similar to some of the previously proposed teaching methods in an education for life context.

However, despite differences in national teacher education programmes, it is likely that most programmes do not cater to the needs required by art of living teachers today. As outlined earlier in this section, art of living teachers require a broad knowledge that draws not only on education and philosophy, but is supplemented with a wider knowledge base in subjects such as anthropology, cultural studies, religions, psychology, sociology, media science, law and ecology. So far, no recognised qualification, either in education, philosophy, sociology or any other subject, requires one to cover aspects of all these areas. However, a study of education or philosophy as a main subject would most likely be a good starting point, as both areas touch on many, if not all, aspects required for art of living classes. In particular, a combination of undergraduate and postgraduate degrees in education would ideally require basic knowledge in most of these areas. A special programme could then intensify this knowledge base and prepare an educationist to become an art of living teacher.

However, more research is needed to make sound and evidence-based propositions for proper teaching methods for both university and school teaching, as well as for proper art of living teacher education programmes.

Summary

Based on the considerations of the earlier chapters, this chapter has focused on the development of practical implications of the art of living on education. Some fundamental aspects of educational content and practice have been explored, with a particular focus on teaching the art of living in school environments. Although this focus is a significant limitation – as discussed earlier, schooling is only a part of education, and an education for life reaches beyond schooling and includes the lifelong development of human beings – it concludes the aims set out for this book by providing a foundation for the development of an education for life concept.

It has been discussed in this chapter that various skills and forms of knowledge are important for the development of an own art of living and a potential good and beautiful life. Among these are the development of a student's hermeneutical faculties, his or her level of *Bildung*, the ability for self-reflection and the support of wisdom through *Bildung* and spirituality in education. Further, it has been argued that an art of living teacher needs to have breadth of knowledge and understanding and that he or she needs to strive for the development of his or her own art of living, including the development of all aspects that are involved, to be able to help students with their own personal growth. Examples have been given how teaching settings (inside and outside of schools) can support the development of a student's and a teacher's art of living and a good life.

Notes

1. www.worldpeacegame.org.
2. See Chapter 5 for more details. A definition of the use of critical thinking in this context can be found in Section 7.3.
3. See Section 5.5 for a definition of the use of "hermeneutical skills".
4. See www.oecd.org/pisa/.
5. See *Kurt Hahn* by Röhrs and Tunstall-Behrens (1970) for a philosophical introduction and www.outwardbound.org/ or www.salem-net.de/ (Salem schools) as examples of implementing outdoor and experience education in schools and other educational settings.
6. Compare the tradition of the German *Bildungsroman* or certain kinds of poetry and novellas, as well as Jesus' way of teaching as described in the Christian Bible.
7. Compare Csikszentmihalyi (2008) and Section 4.5 in terms of connections between control over consciousness, the experience of enjoyments and one's personal well-being.
8. 'Art of living' teacher might be slightly misleading, as it has been established that an art of living cannot be taught directly, but only supported in development. However, for practical reasons this term will be used here.
9. Anonymous group feedback is a method where all participants stick a plain piece of paper on their back and get a coloured felt pen in their hand. Then all

participants will walk around and write positive messages on the pieces of paper of people they wish to tell something positive. It is important to emphasise that only positive and encouraging feedback is permitted. As this feedback is anonymous, students are less likely to be embarrassed and more open to express heartfelt praise without fear. This exercise, when repeated every so often, can also teach students to be more open with praise and to express emotions and support, as they will learn how good positive feedback feels and that it also can feel good to give positive feedback.
10 See Rittelmeyer (2012), Collard (2011), Schumacher (2006) and Hetland and Winner (2001) for summaries of research in the field of arts education and its impact on general academic achievement.

10 Conclusion

In the course of this book, various concepts and approaches to an art of living and a good life have been discussed and a description of these terms, based on Schmid's work, has been given: "the art of living is the wholeheartedness of the attempt, out of [. . . the responsibility for one's own life] to acquire one's life in good time and maybe even make a 'beautiful life' out of it" (2000b, 7). Schmid's notion of a beautiful life has been shown to emphasise the individual-based approach to living a good life, as well as to underline the artful character of shaping one's own life into what one could perceive as a beautiful and good one. However, it has also been pointed out that the development of an individual art of living is always dependent on and influenced by the social context and society one is living in.

As an extension, or counterpart, to philosophical considerations about the art of living, a review of (positive) psychology research has clarified various terms and concepts in the field of emotions, including the notions of happiness, pleasures, enjoyments, flow and subjective well-being. Parallels between philosophical theories and quantitative research findings have been revealed, as well as points of contrast. Aristotle's (n.d./1996; n.d./2002) idea of *eudaimonia*, for example, has proven to be distinct from Seligman's (2010) and Csikszentmihalyi's (2008) theory of gratifications and enjoyments. However, the concept of enduring happiness, which can be influenced positively through enjoyments, could be closely linked with *eudaimonia*, and is, if not necessarily the utmost goal of human beings, at least a strong motivational factor for most people. In further research, a more detailed comparison of Feldman's notion of attitudinal pleasures, Csikszentmihalyi's notion of enjoyments, the concept of enduring happiness and Aristotle's idea of *eudaimonia* could clarify some of the difficulties in comparing these concepts, as pointed out in this study, and might provide a better understanding of parallels and differences between these concepts.

Apart from enjoyments created by flow experiences, harmony and meaning in life have been discussed as relevant for living a good life. To have meaning and to create meaning for one's own life is significantly important in positive psychology and in Schmid's concept *Lebenskunst* alike. Additionally, Csikszentmihalyi's understanding of control over consciousness holds many parallels to Foucault's concept of the care of the self and Schmid's concept of the labour of care: in each case, one has to take responsibility for one's own life and one's own self and actively shape one's mind and one's life.

Further, approaching the art of living and the good life from an educational perspective, a discussion of possible aims in education, drawing on Dewey (2001) and Peters (1973), concluded that a possible end of education could be to enable pupils to develop their own art of living, to help them to live the best life possible, according to their individual judgement and under the circumstances they are living in. This end of education has then been split into four more practical aims that together can lead to the development of an own art of living: (i) to grow and develop students' capabilities; (ii) to help them make sense of the world and the culture they are living in; (iii) to encourage them to reflect upon their own selves, their beliefs and values; and (iv) to support them to flourish in a way that enables them to actively shape their own lives into potentially good and beautiful ones.

To accomplish these aims in education, an evaluation of Schmid's concept showed the importance of essential skills and knowledge to develop an individual art of living, such as being self-receptive, self-reflective and self-productive; the faculty of hermeneutics to identify interrelations in the world; *Bildung*, in the meaning of knowledge, self-cultivation and practical wisdom; and a prudent care of the self. Although some inter-cultural aspects have been taken into account, more needs to be done to review Schmid's theory of the art of living in relation to non–Western European cultural and social settings. Also, on a fundamental level, questions that need to be explored further in this context are: How much *Bildung* is necessary to live a good and beautiful life? Do necessary skills for developing an art of living differ between societies? How does Schmid's focus on an active and artful shaping process of one's own life relate to lives that are considered as good or beautiful ones by the individuals living them but seem to come to pass "naturally," that is, in a less active and conscious way? Is this natural coming to pass of beautiful lives possible at all, or should they be considered virtuosic lives, lived by truly artistic art of living practitioners? I have touched on aspects that can lead to answers to these questions, but more needs to be done in this direction beyond the scope of this book.

A further topic discussed in this context has been choice and freedom in relation to education. It has been shown that the increase of opportunities and necessary choices today has de-liberating consequences and reduces the experienced amount of freedom for individuals. An education for life needs to take these changes into account: it needs to make students aware of these difficulties; provide knowledge about the different types of choices, such as particular choices and fundamental choices; and it needs to enable students to make prudent choices and to know when to choose and when to rely on habits to reduce the need for continuously having to make conscious decisions.

To prepare for a discussion about the role of schooling in education and for society, a review of the relation between education and schooling has been presented on the basis of the German understanding of *Pädagogik* [pedagogy/education], which is understood as a combination of *Erziehung* [upbringing], *Bildung* [self-cultivation] and *Entfaltung* [flourishing]. Various implications of these aspects of education for schooling have been discussed, such as to provide students with a general humanistic education, to prepare them for lifelong learning and to enable them to continuously shape their own self to acquire *Bildung*, which is closely related to Schmid's concept of the art of living. Further, education (not schooling) has been presented as potentially occurring everywhere and anytime. In this understanding, education reaches far beyond schooling; schooling is only a part of education and not necessarily the most important one for living a good and beautiful life. However, as mentioned previously, I have limited the discussion here mainly to considerations of implications for schooling. Other relevant areas, such as early childhood or adult education, and their relation to an education for life need to be explored further in subsequent theoretical and practical research.

Finally, first steps have been taken to develop an education for life concept that is based on Schmid's concept of the art of living and refocuses on the personal human development of students to live a good and beautiful life. Various aspects of pedagogical content and practice have been reviewed in light of the earlier discussions, including areas such as hermeneutics; *Bildung*; wisdom; spirituality; and mind-sets, beliefs and attachments. Further, requirements for teaching the art of living have been discussed, including personal and professional characteristics of art of living teachers, teaching methods, teaching settings, the wider school context and teacher education for art of living teachers in particular and teachers in general.

The main argument in this book is that the personal development of human beings and their ability to live a good and beautiful life as described in Schmid's art of living concept should be the key focus of educational theory and practice. Following Dewey, the only possible overall vision for educational intervention should be the best possible realisation of humanity. According to the German *Bildung* idealists, this can only be achieved through the perfection of each individual through *Bildung*. Taking into account Lauxmann's argument, wisdom is as important as *Bildung* for the good of human beings and societies alike. According to Dewey, educated and autonomous citizens are crucial for a democratic society, and as Lauxmann states, wisdom brings forth the good for the person who is wise and the people around him or her. Hence, *Bildung* and wisdom are important for individuals to develop their own art of living and to become active democratic citizens.

It has been argued that wisdom cannot be taught directly, but it can be supported through the development of a student's ability for practical wisdom and the development of his or her spirituality, for example, through meditative practice and (self-)awareness. To further one's *Bildung*, self-reflection and the ability for lifelong learning and self-*bildung* are important and need to be supported in formal and informal educational settings.

However, educational institutions, such as kindergartens, schools and universities, are mainly shaped by the dominant discourses of the society they are situated in. Therefore, one ought to ask the question: In which society do we want to live? Are current values of money, power and influence more important than happiness, well-being and personal development? (That the earlier three do not lead to the latter ones has been discussed, for example, in Chapter 6.) To come back to Liebau's question as stated in Chapter 1: it is not education that should cater for the reproduction of society as it currently is, but society should provide an education that allows human beings to develop their own art of living and to live the best life possible under the circumstances they are living in. This could promote the development and improvement of individuals and society alike, as envisioned by Dewey, Lauxmann, German *Bildungs* Idealists and many others. After all, societies should care as much for the good of their people as the people should care for a thriving society. One could ask what value a society has that does not have the happiness and good life of its people at heart. The mantra of economic growth has been a means to a greater end of a flourishing society and a better life for its people. However, we ought not to forget what the means and what the ends are. An increase in wealth in many current societies does not increase their people's happiness and satisfaction with life, as has been argued earlier.

In this book, I explored and discussed a range of philosophical, psychological and educational theories to develop a foundation on which an educational theory based on the art of living can be built. Such an "education for life" theory might not necessarily be different in vision from other educational theories, but it can provide a more holistic and universal approach to living a good life for each individual, as well as an approach to "the best possible realization of humanity as humanity" (Dewey 2001, 100).

Bibliography

Aristotle. n.d./1996. *The Nicomachean Ethics*. Edited by T. Griffith. London, England: Wordsworth Editions Limited.
———. n.d./2002. *Nicomachean Ethics*. Edited by J. Sachs. Newburyport, MA: Focus Publishing.
Aylesworth, G. 2005. "Postmodernism." In *The Stanford Encyclopedia of Philosophy*, edited by E. N. Zalta. Stanford, CA: Stanford University. Retrieved from https://plato.stanford.edu/entries/postmodernism/
Bauman, Z. 2000. *Liquid Modernity*. Malden, MA: Blackwell Publishers.
Beck, A. T. 1999. *Prisoners of Hate*. New York, NY: HarperCollins.
Bénabou, R., and J. Tirole. 2003. "Intrinsic and Extrinsic Motivation." *The Review of Economic Studies* 70 (3): 289–520.
Berlant, L. 2011. *Cruel Optimism*. Durham, NC: Duke University Press.
Bieri, P. 2006. *Das Handwerk der Freiheit: Über die Entdeckung des eigenen Willens*. Frankfurt, Germany: Fischer Verlag.
Biesta, G. J. J. 2006. *Beyond Learning: Democratic Education for a Human Future*. Boulder, CO: Paradigm Publishers.
Bobzien, S. 2006. "Moral Responsibility and Moral Development in Epicurus' Philosophy." In *The Virtuous Life in Greek Ethics*, edited by B. Reis, 206–29. Cambridge, England: Cambridge University Press.
Boniwell, I. 2008. *Positive Psychology in a Nutshell*. London, England: PWBC.
Bryant, F. B. 2003. "Savoring Beliefs Inventory (SBI): A Scale for Measuring Beliefs About Savouring." *Journal of Mental Health* 12 (2): 175–96.
Buckman, P., ed. 1973. *Education Without Schools*. London, England: Souvenir Press.
Burke, B. 2000. "Post-Modernism and Post-Modernity." In *The Encyclopaedia of Informal Education*, edited by M. K. Smith. www.infed.org/biblio/b-postmd.htm.
Butler, R., and N. Mordecai. 1986. "Effects of No Feedback, Task-Related Comments, and Grades on Intrinsic Motivation and Performance." *Journal of Educational Psychology* 78 (3): 210–16.
Cassebaum, A. 2003. "Revisiting Summerhill." *The Phi Delta Kappan* 84 (8): 575–8.
Codd, J. A. 1993. "Neo-Liberal Education Policy and the Ideology of Choice." *Educational Philosophy and Theory* 25: 31–48.
Collard, P. 2011. "Whole School Change: Die Wirkung von Creative Partnerships." In *Lebenskunst Lernen in Der Schule: Mehr Chancen Durch Kulturelle Schulentwicklung*, edited by T. Braun, 219–27. München, Germany: Kopaed-Verlag.
Cosmides, L., and J. Tooby. 2000. "Evolutionary Psychology and the Emotions." In *Handbook of Emotions*, edited by M. Lewis and J. M. Haviland-Jones, 91–115, 2nd ed. New York, NY: Guilford.

Csikszentmihalyi, M. 2008. *Flow: The Psychology of Optimal Experience*, Modern classics ed. New York, NY: Harper Perennial.

Daniel, M.-F., and E. Auriac. 2011. "Philosophy, Critical Thinking and Philosophy for Children." *Educational Philosophy and Theory* 43 (5): 415–35.

Danner, D., D. Snowdon, and W. Friesen. 2001. "Positive Emotions in Early Life and Longevity: Findings From the Nun Study." *Journal of Personality and Social Psychology* 80: 804–13.

Deci, E., R. Koestner, and R. Ryan. 1999. "A Meta-Analytic Review of Experiments Examining the Effects of Extrinsic Rewards on Intrinsic Motivation." *Psychological Bulletin* 125 (6): 627–68.

Deci, E., and R. Ryan. 1985. *Intrinsic Motivation and Self-Determination in Human Behavior*. New York, NY: Plenum Press.Dennett, D. C. 2003. *Freedom Evolves*. New York, NY: Viking Press.

Dewey, J. 1963. *Experience and Education*. New York, NY: Collier.

———. 2001. *Democracy and Education*. Edited by Jim Manis. Electronic Classics Series. Hazleton, PA: The Pennsylvania State University.

Easton, M. 2006. "The Politics of Happiness." *BBC News* 22 May. http://news.bbc.co.uk/2/hi/programmes/happiness_formula/4809828.stm

Education Scotland. n.d./2013. *Curriculum for Excellence*. www.educationscotland.gov.uk/Images/all_experiences_outcomes_tcm4-539562.pdf.

Ellsworth, E. A. 1997. *Teaching Positions*. New York, NY: Teachers College Press.

———. 2005. *Places of Learning*. New York, NY: Routledge.

Emmons, R. A., and M. E. McCullough. 2003. "Counting Blessings Versus Burdens: An Experimental Investigation of Gratitude and Subjective Well-Being in Daily Life." *Journal of Personality and Social Psychology* 84 (2): 377–89.

Evans, J. 2008. "Teaching Happiness: The Classes in Wellbeing That Are Helping Our Children." *Times Online* 18 Feb. www.thetimes.co.uk/tto/education/article1799879.ece.

Feldman, F. 2004. *Pleasure and the Good Life: Concerning the Nature, Varieties and Plausibility of Hedonism*. New York, NY: Clarendon.

Foucault, M. 1984. *The Care of the Self*. Vol. 3. The History of Sexuality. London, England: Penguin Books.

Gadamer, H.-G. 1975. *Truth and Method*. New York, NY: The Seabury Press.

———. 1978. *Die Idee Des Guten Zwischen Plato Und Aristoteles*. Heidelberg, Germany: Carl Winter Universitätsverlag.

Gane, N. 2001. "Zygmunt Bauman: Liquid Modernity and Beyond." *Acta Sociologica* 44 (3): 267–75.

Gardner, H. 2006. *Five Minds for the Future*. Boston, MA: Harvard Business School Press.

Grayling, A. C. 2006. *The Form of Things: Essays on Life, Ideas and Liberty in the Twenty-First Century*. London, England: Weidenfeld & Nicolson.

Hall, C. S., and G. Lindzey. 1957. "Rogers' Self Theory." In Calvin S. Hall, Gardner Lindzey, John B. Campbell (eds.), *Theories of Personality*, 467–502. New York, NY: John Wiley & Sons.

Heatherton, T. F., A. C. Krendl, C. N. Macrae, and W. M. Kelley. 2007. "A Social Brain Sciences Approach to Understanding Self." In *The Self*, edited by C. Sedikides and S. J. Spencer, 4–16. New York, NY: Psychology Press.

Helene Lange Schule Wiesbaden. 2012. *Schulprogramm Helene-Lange-Schule Wiesbaden*. http://helene-lange-schule.templ2.evision.net/fileadmin/downloads/Schulprogramm 2012 Arial Homepagefassung.pdf.

Hetland, L., and E. Winner. 2001. "The Arts and Academic Achievement: What the Evidence Shows." *Arts Education Policy Review* 102 (5): 3–6.
Hüther, G. 2013. "Jedes Kind Ist Hoch Begabt." *Bildung + Innovation.*
Illich, I. D. 1972. *Deschooling Society.* London, England: Calder & Boyars.
Isen, A. 2000. "Positive Affect and Decision Making." In *Handbook of Emotions*, edited by M. Lewis and J. M. Haviland-Jones, 417–35, 2nd ed. New York, NY: Guilford Press.
Kant, I. 1997. *Groundwork of the Metaphysics of Morals.* Edited by Mary Gregor. New York, NY: Cambridge University Press.
———. n.d./1900. *Kant on Education.* Edited by Annette Churton (Trans.). Boston, MA: D. C. Heather & Co.
Kierkegaard, S. 2000. *The Essential Kierkegaard.* Edited by H. V. Hong and E. H. Hong. Princeton, NJ: Princeton University Press.
Korthagen, F. A. J. 2010. "Situated Learning Theory and the Pedagogy of Teacher Education: Towards an Integrative View of Teacher Behavior and Teacher Learning." *Teaching and Teacher Education*, 26 (1): 98–106.
Kraut, R. 2010. "Aristotle's Ethics." In *The Stanford Encyclopedia of Philosophy*, edited by Edward N. Zalta. http://plato.stanford.edu/archives/sum2010/entries/aristotle-ethics/.
Laozi. n.d./1993. *Tao Te Ching.* Edited by B. Watson, S. Addiss, and S. Lombardo. Indianapolis, IN: Hackett Publisher.
Larner, W. 2000. "Policy, Ideology, Governmentality." *Studies in Political Economy* 63: 5–25.
Lau, N. 2009. "Cultivation of Mindfulness: Promoting Holistic Learning and Wellbeing in Education." In *International Handbook of Education for Spirituality*, Care and Wellbeing, edited by M. de Souza, L.J. Francis, J. O'Higgins-Norman, and D.G. Scott, London, England: Springer Science+Business Media B.V.
Lauxmann, F. 2004. *Die Philosophie Der Weisheit: Die Andere Art Zu Denken.* München, Germany: dtv.
Liebau, E. 1999. *Erfahrung und Verantwortung: Werteerziehung als Pädagogik der Teilhabe.* Weinheim; München, Germany: JuventaVerlag.
Lin, Y. 1976. *The Importance of Living.* New York, NY: Buccaneer Books.
Lipnevich, A. A., and J. K. Smith. 2008. "Response to Assessment Feedback: The Effects of Grades, Praise, and Source of Information." Princeton, NJ: Educational Testing Service.
Lister, I. 1973. "Getting There from Here." In *Education Without Schools*, edited by P. Buckman, 20–8. London, England: Souvenir Press.
Loewenstein, G. 2007. "Defining Affect." *Social Science Information* 46 (3): 405–10.
Long, A. A. 2006. *From Epicurus to Epictetus – Studies in Hellenistic and Roman Philosophy.* New York, NY: Oxford University Press.
Luck, S. J., and S. P. Vecera. 2002. "Attention." In *Stevens's Handbook of Experimental Psychology*, edited by S. Yantis and H. Pashler, 1: Sensation and perception, 235–86. New York, NY: John Wiley & Sons.
McConnell, A. R., and L. M. Strain. 2007. "Content and Structure of the Self-Concept." In *The Self*, edited by C. Sedikides and S. J. Spencer. New York, NY: Psychology Press.
Mackendrick, P. 1952. "Education for the Art of Living." *The Journal of Higher Education* 23 (8). Ohio State University Press: 423–56. www.jstor.org/stable/1977095.
McNamee, S. J., and R. K. Miller. 2004. "The Meritocracy Myth." *Sociation Today* 2 (1).
Marois, R., and J. Ivanoff. 2005. "Capacity Limits of Information Processing in the Brain." *Trends in Cognitive Sciences* 9 (6): 296–305.

Maurois, A., and G. Robert. 1940. *The Art of Living*. London, England: English Universities Press.
Maxwell, N. 2007. *From Knowledge to Wisdom: A Revolution in the Aims and Methods of Science*, 2nd ed. London: Pentire Press.
———. 2012. "Arguing for Wisdom in the University: An Intellectual Autobiography." *Philosophia* 40: 663–704.
Mello, A. de. 1992. *Awareness – The Perils and Opportunities of Reality*. Edited by J. Francis Stroud. New York, NY: Doubleday.
Merton, R. K. 1957. *Social Theory and Social Structure*. Glencoe, IL: The Free Press.
Ministry of Education. 2007. *The New Zealand Curriculum*. Wellington, New Zealand: Learning Media.
Morris, I. 2009. *Teaching Happiness and Well-Being in Schools*. London, England: Continuum International.
Müller-Commichau, W. 2007. *Lebenskunst Lernen*. Baltmannsweiler, Germany: Schneider.
Nakagawa, Y. 2009. "Awareness and Compassion for the Education of Enlightenment." In *International Handbook of Education for Spirituality, Care and Wellbeing*, edited by M. edited by M. de Souza, L.J. Francis, J. O'Higgins-Norman, and D.G. Scott, London, England: Springer Science+Business Media B.V.
Nehamas, A. 1998. *The Art of Living: Socratic Reflections from Plato to Foucault*. Berkeley, CA: University of California Press.
Neill, A. S. 1992. *The New Summerhill*. Edited by A. Lamb. London, England: Penguin Books.
Noddings, N. 2005. *Happiness and Education*. Cambridge, UK: Cambridge University Press.
Nussbaum, M. C. 2000. *Women and Human Development: The Capabilities Approach*. Cambridge, UK: Cambridge University Press.
———. 2001. *The Fragility of Goodness: Luck and Ethics in Greek Tragedy and Philosophy*. New York, NY: Cambridge University Press.
Nussbaum, M. C., and A. K. Sen. 1993. *The Quality of Life*. Oxford, UK: Oxford University Press.
Ozolins, J. T. 2011. "Reclaiming Paedeia in an Age of Crises: Education and the Necessity of Wisdom." In *PESA Conference Proceedings, 1–4 Dec*. Auckland, New Zealand.
Perry, J. 2002. *Identity, Personal Identity, and the Self*. Indianapolis, IN: Hackett Publishing Company.
Pestalozzi, J. H. 1997. *Pestalozzi über Seine Anstalt in Stans*. Weinheim; Basel, Germany: Belz Verlag.
Peters, M. A., and J. D. Marshall. 1996. *Individualism and Community: Education and Social Policy in the Postmodern Condition*. London, England: Falmer Press.
Peters, R. S. 1973. *Authority, Responsibility and Education*. New York, NY: Paul S. Eriksson.
Plato. n.d./2003. *The Last Days of Socrates*. Edited by Harold Tarrant. London, England: Penguin Books.
Plutchik, R. 2002. *Emotions and Life*. Washington, DC: American Psychological Association.
Raapke, H.-D. 2006. *Montessori Heute: Eine Moderne Pädagogik Für Familie, Kindergarten Und Schule*. Hamburg, Germany: Rowohlt Taschenbuch Verlag.
Ramberg, B., and K. Gjesdal. 2011. "Hermeneutics." In *The Stanford Encyclopedia of Philosophy*, Summer 2009 ed., edited by Edward N. Zalta. Stanford, CA: Stanford University.

Rathunde, K. 1988. "Optimal Experience and the Family Context." In *Optimal Experience: Psychological Studies of Flow in Consciousness*, edited by M. Csikszentmihalyi and I. S. Csikszentmihalyi, 342–63. New York, NY: Cambridge University Press.

Redelheimer, D., and S. Singh. 2001. "Social Status and Life Expectancy in an Advantaged Population: A Study of Academy Awardwinning Actors." *Annals of Internal Medicine* 134 (10): 1001–3.

Rittelmeyer, C. 2012. *Warum Und Wozu ästhetische Bildung?* Oberhausen, Germany: Athena-Verlag.

Rizvi, F. 2012. "Keynote: Mobilities Paradigm and Its Challenges for Comparative Education." In *40th Annual Conference of Anzcies, 28 Nov 2012*. Christchurch, New Zealand: The Australian; New Zealand Comparative; International Education Society.

Roberts, P. 2004. "Neo-Liberalism, Knowledge and Inclusiveness." *Policy Futures in Education* 2 (2): 350–64.

———. 2012. "Keynote: A Golden Age? Dostoevsky, Daoism and Education." In *Philosophy of Education Society of Australasia Conference, 7–10 Dec 2012*. National Chiayi University, Taiwan.

———. 2013. "Happiness, Despair and Education." *Studies in Philosophy and Education* 32 (5), 463–75.

Roberts, P., and J. Codd. 2010. "Neoliberal Tertiary Education Policy." In *Another Decade of New Zealand Education Policy: Where to Now?* edited by M. Thrupp and R. Irwin, 99–110. Hamilton, New Zealand: Wilf Malcolm Institute of Educational Research.

Roberts, P., and M. A. Peters. 2008. *Neoliberalism, Higher Education and Research*. Rotterdam, The Netherlands: Sense Publishers.

Roger, D. 1998. "Stress, Health and Personality: A New Perspective." *Complementary Therapies in Nursing and Midwifery* 4 (2): 50–3. doi:10.1016/S1353-6117 (98)80026-7.

Röhrs, H., and H. Tunstall-Behrens, eds. 1970. *Kurt Hahn*. London, England: Routledge & Kegan Paul.

Roth, G. 2001. *Fühlen, Denken, Handeln: Wie das Gehirn unser Verhalten steuert*. Frankfurt, Germany: Suhrkamp.

Rousseau, J.-J. n.d./2004. *Emile*. Project Gutenberg.

Rutter, M. 1980. "The Long-Term Effects of Early Experience." *Developmental Medicine & Child Neurology* 22: 800–15.

Scherer, K. R. 2005. "What Are Emotions? And How Can They Be Measured?" *Social Science Information* 44 (4): 695–729.

Schmid, W. 2000a. *Philosophie der Lebenskunst: Eine Grundlegung*. Frankfurt, Germany: Suhrkamp.

———. 2000b. *Schönes Leben? Eine Einführung in die Lebenskunst*. Frankfurt, Germany: Suhrkamp.

Schumacher, Ralph, ed. 2006. *Macht Mozart schlau? Die Förderung kognitiver Kompetenzen durch Musik*. Berlin, Germany: Bundesministerium für Bildung und Forschung.

Schwartz, B. 2004. *The Paradox of Choice: Why More Is Less*. New York, NY: ECCO.

Schwartz, B., and K. Sharpe. 2010. *Practical Wisdom – The Right Way to Do the Right Thing*. New York, NY: Penguin Books.

Seligman, M. E. P. 2010. *Authentic Happiness: Using the New Positive Psychology to Realise Your Potential for Lasting Fulfillment*. London, England: Nicholas Brealey Publishing.

———. 2011. *Flourish: A Visionary New Understanding of Happiness and Well-Being*. New York, NY: Free Press.

Snook, I., and J. O'Neill. 2010. "Social Class and Educational Achievement: Beyond Ideology." *New Zealand Journal of Educational Studies* 45 (2): 3–18.

Solomon, R. C., and L. D. Stone. 2002. "On 'Positive' and 'Negative' Emotions." *Journal for the Theory of Social Behaviour* 32 (4): 417–35.

Sorabji, R. 2006. *Self. Ancient and Modern Insights About Individuality, Life, and Death*. Oxford, England: Oxford University Press.

Sorokin, P. 1962. *Social and Cultural Dynamics*. New York, NY: Bedminster.

Soutter, A. K., A. Gilmore, and B. O'Steen. 2011. "How Do High School Youths' Education Experiences Relate to Well-Being? Towards a Trans-Disciplinary Conceptualization." *Journal of Happiness Studies* 12 (4): 591–631.

Souza, M. de. 2009. "Promoting Wholeness and Wellbeing in Education: Exploring Aspects of the Spiritual Dimension." In *International Handbook of Education for Spirituality, Care and Wellbeing*, edited by M. de Souza, L.J. Francis, J. O'Higgins-Norman, and D.G. Scott. London, England: Springer Science+Business Media B.V.

Strawson, Galen, ed. 2005. *The Self?* Oxford, England: Blackwell Publishing.

Suissa, J. 2008. "Lessons From a New Science? On Teaching Happiness in Schools." *Journal of Philosophy of Education* 42 (3–4): 575–90.

Suntum, U. van, and A. Prinz, and N. Uhde. 2010. "Lebenszufriedenheit Und Wohlbefinden in Deutschland: Studie Zur Konstruktion Eines Lebenszufriedenheitsindikators." 259. DIW Berlin, The German Socio-Economic Panel (SOEP). http://ideas.repec.org/p/diw/diwsop/diw_sp259.html

Tarrant, H. 2003. "Introduction to Phaedo." In *Plato – The Last Days of Socrates*, 99–115. London, England: Penguin Books.

Taylor, C. 1989. *Sources of the Self: The Making of the Modern Identity*. Cambridge, MA: Harvard University Press.

Tucker, M. E. 2003. *Confucian Spirituality*. Edited by T. Weiming and M. E. Tucker. New York, NY: The Crossroad Publishing Company.

UK Qualifications and Curriculum Development Authority. 2012. *The Aims of the Curriculum*.

United Nations. 1948. *The Universal Declaration of Human Rights* New York, NY.

Vaughan, M., ed. 2006. *Summerhill and A. S. Neill*. New York, NY: Open University Press.

Weinsheimer, J. 1985. *Gadamer's Hermeneutics*. New York, NY: Vail-Ballou Press.

Werfhorst, H. G. van de, and R. Andersen. 2005. "Social Background, Credential Inflation and Educational Strategies." *Acta Sociologica* 48 (4): 321–40.

Wilkinson, R., and K. Pickett. 2010. *The Spirit Level: Why Equality Is Better for Everyone*. London, England: Penguin Books.

Worthington, E. L. Jr. 2006. *Forgiveness and Reconciliation: Theory and Application*. New York, NY: Brunner-Routledge.

Index

ABCDE model 45–6
aesthetic emotions 26
affect dispositions 23, 24
alienation 52, 99, 104
anomie 52, 104
Apology (Socrates) 10, 22n6
aretê, concept of 9, 10, 17
Aristotle 7, 8, 34, 46–7, 86, 140, 147; eudaimonia 8, 9, 16–18, 29, 40, 56, 110, 157; *Nicomachean Ethics* 14, 16, 18; phronesis 20, 35, 67
art of living 107; art of irony 87–8; art of rage 86–7; conscious use of time 84–5; de-schooling and 126–30; descriptions of 73–4; education for 89–90; end of education 110–15; focus on individual 2–4; foundational theory of 8, 21n3; fundamental questions 74–7; importance of, for education 115–18; interpretations of 6–8; living experimentally 85–6; negative thinking 88–9; pedagogical approach for teaching 149–51; philosophy of 69–71; reasons for educational approach 109–10; relevance of 94–7; relevance of positive psychology 38–9; requirements for teaching 147–55, 155n8; Schmid's concept 6, 8, 21, 35; and schooling 130–1; social influences on individual 103–5; teaching settings 151–3; term 6
art of rage 86–7
askesis 70, 79, 106
attention 49
attention deficit hyperactivity disorder (ADHD) 51–2
attitudes, defining 24
attitudinal hedonism 15–16
attitudinal pleasure 13, 27–8
Authentic Happiness (Seligman) 3, 39

autonomic hermeneutics 83
autotelic 49
awakening, concept of 33–4

Bakewell, Sarah 85
beautiful life 16, 35, 36, 61, 103, 107, 121, 157
Bieri, Peter 64
Bildung 82, 89, 90, 105, 113–15, 117–19, 122, 123, 132, 137–9, 148, 158–60
Bourdieu, Pierre 154
Buckman, Peter 126
Buddhism 9, 44, 106, 140, 146

care of the self: control over consciousness and 105–6; development of habits 79–80; enjoying pleasures 80; Foucault 7–8, 9, 20–1; labour of care 78–82; living with death 81–2; meaning of pain 80–1; Schmid's concept of 48, 77–8
The Care of the Self (Foucault) 7–8, 20–1
choice 42, 91n7, 91n8; art of living and 65–6; education and 67–8; and freedom 62–8; problems of 63–5; types of 67
Christianity 9, 140
Confucianism 140
Confucius 9, 140
consciousness, control over 105–6
contentment 30, 48
credential inflation 129
critical thinking 1, 7, 105, 110, 117, 136
Cruel Optimism (Berlant) 146
Csikszentmihalyi, Mihaly 2, 22n9, 28, 30, 38–9
Curriculum for Excellence, Scotland 31

Index

Dalai Lama 147
Dao De Jing 140
Daoism 140
death, to live with 81–2
de Mello, Anthony 8, 33–4, 145–6
Democracy and Education (Dewey) 110
Dennett, Daniel C. 64
Deschooling Society (Illich) 126
desire death, concept 11
despair, suffering and 33–4
Diogenes 140
Dostoevsky, Fyodor 33, 137, 140

education: approach to art of living 109–10; art of living 82–90, 107; art of living and schooling 130–1; choice and 67–8; de-schooling and art of living 126–30; end of 110–15; German understanding of 4; hermeneutics 82–4; importance of art of living for 115–18; and schooling 123–5; society and 1; spirituality and 142–5
educational critique, Schmid's concept *Lebenskunst* 118–21
education for life 4, 130, 158–60; concept 133; implications for teacher education 153–5; pedagogical content and practice 134–46; skills and knowledge 134–6; teacher personality 147–9; teaching settings 151–3; *see also* pedagogy
Emile (Rousseau) 111, 122n3
emotional concepts: defining 26–31; happiness and eudaimonia 28–9; joy and enjoyments 29–30; satisfaction and contentment 30; sensational and attitudinal pleasures 27–8; well-being and subjective well-being 30–1
emotions: classification of 25–6; defining 23–5; enhancing positive 45–6; future 42–3; good life 34–6; past 42; positive and negative 31–3; present 43–4; subjective well-being and 40–4; suffering and despair 33–4
enduring happiness 39; enhancing 46–7; working formula 40
energy 51–3
enjoyments 29–30, 43–4
Enlightenment 123
Entfaltung (flourishing) 123, 125, 132
Epictetus 7
Epicurus 22n9; hedonism 7, 9, 13–15

Erfahrung und Verantwortung (Experience and Responsibility) (Liebau) 1
Erziehung (upbringing) 123–5, 132
ethics: art of living 71–3; hierarchy of 72
eudaimonia (happiness) 8, 9, 13, 16–18, 28–9, 32, 40–1, 46, 56, 61, 97, 107, 110, 133, 157
Evans, Jules 3
Experience and Education (Dewey) 150

fabricando fabricamur 73
feeling, defining 23–5
Feldman, Fred 13, 15–16, 27
Finland school system of 5n9
flourishing [*Entfaltung*] 123, 125, 132
flow 47, 48–52; conditions and characteristics of 49; core aspects of 51; description 49–50; limitations of optimal experience 51–2; reason for 48–9; social and cultural perspectives 50–1
Flow (Csikszentmihalyi) 39, 102
forgiveness 42, 45
Foucault, Michel 7–8, 9
foundational theory, art of living 8, 21n3
freedom 61–2, 91n8; choice and 62–8
fundamental choice 67, 152
fundamental hermeneutics 83

Gadamer, Hans-Georg 82, 136; good life 34–5
Geelong Grammar School 3, 133
Gibbings, Robert 6
Glücks-BIP [happiness-GDP] 3
Goethe 137
golden rule 19
good life 104, 121; concepts and definitions of 97–8; emotions of 34–6; Kant's definition of 19; measuring and values 97–8, 108n3; term 25, 37n1, 61; values and norms 8
gratifications 43–4, 46–7
gratitude 42
Groundwork of the Metaphysics of Morals (Kant) 18, 19

Hahn, Kurt 150
happiness 3; defining 28–9; enduring 46–7; happiness formula 3

happy life 8, 18, 26, 27, 98, 104
harmony, meaning in life and 55–6
hedonism 27; Epicurus 7, 9, 13–15; intrinsic attitudinal 15–16; today 15–16
hermeneutical circle 136
hermeneutics 116–17, 122; art of living 82–4; role for art of living 136–8
Hesse, Herman 137
Hinduism 140
The History of Sexuality (Foucault) 20
Hoddings, Nel 133
hope 42–3
How to Live (Bakewell) 85
human nature 26, 35, 95, 99, 148
Hunter, John 135
Hüther, Gerald 150

ideology, freedom and choice 63
Illich, Ivan 126
individual focus, art of living 2–4
individuality 2
interpersonal stances 24
intrinsic attitudinal hedonism 15–16
irony, art of 87–8
Isen, Alice 41
Islam 9, 140

joy 29–30
Judaism 140

Kant, Immanuel 7, 9, 18–20, 34, 86, 123, 138

labour of care 62
Lange, Helene 127, 133
Lauxmann, Frieder 129, 140–2
Lebensgestaltung (shaping-of-life) 131
Lebenskunst (art of living) 2–4, 6, 21, 56, 116; care of the self 77–82; choice and freedom 62–8; educational critique of 118–21; educational perspective 82–90; education for 89–90; hermeneutics 82–4; quest for new 68–77; Schmid's approach 59–62; techniques for 84–9
Lebenswissen (life-knowledge) 76, 84, 92–3n40
Liebau, Eckard 1, 123
life-knowledge 135, 138–9; *Lebenswissen* 76, 84, 92–3n40
life-pedagogy 130

life satisfaction 3, 30, 31, 42, 45, 65; *see also* education for life
liquid modernity 60

Mackendrick, Paul 7
Mandela, Nelson 147
Mann, Thomas 137
market knowledge 59
Maslow, Abraham 22n10, 54, 95
Maurois, André 6
Maxwell, Nicholas 140–2
meaningful life 53, 97
meaning in life 52–6; harmony and 55–6; purpose 53–4; resolve 54–5
measures, values and 97–8, 108n3
media-literacy 96, 108n2
mindfulness 44, 144, 146
modernity, Schmid's approach 59–62, 105
momentary happiness 39
Montaigne 9, 86
Montessori, Maria 133, 150
moralism 71, 72
morality 12, 18, 71–3, 148
morally good life, Kant 18–20
Morris, Ian 151
Mother Teresa 35
Müller-Commichau, Wolfgang 29

negative thinking 88–9
Nehamas, Alexander 2, 10
Neill, A. S. 133, 153
New Zealand 58–9, 153; New Zealand Health curriculum 31
Nicomachean Ethics (Aristotle) 14, 16, 18
Nussbaum, Martha 2

optimal experience 49; limitations of 51–2
oracle of Delphi 10, 96, 106
"the Other" 2, 5n3, 67, 80, 103, 115

The Paradox of Choice (Schwartz) 64
particular choice 67
Pearse, Richard William 42
pedagogy 123, 125, 132; *Bildung* 138–9; education for life 134–46; hermeneutics 136–8; implications for teacher education 153–5; mind-sets and attachments 145–6; requirements for teaching art of living 147–55; skills and knowledge 134–6;

Index

spirituality and education 142–5; teaching the art of living 149–51; wisdom 140–2; *see also* art of living
permanence 43
personal happiness 9
pervasiveness 43
Pestalozzi, J. H. 133
Peters, R. S. 113
Phaedo (Plato) 10, 11
philosophy 59, 140–1: ancient Greek 7, 20; art of living 69–71, 107; Bieri's 64; for children 136; concept of philosopher's virtue 12–13; de Mello's 8, 146; Eastern 142, 145; education and 154; Epicurean 13–14, 80; Kant 19; Schmid's 3, 21, 38, 61, 68, 90–1, 100, 102, 118, 122; Socrates 9–13; Stoic 106; Western 145
phronesis, Aristotle's' notion of 20, 35, 67
Places of Learning (Ellsworth) 128
Plato 7, 9, 10, 34–5
Pleasure and the Good Life (Feldman) 15
pleasures 43–4; sensational and attitudinal 27–8
positive education 5n8
positive psychology 3, 5n8, 31, 107; happiness and well-being 26; relative for art of living 38–9; relevance of 94–7; self-concept of 100; social influences on individual 103–5; subjective well-being and positive emotions 40–4; usage of terms 39–40
postmodernity, Schmid's approach 59–62
power 51
practical hermeneutics 83
practical wisdom: *Bildung* and 119, 122, 138–41, 158; concept of 35, 67; development of 88, 159; ethics of 72; prudence and 2, 14, 20, 36, 72, 76, 80, 103, 105, 114–15, 117–18, 121, 143; wisdom and 140–1
preferences 23–4
pre-meditation 87
psychological growth 47

rage, art of 86–7
raw feels 44
REACH (recall, empathise, altruistic, commit and hold) 45
reality 82, 88, 92n36

reflective art of living 69, 91n13
reformulation 106
religion 8, 71–2, 94–6, 98, 120, 130, 133
Roberts, Peter 33, 34, 140
Rogers, Carl 100–1, 108n10
Roth, Gerhard 63
Rousseau, J.-J. 111, 122n3

satisfaction 30
satisficing 66
savouring the present 44
Schmid, Wilhelm 2, 8, 21
school curricula 1
Schwartz, Barry 64–6
self: concepts of 98–103; *see also* care of the self
self-alienation 99
self-awareness 77–8, 99, 116, 149
self-*bildung* 48, 90, 119, 124–5, 139
self-concept 128; positive psychology 100; Rogers' theory 100–1, 108n10
self-cultivation 119, 125, 139, 158
self-formation 4, 139
self-fulfilling prophecy 43, 89
self-knowledge 54, 136
self-mastery 66, 78, 106, 107
self-receptive 78, 116, 158
self-reflection 26, 29, 80, 87–8, 90, 116–17, 131, 136, 139, 146, 149, 151
self-sacrifice 112
Seligman, Martin 3, 25, 28, 38–9, 45–7
Seneca 7, 9, 86
sensational pleasure 27–8
sensitive choice 67, 68
Shakespeare, William 137
shaping-of-life (*Lebensgestaltung*) 131
signature strengths, core virtues and 47–8
A Social Brain Sciences Approach to Understanding the Self (Heatherton *et al*) 100
Socrates 7, 9, 140, 147; art of living 69; philosophic life 9–13
Sorokin, Pitrim 53
Souza, Marian de 144
spirituality: education and 142–5; spiritual self-perfection 112
Stoicism 9, 70; philosophy 106
subjective well-being 30–1, 40; emotions about the future 42–3;

emotions about the past 42; emotions about the present 43–4; positive emotions and 40–4
suffering and despair 33–4
suppression and slavery 52

Taoism 106
Tarrant, Harold 10, 11
teaching: anonymous group feedback 149, 155–6n9; art of living 147–55; pedagogical approaches for 149–51; settings and school context 151–3; teacher education 153–5; teacher personality 147–9
Teaching Happiness and Well-Being in Schools (Morris) 151
Thomas, Dylan 46
true liberation 60

UK Qualifications and Curriculum Development Authority 31
upbringing [*Erziehung*] 123–5, 132
utilitarian emotions 26

values, measuring and 97–8, 108n3
virtuous activity of the soul, Aristotle 96
virtuous life 9, 18, 35
vita activa 54
vita contemplativa 54

well-being 30–1; centre 3; *see also* subjective well-being
Wellington College 3, 133
wisdom 140–2
World Peace Game (Hunter) 135

Zen Buddhism 106